Chile's Allende

Chile's Allende

Life and Revolutionary Legacy

Victor Figueroa Clark

First published in September 2023

LeftWord Books
2254/2A, Shadi Khampur
New Ranjit Nagar
New Delhi 110008
INDIA

LeftWord Books and Vaam Prakashan are imprints of
Naya Rasta Publishers Pvt. Ltd.

leftword.com

ISBN   978-93-92018-51-0 (paperback)
            978-93-92018-49-7 (e-book)

Digital print edition, July 2024

Visit website

For
Emilio,
my family,
and
anti-imperialists everywhere.

'Deep passion which cannot be uprooted or shaken is, therefore, the foundation of everything. Without it, even if he is the wisest of men, if he is the most honest of men, he would not have the strength to carry on to the end the fight against the terrible socio-political power which oppresses us all.'
— Bakunin

'There are men who struggle for a day, and they are good. There are others who struggle for a year, and they are better. There are some who struggle many years, and they are better still.
But there are those who struggle all their lives, and these are the indispensable ones.'
— Bertolt Brecht

' ... nothing is harder to organise, more likely to fail, or more dangerous to see through, than the introduction of a new system of government.'
— Niccolo Machiavelli

'Does materialist dialectics leave external causes out of account? Not at all. It considers external causes to be the condition of change and internal causes are the basis of change, external causes taking effect through internal causes.'
— Mao Zedong

'After the aerial bombardment, the tanks went into action — many tanks — to intrepidly fight against one man: the President of the Republic of Chile, Salvador Allende, who waited for them in his office with no company other than his great heart swathed in smoke and flames.'
— Pablo Neruda

'Takes more than guns to kill a man.'
— 'The Ballad of Joe Hill'

Contents

Preface

In 2013 a shorter and less complete version of this text was published in the UK by Pluto Press as part of their 'Revolutionary Lives' series. Some might consider that everything that could have been said has been said in this earlier text, so why have I returned to the subject now, ten years later? The answer is that in these ten years, the relevance of Allende's life to Chilean history has become increasingly clear both in Chile and further afield.

In 2019, Chilean society erupted in a wave of protests that transformed the political landscape, with the figure of Allende and his Popular Unity (*Unidad Popular*, UP) government looming large over the proceedings. The socio-economic crisis and political machinations since 2019, including the election of a timidly progressive President, Gabriel Boric, provide a modern echo of previous episodes in Chilean politics and highlight how consistent some of the tensions in revolutionary thought and practice have been through time.

Beyond Chile, the period after 2013 saw a left-wing upsurge in some Western countries, epitomised by Bernie Sanders and Jeremy Corbyn in the Anglosphere, by Jean-Luc Mélenchon in France, and Podemos in Spain. While Melenchon remains politically relevant and Podemos shares power in Spain, in the Anglosphere, the socialist upsurge resulted in total defeat and the subsequent retreat of progressive forces. Both in defeat and where they continue to struggle, lessons of Chile's Left, and of Allende's leadership remain relevant, partly because they consciously refer back to it themselves.

Across Latin America, the period after 2013 saw imperialism back rebellions against progressive governments in Venezuela,

Nicaragua, Cuba, and Bolivia, as well as what could be called the 'judicial-legislative overthrows' of Leftist governments in Brazil, Argentina, Ecuador and most recently, Peru. The strategy largely failed, and left-wing governments have returned to government in Brazil and Argentina, while Colombia and Mexico have also joined the progressive ranks. In all these cases, the relationship between state and society, between institutions and masses, and between violence and coercion has been tested in ways that would have been familiar to Allende. That they have survived is in part due to the lessons these movements and leaders have drawn from the Latin American past, including the UP.

The questions I was asked during these ten years have indicated the need for a new text that could clearly highlight the political, ideological, theoretical, and practical lessons of the Chilean experience for a new generation of socialists with their own (often bitter) experiences of struggle.

This book is, therefore, the outcome of a long process of consideration, examination of new source material, and intellectual labour to connect the various points of relevance for the modern socialist so as to provide a text that is interesting, inspiring, but also of practical use — particularly to those just beginning the process of their political awakening.

What is socialism? What is imperialism? What is the relationship between the national and international? Between the general good and the particular need? What do we use power for? What should define the relationship of the revolutionary to the state and to its institutions? Does this change with a change of government?

These and many more questions are touched upon here in ways that hopefully provide food for thought and, just as important, energy for action, which is why I am so happy that the text is being published by a publisher like LeftWord Books, whose readership is in the vanguard of the struggle.

¡Venceremos!

Introduction

Most politicians are known for what they did in life rather than for the way they died. In this, as in so many things, Salvador Allende was an exception. More people know about his overthrow than about his government, or how he became the President of Chile. Allende's life, like that of so many other revolutionaries, has been stripped of context and reduced to a symbolism of his last moments surrounded by the smoke and flames of a bombed and burning Presidential Palace.

Allende's last words to the Chilean people were probably the greatest words of farewell ever uttered by a political leader, and they had an immense impact on people around the world. Yet there is much more to the life of Salvador Allende than the last seven hours or even the last three years of his life. These years were the culmination of his political ambitions and the triumph of his political methods, but they were also the last stage in a long process of struggle and organisation that had its roots at the beginning of the twentieth century, around the time Allende was born. Allende's death and the overthrow of his government are often told as a dramatic tragedy, but Allende's significance for Chile and the wider world also lies within the story of his life, intertwined with the history of the popular movement he led.

Chile's UP government was of tremendous interest during the early 1970s. The successful implementation of a 'peaceful road' happened to chime with the USSR's public recognition that a 'peaceful road to socialism was possible, and it was of great interest to a Western European and North American Left that shared its political methods, if not always its revolutionary goals. The Chilean process was also of great interest to the Third World and the countries of the Non-Aligned Movement, who recognised in Allende's Chile a country that struggled with the same problems of exploitation and under-development. Allende's victory in September 1970 was, therefore, an event of global importance, which inadvertently and inevitably dragged Chile towards what one of Allende's erstwhile friends called 'the precipice of the Cold War.'[1]

Allende's victory was just as important to his ideological opponents. For the Chilean elite, it marked the failure of constitutional means to hold back social pressure for fundamental changes. For Christian Democrats, it highlighted the abject failure of their 'revolution in liberty', the effort to make deep social changes within capitalism while staying aligned with the US. Further afield, it was also the death knell of Washington's Alliance for Progress, a decade-old programme of economic and military measures designed to prevent revolution in the region and ostensibly promote development through free trade and political liberalism. By the late 1960s, it was clear that while it had successfully prevented revolution, often through dictatorship and repression, it had failed to achieve anything else. With its relatively well-developed political system and strongly rooted political parties, Chile was an important example of a civilian US-aligned government. Allende's election thus hit an exposed nerve. The US had been actively preventing a Marxist government in Chile since the early 1960s, spending millions of dollars and penetrating Chilean politics at every level. This made it even worse that Salvador Allende, a self-proclaimed Marxist, had been elected, and to top it all, one of the main pillars of his government was the region's largest and best-organised Communist Party (Partido Comunista, PC). The US had helped overthrow Latin American governments for much less.

It was not just the failure of the Alliance for Progress and

---

[1] Frei to Allende, quoted by Valdés in Gabriel Valdés, *Sueños y memorias*, (Santiago: Taurus, 2009), p. 210.

its efforts to subvert Chilean democracy that irked the United States. Allende's government had an economic and foreign policy programme that put it on a collision course with Washington. The nationalisation of copper and other natural resources created an example that could be emulated by many other Third World countries, and its foreign policy directly challenged the US's efforts to align Latin American countries behind Washington by claiming Chile's inalienable right to determine its own foreign policy, free of US dictates — a complete rejection of the Monroe Doctrine that had justified US interventionism in Latin America since 1823. For the US, the appearance of a Marxist government was completely unacceptable. Détente between superpowers was one thing, allowing Chile to 'go Communist' — as Kissinger put it — was another.

The US government was not the only enemy of the UP. Other right-wing regimes, transnational corporations, and individual businessmen from around the world were also opposed. There was particular opposition in Brazil, when in 1964, the military had overthrown João Goulart, a president with similar aspirations to Allende. The UP was, therefore, at the centre of an ideological conflict that went beyond spheres of influence and economic interest and to the heart of a global struggle.

The UP government and its overthrow were thus a defining moment of Cold War politics. It frightened and inspired in equal measure. In Italy, its overthrow led to the 'historic compromise' between Communists and Christian Democrats and, in France, to the construction of a Socialist-Communist coalition led by François Mitterrand. In many countries, it radicalised young people and provided evidence of the futility of the 'peaceful road'. Many people learned from studying the UP and its overthrow, and many more also heard about it first-hand from the hundreds of thousands of Chileans that the dictatorship forced into exile. Chile, thus became a global revolutionary reference.

Allende's government also has an important historical and

ideological significance. It has been a key reference point for today's progressive Latin American governments, with Venezuela the best-known example. All the socialist governments of the early twenty-first century won through electoral means and, to one degree or another, attempted gradual transformations of society and economy. Although in a different period in history, they, too attempted to build forms of socialism. In this process, the spectre of Chile has loomed large and history has seemed to repeat itself — US-funded opposition, bosses' lock-outs, 'lawfare', efforts to split trade unions and the popular movement, coups promoted in the military, media hysteria and political pressure in the international arena. Several of these governments succumbed to these pressures, including Bolivia, most recently. Nevertheless, their success in resisting these challenges over many years owed much to lessons learned from Allende's overthrow.

As the first of its kind, Allende's UP government will always be a reference point for any parliamentary transition towards socialism because it was the first-time revolutionaries successfully laid their hands on the levers of power through democratic elections and was subsequently an early example of the modern techniques of forced regime change.

However, in retrospect, the Chilean case is a stark illustration of the simple truth that democratic revolutions are extremely vulnerable to external interference. If we examine the historical record, all third-world regimes espousing socialism faced violent challenges internally and externally. Those that have survived used violence against their (often foreign-backed) opponents at some point, often as a last resort, but at significant cost to their socialist and democratic credentials among western socialists, although not notably elsewhere. The historian Domenico Losurdo identified this as one of the major faultlines separating Western and non-Western Marxism.[2]

---

[2] Domenico Losurdo, *El Marxismo Occidental*, (Madrid: Editorial Trotta, 2019).

More recently, progressive governments, particularly in Latin America, have been far more conscious of the dangers inherent in the use of coercion, and have sought to avoid it. But even here, states such as Venezuela and Nicaragua have been obliged to use police to contain the opposition violence. Nevertheless, these experiences highlight the tense dynamic between coercion and legitimacy, which was key to Allende's Chile as well. The UP, therefore, stands perhaps as an example of the type of challenges that are faced by any government seeking to build socialism in a capitalist world and a reminder of the heavy costs of failure.

Salvador Allende was a tireless champion of Latin American integration and self-determination, picking up the legacy of the liberators of Chile, and by extension, the legacy of Simón Bolívar. Allende helped establish the Andean Pact, and in a region full of dictatorships, he sought to build foreign relations based on mutual respect and non-interference. The UP was, therefore, an ideological precursor to the integrationist efforts being made in the region today.

In Chile, Allende's life and legacy were forbidden topics during the long dictatorship that followed his overthrow. Yet the two processes have created modern Chile. Pinochet's regime was the antithesis of Allende's, but it was unable to extinguish the memory of UP, and it was unable to destroy what one of the junta members called 'the cancer of Marxism'. Nor did it completely undo Allende's lifelong project to nationalise the copper industry, which remains the mainstay of the Chilean economy. Therefore, the story of Allende's life and the story of the popular movement that he helped to shape is key to understanding what Chile is today.

Henry Kissinger once told a visiting Chilean foreign minister, 'Nothing important can come from the south. History has never been produced in the South ... '.[3] Yet Allende's political thought, and his efforts to build a revolutionary coalition remain relevant

---

[3] Kissinger speaking to Gabriel Valdés, Chilean Foreign Minister, June 1969.

wherever there are people seeking to transform their societies away from capitalism. It was this potential that was one of the causes of Allende's overthrow.

The 1970s was an ideologised period, and the language of Marxism was well known hotly debated by left-wingers. In his own time, Allende was called a 'reformist' and was accused of 'parliamentarism'. Today, in a world with far less ideological clarity but with a more objective distance from the events described, we can see the revolutionary content of his thought more clearly, away from what Allende called 'the cold maze of theory'.[4] Throughout his life, Allende pushed for a process of revolutionary reformism, a democratic revolution, to achieve a qualitative change in society in order to begin the process of socialist transformation. Although others often misunderstood him, he never lost sight of this goal. Allende's life shows that political compromises do not have to be reformist or aimed at preserving capitalism and that, in fact, reforms, by building upon and within existing structures, can become a revolutionary 'perestroika', avoiding the carnage and waste of violent change.

Allende came to lead a vast popular movement, which had three main motors — the country's two Marxist parties, and its unified trade union movement. As the century progressed, Chile developed a rich network of social and political organisations and a profound political culture. Although positioned within the Left, Allende was able to appeal to those beyond the popular movement, and this is why he became its pre-eminent figure. Throughout his life, Allende sought to 'cultivate consciousness', and how Allende was able to do so is the story of the breadth of his political vision, the energy of his political methods, and the charisma of his personality.

In a measure of his importance to Chile, in 2008 — 100 years after his birth — the Chilean public voted Allende as the greatest

---

[4] Speech to the students of the Universidad de Concepción, 4 May 1972.

Chilean in history. Throughout the years, since his death, Chileans continue to lay flowers on his grave and leave letters and cards addressed to him. During and since the October 2019 *Estallido Social* uprising, Allende's image and ideas have flared bright again, inspiring some as a symbol of a Chile that was and yet could be.[5] Nevertheless, there are Chileans who fear this *Allendista* comeback. Even today, Chileans remain divided by the twin legacy of the UP and the dictatorship that consumed it.

Allende feared civil war because of the 'tremendous and painful' social and economic scars it would leave while destroying the 'national community'. Yet despite his efforts, Chile was subjected to brutal one-sided violence from which it has yet to recover. The brutality unleashed by the military eventually provoked a response in kind from the organisations of the Left after Pinochet attempted to institutionalise his rule through a new constitution in 1980. This left-wing violence was intended to support and motivate the mass mobilisations that grew in scale until, by 1986, they were regularly drawing hundreds of thousands. According to US Intelligence, this created 'a substantial threat to political stability in Chile', and they feared that an all-out insurgency could develop that might lead to 'civil war on the Central America pattern' whereby the Communists would 'stand a good chance of reaching power'.[6]

During the mid-1980s, most of the poor neighbourhoods around Santiago and other cities could only be accessed by the regime in military operations. The electricity network was regularly sabotaged, plunging vast areas of the country into darkness. The unrest culminated in the effort to assassinate Pinochet on 7 September 1986, which, it was hoped, would lead to a popular uprising. The attempt failed, and the PC, under pressure from the rest of the opposition, withdrew from violent confrontation.

---

5   *Estallido Social*: (lit.) Social Outburst.
6   CIA Research paper, 'The Chilean Communist Party and Its Allies: Intentions, Capabilities and Prospects', May 1986, Box 91703, Flower, Ludlow 'Kim' Files, Ronald Reagan Library.

The result was that the Pinochet dictatorship ended on terms that preserved its essence. Some of the forms of democracy, such as elections, were introduced, but the dictatorship's authoritarianism was hardwired into a system explicitly designed to prevent another UP-type of government permanently.

For Allende, democracy had been a way to channel and institutionalise dissent so that violent conflict was avoided. For Pinochet's ideologues like Jaime Guzmán, it was a straitjacket to contain popular demands. The political defeat of the social movement, which had sought to overthrow the dictatorship, along with Chile's foreign investment-funded economic growth during the 1990s, mitigated the social impacts of this process. Nevertheless, every subsequent social or political struggle came up against Pinochet's constitution. By the early years of the twenty-first century, large segments of society — students, pensioners, environmentalists, workers, and indigenous peoples — had experienced this. In the context of institutionalised inequality and democratic deficits, the system became increasingly corrupt, and the population increasingly alienated.

The memory and legacy of Allende's government underlay the social mobilisation of the 1980s, which in the eyes of many of its participants, sought to re-establish a democracy that would re-start a UP-type process. Today, the legacy of that protest movement has itself not entirely disappeared. The constitutional essence of Chile's problems could not be obscured forever. Also, opposition to Chile's neoliberal model grew in size and militancy until it exploded in the 'Chilean October' of 2019, smashing the ideological basis of the system and forcing a process of change which is still in the midst of contestation. As one recent protest meme read, 'Allende didn't die, he has returned made [of] millions [of people]'.

Allende's government recognised that violence could be as much socio-economic as physical. In its programme, it stated, 'violence is when alongside those with luxury housing, much of the population lives in squalor, and others have no home;

violence is that while some throw food away, others can't feed themselves.'[7] It is here, in this long legacy of violent dictatorship and institutionalised socio-economic violence, that we have to ask questions about the effectiveness of Allende's methods, about the potentially contradictory role of his humanism, and question, whether or not he may have wrongly prioritised democracy over socialism. These questions remain relevant today, wherever people struggle for social change and are confronted by the opposition of local and international elites.

Allende has remained a figure of fascination in Chile and throughout the Spanish-speaking world. Yet, few biographies of Allende exist in English, most of which were written shortly after his death in 1973. Naturally, the emphasis of these works was on the final years of his life, and there was an inclination to make the books serve the purpose of solidarity with the victims of the coup. Some aspects of his life, most notably regarding his character and personality, were ignored or overlooked. The many memoirs that friends and collaborators have published in the years since, allow us today to fill out the picture of Allende's life as a politician and man. Now we can have a much richer, livelier, more human version of this extraordinary man who did so much to shape the destiny of his country and, by doing so, has influenced Latin America and the World.

* * *

Chile, the land of Salvador Allende's birth, is a long and narrow country that stretches 5,000 kilometres from the desert border with Peru, down through a warm central region, onwards through a temperate southern zone where it begins to break up into islands and fjords. Far to the south, a short distance from Antarctica, it ends in the windswept and rainy plains of Tierra del Fuego. Isolated from the rest of Latin America by deserts and the mountainous

[7] Basic Programme of the Popular Unity, 1970, p. 5.

spine formed by the high Andes and facing the vastness of the Southern Pacific Ocean, Chileans have something of an island mentality. Chile's isolation and distance from world events have made Chileans somewhat self-conscious of their provincialism and very proud of those who have achieved international recognition.

Chile's original indigenous inhabitants, the Araucanían Mapuches, fiercely defended their independence for 300 years. Their courage and intelligence were admired by Spaniards, such as the sixteenth-century poet Alonso de Ercilla, who wrote that Chile produced people 'so remarkable, so proud, gallant and martial, that they have never by king been ruled nor to foreign dominion submitted.' Chile was a frontier country, and from war and trade, the new *mestizo* Chilean arose — a mixture of the Indigenous and Spanish peoples.[8] After independence in 1818, new communities arrived from an industrialising and convulsed Europe. Although the majority of these immigrants were Germans, among them was also Allende's Belgian grandfather Arsene Gossens. Yet, despite this immigration, Chile's population remained remarkably homogenous, with only 4 per cent of the population being foreign-born in 1907.[9]

The vast majority of these people worked the land and toiled in the cities, or in mines and nitrate fields. Two contradictory stereotypes arose to describe the typical Chilean: the *roto*, and the *huaso*. The *roto* (lit. 'the broken one'), the archetypal urban worker, tough, stubborn, cunning, opportunistic, and uncouth. A dark-skinned *mestizo*, the *roto* was admired as a symbol of *chilenidad* (chileanness), the 'ethnic basis of the Chilean nation'.[10] Yet at the same time, the *roto* was scorned for his poverty and ignorance,

---

[8] *Mestizo*: A racially mixed person, especially of Indigenous and European heritage. Initially one of the several colonial racial categories in Spanish and Portuguese America.

[9] Brian Loveman, *Chile: The Legacy of Hispanic Capitalism*, (New York: OUP, 1988), p. 42.

[10] Alberto Cabero, 'El roto', in *El Caracter Chileno*, ed. Hernan Godoy Urzua (Santiago: editorial universitaria, 1991), p. 380.

and for his lack of respect for the law, for his propensity to violence and rebellion, and for drunkenness. All ranks of society saw something of the *roto* in themselves, and so, as Brian Loveman has described, the *roto* is 'a complex symbol of *chilenidad*, that signifies both the misery of the poverty-stricken worker and the *viveza* (opportunism) of those who benefit from his toil.'[11]

The *huaso* was originally a poor rural worker and cowboy of a 'primitive roughness', within whom the 'screaming of the Indian' subsisted.[12] Increasingly, rural landowners began to associate with this symbol of Chilean identity, completing it with flamboyant ponchos, ornate wooden stirrups and silver spurs. These stereotypes developed through the nineteenth century and were symbolic of Chile's increasing reliance on its growing mining industry and the agriculture of its central valley. This was the *pueblo* — the people — who, during the nineteenth century, had begun to mobilise to improve their quality of life.

The Chile that Allende grew up in was the product of events that occurred during the late nineteenth century. Towards the end of this century, Chile had come into conflict with its northern neighbour, Bolivia, over the allocation of income from nitrate mines located in Bolivian territory but mostly manned and owned by Chileans. In 1879, the conflict escalated into war as Bolivia sought to impose taxes on foreign-owned mines, including Chilean ones. Chilean troops, backed by Britain, moved north and rapidly conquered Bolivia's maritime provinces. Peru, which had a secret treaty with Bolivia, entered the war but was also defeated. By 1883, Chilean forces had occupied Lima. The result of the war was the annexation of Bolivia's maritime province, as well as some of Southern Peru. Chile continued to occupy the Peruvian province of Tacna until 1925 when it was evacuated after the failure of a long-running and unpopular process of 'Chileanisation'. The conflict left Chile in possession of the Atacama Desert, with its immense

---

[11] Loveman, p. 43.
[12] Tomás Lago, 'Asi es el huaso' in *El caracter chileno*, p. 390.

mineral riches, and a heightened sense of Chilean superiority over its neighbours, reinforcing ideas regarding the martial qualities of the 'Chilean race'. The Chilean army then turned south, and troops fresh from the deserts of the north completed the subjugation of the Mapuche indigenous people, opening up their lands for colonisation.

The War of the Pacific stimulated the industrialisation of Chile, thanks to the need to supply the army. After the war, the workforce dedicated to nitrates and other forms of mining in the north expanded rapidly as both Chilean and foreign companies moved in. Chile experienced a population shift northwards at the same time as this workforce became recognisably proletarian. Meanwhile, the growth of industry and mining also stimulated changes within the elite. The new industrial elites sought greater political representation than Chile's aristocratic and the system allowed them. By the 1880s, many of these wealthy mine owners had begun to question free trade, and were beginning to argue for forms of protectionism for Chile's nascent industry. The elite was also divided over religious issues, and the role of the Catholic Church in society.

In 1886, José Manuel Balmaceda came to the Presidency, initiating the largest programme of public works yet seen with income from the nitrate mines. However, Balmaceda gradually alienated the landowning aristocracy as well as a large number of Chilean nitrate impresarios, who feared his talk of the creation of a national nitrate company. This also threatened foreign nitrate barons, most notably, John Thomas North. North then began to use his fortune to undermine Balmaceda's government. Balmaceda did not seek mass political support, and his repression of Chile's first general strike in 1890 lost him much of what he had. Personality conflicts and problems dispensing patronage among his Liberal followers then ensured Balmaceda's increasing isolation.[13] In 1891,

---

[13] See Maurice Zeitlin, *The Civil Wars in Chile*, (Princeton: Princeton University Press, 1984), Hernán Ramírez Necochea, *Balmaceda y la contrarrevolucion*

Congress declared his government unconstitutional, and the navy rebelled; a short and bloody civil war followed, and Balmaceda's forces were defeated.

Following 1891, Chile was governed by a 'parliamentary republic' where most powers lay with parliament and 'elite interest groups dressed up as political parties vied for power and state patronage.'[14] Although restrictive in many ways, the parliamentary republic, founded by the revolution against Balmaceda's 'tyranny', did allow the development of free speech and some level of political opposition. The state's role in the economy was reduced, and foreign investment in nitrates increased. Thanks to income from nitrates, taxes were gradually withdrawn. The income from mining and nitrates continued to stimulate development, and urbanisation increased, as did the role of mining in the economy. By 1907, 44 per cent of the population was urban. Chilean society was overwhelmingly poor, uneducated, had no political representation and lived in extreme insecurity. By 1913, more than half of the deaths recorded in Chile were infants under five years of age.[15] The social question became increasingly important, yet the parliamentary governments of the elite did not develop any social policies.

Meanwhile, workers' organisations expanded. Ever since independence, some people had sought to make true its lofty ideals. By the middle of the nineteenth century, this, combined with the radicalising effects of the 1848 revolutions in Europe, led to the first recognisably modern 'left-wing' organisations, such as The Society for Equality, founded at the end of 1850.[16] Then in 1887, the Democratic Party (*Partido Democrata*) was founded

de 1891, (Santiago: Ed. Universitaria, 1958).

[14] Edwin Williamson, *The Penguin History of Latin America*, (London: Penguin, 1998), p. 485.

[15] Loveman, p. 208.

[16] Luis Sicilia, *Luis Emilio Recabarren*, (Buenos Aires: Capital Intellectual, 2007), p. 33.

to seek 'political, economic and social liberation of the people'.[17] As a response to poverty and injustice, and under the influence of socialist and anarchist ideas, worker organisation and unrest grew during the same period. Workers' cooperatives, fraternities and incipient trade unions were founded, and by the turn of the century, strikes were commonplace. Lacking any social policies, the establishment responded with massacres of — workers in Valparaíso (1903), dockworkers in Antofagasta (1906) and nitrate workers in the infamous massacre at Iquique (1907). Repression was unable to prevent further popular mobilisation, and in 1907, workers founded the Federation of Chilean Workers (*Federación Obrera de Chile*, FOCH). Then in 1912, workers who were disillusioned with the Democratic Party founded the Socialist Workers' Party (*Partido Obrero Socialista*, POS), led by Luís Emilio Recabarren, a printworker originally from Valparaíso.

By the early twentieth century, discontentment with how things were, was no more confined to the popular classes. Thirty years of studies, reports and investigations into the dire poverty of the masses had led many to seek some form of reform. Such obvious injustice cried out for change. The middle class was also unhappy at their exclusion from politics and at the routine injustices of Chilean society. Abroad, the Mexican and Russian revolutions showed that radical change was possible, and it inspired Chilean youths such as Vicente Huidobro, who wrote:

> See how those steppes shake off their hands,
> Millions of workers have at last understood
> And raised the banners of their Aurora to the skies.
> Come! Come!
> We await you, for you are hope, the only hope,
> The last hope.[18]

---

[17] Loveman, p. 194.
[18] Vicente Huidobro, *Altazor*, Canto I.

Thousands of people, including some of Chile's greatest figures, such as its Nobel Prize winning poets — Pablo Neruda and Gabriela Mistral — shared this discontent and helped create new political movements. These men and women were products of a country undergoing immense socio-economic transformations at the beginning of the twentieth century and buffeted by the winds of change blowing across the world.

Most of Allende's peers looked to Europe, and prized rationalism, a solid education and high culture. They had benefited from the evolution of the Chilean state and from Chile's uneven and unjust economic development. In particular, they were products of a well-developed education system, albeit one out of sync with a conservative political system. This generation could still hear the distant echoes of the ideals of independence. Born during the death throes of the old oligarchic society, Allende was shaped by an age where new social classes fought for their share of the nation's wealth and for a say in how society was run. It was a period in which people were moved by great ideals, where revolution was not a utopic dream but an evident possibility.

Like many people across the world, Allende's thinking was shaped by the great ideology of the age, Marxism. It came to offer him a means of interpreting history, but also a way to end the alienation suffered by the vast majority of people. By freeing the people from exploitation, socialism also offered a way to liberate the oppressors, thus making real the ideals expressed in the American and French Revolutions. Allende lived his life in the cause of these ideas, and if he sought power, it was to bring about the changes that would make such a country and such a world possible. By doing so, he changed Chile and made an indelible mark on its people and its history.

Early Life and Youth

A person who is fond of courage but who despises poverty
will become rebellious.
— Confucius

I shall do nothing unsocial, but rather look to the good of
my kin and have every impulse directed to the common
benefit and diverted from its opposite.
— Marcus Aurelius

Salvador Allende Gossens was born on 26 June 1908 in the port city of Valparaíso.[1] He was the fourth child of Salvador Allende Castro and Laura Gossens Uribe, but the two babies that preceded him died in infancy. As was then the tradition in Chile, Allende was named after his deceased elder sibling, Salvador. His sister, Laura, born three years later, was similarly named after her elder sister. His was an established middle-class professional family of distinguished radical lineage. On his father's side, Allende was descended from a long line of revolutionary masons — men imbued with the ideals of the Latin American independence struggles, the French and American revolutions and an interest in secular education and modernisation.[2] His great-grandfather,

---

[1] In Hispanic cultures, the paternal surname precedes the maternal one but both are retained. There is some debate as to whether Allende was in fact born in Santiago since a birth certificate asserting this has been unearthed. However, Allende always spoke of himself as a citizen of Valparaíso and moreover, it was common at the time not to register children immediately and it may be that Allende was registered in Santiago after actually having been born in Valparaíso.

[2] The liberators of Latin America organised themselves in the Lautaro Lodge to fight for Independence. This then developed into the Chilean freemasonry,

José Gregorio Allende Garcés, was one of the three Allende Garcés brothers, famed for their valour and had fought alongside Chile's independence hero — Bernardo O'Higgins. When O'Higgins was forced into exile, José Gregorio followed him there, fighting alongside José de San Martin (the liberator of Argentina, Chile and Peru) and Simón Bolívar. His two brothers, Salvador Allende's great uncles, remained in Chile fighting the Spanish alongside the legendary guerrilla leader, Manuel Rodríguez.

José Gregorio's son, Ramón Allende Padín, Salvador Allende's grandfather, became a renowned doctor, freemason and politician of the Radical Party at a time when the Party was the leading force for social change. He became famous for his charity and for providing medical assistance to the poor. He was elected to Congress in 1876, campaigning vigorously for the separation of Church and State at a time when the Catholic Church dominated Chilean politics. He gave up the safety of his office to create the Chilean army's medical services in the 1879-1883 war with Peru. This war changed the socio-economic balance in Chile and led to the strengthening of Chilean Liberalism. After the war, Ramón Allende founded Chile's first secular school and became the dean of the Medical School of the University of Chile, as well as being re-elected to the Senate. Shortly before his death, he was elected Grand Master of the Chilean freemasons. His renown was such that his funeral was attended by all the leading political figures of the day, and among his coffin-bearers were two future presidents of Chile — José Manuel Balmaceda and Ramón Barros Luco. Ramón Allende's political views and his red hair led to him being nicknamed 'Red Allende', which his grandson took great pride in.[3]

Although not as distinguished as Ramón Allende Padín, Ramón's son Don Salvador Allende Castro, was also a man of radical political views, a lawyer and a freemason. Reputedly a

which therefore had close links with enlightenment ideas and the struggle for independence.

[3] Salvador Allende interview with Julio Lanzarroti.

charismatic man, with a talent for rhyming and mischievous poetry, Salvador Allende Castro was a former soldier who had fought for the Liberal president José Manuel Balmaceda in the brutal 1891 civil war that cost 30,000 lives. Balmaceda was overthrown in a naval rebellion supported and partly financed by British nitrate magnates who opposed his measures to tax the trade in order to finance the industrialisation and modernisation of Chile.[4] Balmaceda promoted the colonisation of the south of the country and invested heavily in infrastructure, upsetting the Chilean landowning and conservative elite by promoting universal suffrage and secular education, and by reforming the political system. Under Balmaceda, the organisations of the working class began to develop, and the Democratic Party — the forerunner of the political parties of the Chilean Left — was founded.[5] The day after his elected mandate ran out, he became a refuge in the Argentinean embassy, and when in the face of defeat, Balmaceda shot himself. In the post-war amnesty, Salvador Allende Castro became a lawyer. His career took off when he was appointed the appeals court lawyer in the Peruvian city of Tacna — where the family lived for several years. However, Allende Castro was famed for his spendthrift ways, and also, with his wages often arriving late, the family was often heavily in debt.

On his mother's side, Salvador Allende was descended from Arséne Gossens, a devout Catholic Belgian immigrant to Chile, who arrived in about 1860 and later married Laura Uribe. Allende's mother, Laura Gossens Uribe, was brought up a religious woman, and the family's Catholic piety led them to take the other side in the 1891 civil war. In August 1891, Salvador Allende's uncle, Arsenio Gossens Uribe, was executed by Balmaceda's troops. Allende's family had thus experienced the divisions and the brutality of civil

---

[4] The British nitrate magnate John Thomas North contributed 100,000 pounds to the rebellion. The rebels' victory made him fantastically rich. British ships also provided coal and other supplies to the rebel forces.

[5] Hernán Ramírez Necochea, *Origen y Formación del Partido Comunista de Chile*, (Moscow: Progreso, 1984), pp. 214-216.

war in his own family, and this was one of the reasons why he later opposed a violent road to revolution.

Allende spent his early childhood in Tacna. It was here he received the nickname that family and old friends had for him — *Chicho* — a mispronunciation of the diminutive of his name (Salvadorchicho instead of Salvadorcito). Tacna remained under Chilean occupation from 1880-1929, and Salvador spent several years in the city, in close proximity to the Chilean army. It was here that he first learned to ride and shoot. In Tacna, Allende attended a mixed school for Chileans and Peruvians and picked up a love of spicy Peruvian cooking while making his first friendships. The children grew up in a tense atmosphere of increasingly active Peruvian resistance to efforts to 'Chileanise' the city. Inspired by teachers' accounts of the independence of the principality of Monaco, some of the children proposed making Tacna independent. It was Allende's first idealist foray into politics.[6] In Tacna, during the scene of intense political debate, the young Allende would regale his family with presidential speeches, one foot atop a small stool. It is possible that Allende was later uncomfortable with his family's role in the administration of occupied Peru, since he rarely spoke of this period.

When young Salvador was ten (1918), the Allende family moved south to Iquique, the capital of the nitrate exporting industry and the scene of the infamous 1907 massacre of nitrate miners. Miners protesting slave-like working conditions demonstrated in the city attracted more and more followers. Foreign mine-owners and their diplomatic representatives were concerned as to whether the state would be able to 'control' the situation, and eventually, up to 3,000 workers were gunned down by the Chilean troops. Among the victims were women and children. Despite the killings, the city retained a reputation for political radicalism, and Iquique was the scene of continual demonstrations. Conservative forces

---

[6] Fredy Gambetta recounts this story in Eduardo Labarca, *Salvador Allende: Biografía Sentimental*, (Santiago: Catalonia, 2007), pp. 30-31.

organised to oppose them. Elías Laferte recalled that in November 1919, a 'Patriotic League' organised a so-called 'procession' through the city. It consisted of an armed mob followed by soldiers and police and a lone priest, who smashed the shops of foreign merchants and beat and intimidated workers.[7] The city was even put under martial law. Although Allende was only ten at the time, a close friend later wrote that Allende had witnessed workers' demonstrations and heard their slogans.[8] The brutal repression of workers' demands helped to undermine the legitimacy of the regime installed after 1891.

In 1919, the Allende family moved once more, this time to the Southern port city of Valdivia, on the old colonial border between the Mapuche nation and the Spanish colony — the scene of heavy German colonisation following the brutal Chilean conquest of the region in the 1880s. Allende attended a school where he was notable for his comparative worldliness and for having a waterproof coat. In 1921, the family returned to Valparaíso, where Allende finished school in 1924. The Chilean education system, funded by the taxation of the British-owned nitrate mines, remained largely secular and progressive. It enjoyed some independence from the government. It was a system that tried to imbue students with modern ideas, and a healthy interest in physical education. Allende thrived at school, becoming national swimming and decathlon champion, and thanks to his prodigious memory and the help of discussions with friends, he achieved high grades without having to dedicate long hours to studying.

Tacna, Iquique, and Valdivia were all somewhat peripheral cities, but Valparaíso was one of the most important ports on the Pacific Ocean until it began a slow decline after the Panama Canal was completed in 1914. It had some 200,000 inhabitants and was

---

[7] Cited in N.M. Lavrov, M.S. Alperovich, V.I. Yermolaev, M.F. Kudachkin (eds), *Ocherki Istorii Chili*, (Moscow: Nauka, 1967), p. 251.

[8] Fernando Alegría, *Allende, Mi Vecino El Presidente*, (Santiago: Planeta, 1989).

a key stopping point for any ship travelling around Cape Horn. It attracted many immigrants, from the British expats — who dominated the nitrate industry and set up the city's first cricket and football clubs — to the Italian anarchists such as Juan (Giovanni) De Marchi, the shoemaker (or carpenter) who Allende recalled lending him his first anarchist and socialist literature and teaching him to play chess after school. De Marchi was one of the leaders of the Valparaíso local of the International Workers of the World (IWW), whose 'atheneum' was not far from Allende's school, a man who had many years of militant labour activism behind him in many countries.[9] Although Allende was only a teen at the time, the influence of De Marchi's anarchism is evident in Allende's attitude towards comradeship and political argument, in which he regularly echoed Bakunin, even in later life.

In 1906, a terrible earthquake hit Valparaíso, and much of its elite left the exposed slopes of the city for the safer and gentler hills of nearby Viña del Mar. By 1921, 'Valpo' had a marked proletarian feel and a well-developed popular movement. The young Allende's life revolved around these two very different cities. In Valparaíso, he socialised with the children of the middle and working classes, whereas in Viña del Mar, he mixed with the offspring of the rich. In Valparaíso, he played football and swam in the sea; in Viña del Mar, he practised marksmanship and riding. In Valparaíso, he learned at the footstool of an anarchist cobbler and in Viña del Mar, Allende listened to Arturo Alessandri — the future President of Chile — and discuss politics with his father, an old university friend. Salvador's elder sister married into the well-respected Grove family, who would also play an important role in Chilean politics and influence the thinking of the young Salvador Allende. The combination of a distinguished family history and an elite

---

[9] A short biography of De Marchi is available on the site of the 'Biographical Dictionary of the Latin American Lefts' [sic] (*Diccionario Biografico de las Izquierdas Latinamericanas*).
https://diccionario.cedinci.org/de-marchi-juan/

upbringing gave the young Salvador a strong sense of his worth and a clearly defined set of behaviours expected of a 'man' of his station. At the same time, his unsettled childhood must have forced him to establish friendships and his social status in each new place, which alongside a natural temper, contributed to the development of a sociable and yet combative personality.

Despite this easy access to wealth and power, his contact with the harsh realities of life in Valparaíso and an increasingly turbulent political atmosphere led him to later identify with the proud proletarian port city and not the gentle avenues of Viña del Mar. In a 1972 interview with Regis Debray, he called himself a proud *porteño* (the name for people from the port of Valparaíso) and Chile's first *porteño* president.

At the age of sixteen, Salvador Allende finished school, a year early, with excellent grades. On the day he received his exam results, Allende's classmates were discussing their future options. When they asked Salvador what he wanted to become, he said, 'I'm going to be the President of Chile.'[10] Allende did not recall his classmates' reactions, but his answer underlined his early interest in politics, his ambition and a self-confidence bordering on arrogance. However, this arrogance was often offset with a lively self-deprecating humour and a love of practical jokes.

Allende had to decide between becoming a lawyer like his father or a doctor like his grandfather. Torn between the two, Allende chose medicine because, like his grandfather, he wanted to 'serve the most poor and needy'.[11] It was not an easy decision; however, in later life, he sometimes expressed regret at not having been permitted to study law alongside his medical studies. On top of having to decide his professional future, Allende was affected by a confusing political situation that led to a period of 'perplexity

---

[10] Gloria Gaitán, *El Compañero Presidente*, (Bogota: Margen Izquierdo, 1973), p. 88.
[11] Alegria, p. 45.

and negativism'.[12] A corrupt Congress, dominated by factions of the elite, ruled the country, and a few families controlled much of the nation's wealth. Yet, the majority of Chileans lived in brutal poverty and faced harsh exploitation — often at the hands of foreign bosses. At the same time, a new middle class was bursting onto the scene, and it thirsted for representation. It was a time of feverish political debate, inspired by the Mexican and Russian revolutions. In Argentina, students in Córdoba rebelled in a campaign to have a say in how the universities were run, but it echoed a broader demand for greater democracy and justice. Their 1918 proclamation had a huge impact across Latin America; it stated:

> Men of a free republic, we have broken the last chain that in the XX century tied us to monarchic and monastic domination. We have decided to call things by their name. [...] From today, we have one shame less and one freedom more. The pains that remain are those of the freedoms we still lack. We are not mistaken. The resonance in our hearts tells us — we are treading the eve of a revolution; we are living an American hour. [...] The youth are no longer asking. They demand that their right to express their thinking in the university bodies, through their own representatives, be recognised. They are tired of supporting tyrants.[13]

The situation in Chile was, therefore, a reflection of international trends. Workers and students, in particular, were actively visualising a better future. What role could a young man from the edges of the elite play in this future? The Federation of Students of Chile (*Federación de Estudiantes de la Universidad de Chile, FECH*) students' federation newspaper — *Claridad* (clarity)

---

[12] Miguel Labarca, *Allende En Persona*, (Santiago: CESOC, 2008), p. 31.
[13] From the 'Manifiesto Liminar', 21 June 1918.

— succinctly expressed the challenge facing the well-to-do youth of Chile in December 1920:

> You are a coward. Yes, a complete coward. And don't think that we are saying this to attract you to this poster. No. Quite simply, you, whoever you are that is reading this, have you noticed how you live? What is it that you do every day? You are silent when convenient. You always ingratiate yourself with the more powerful. You opine like everyone else. When have you ever raised your voice against the scandalous infamy around you? When? Look back at your life. Tomorrow or maybe the day after, you may die, and what purpose have you served? Do you know what, the society we live in, is this capitalist society? Do you know what the society is that we push for and that you try to delay? No doubt you think the same as *El Mercurio, La Nacion, El Diario Ilustrado*, etc., the same as the newspaper you read every day.[14] Learn for yourself man. Don't be a puppet. Have some shame. Use your own head, that's what it's there for. Find out. Investigate. Don't be fearful. And don't leave calmly after reading this. In vain, you try to be deaf. You are a coward, at the mercy of he who pays you best, or shouts at you loudest. Don't fool yourself. When have you ever said anything that could jeopardise you? Because of docile individuals like you, the world is unliveable with swine.[15]

For Allende, the transition between a youthful interest in politics and political activism had only just begun. Across the world, humanity seemed on the verge of something new, and yet Chile remained stuck in the past. Demands for change were greeted with repression, as in the notorious 1918 Jaramillo Law that

---

[14] Chilean newspapers of the day. *El Mercurio* remains a bastion of conservatism.

[15] Cited in Jorge Arrate and Eduardo Rojas, *Memoria de la izquierda chilena*, (Santiago: Grupo Zeta, 2003), Vol. 1, p. 110.

echoed the Dillingham-Hardwick Act in the US and allowed the expulsion of 'foreign subversives' and legalised armed repression of demonstrations. Similar measures were undertaken across the region.

In February 1920, Argentina hosted a conference of police chiefs from across Latin America in order to discuss measures against 'Bolshevik agitators, troublemakers and anarchists'. In his speech, the Chilean delegate, L. Rodríguez, spoke of the extreme danger posed by the 'growing influence of the Russian Bolshevik revolution and its decrees.' Echoing the Operation Condor of the 1970s, the conference agreed on mechanisms for the arrest and later handover of revolutionaries.[16] Despite these measures, the pressure for change kept building.

Unlike many of his contemporaries, the young Allende had been exposed to the social inequality of Chilean society, and he knew the conditions people lived in far beyond the bay of Valparaíso. He had begun to question the status quo, but he needed time to think. As a remedy to his 'negativism' and to acquire some discipline, Allende prescribed himself a period in the ranks, postponing his entry into the University of Chile's medical school by a year. It was unheard of for a young man of his class to do this. Many even measured their social status by how easily they avoided their nominally compulsory service, but even as a young man, Allende was an independent thinker. He duly joined the *Coraceros* cavalry regiment of the Chilean army, based in Viña del Mar, where he polished the riding skills that were very useful during his many electoral campaigns in remote areas and improved his marksmanship. He ended his military service with a few weeks in Tacna, this Peruvian city that was still occupied by Chile.

His military experience was to mark Allende for life, and unlike many on the Left, he was always comfortable with the military world. However, it did not sit well with his radical

---

[16] N.M. Lavrov et al., *Ocherki Istorii Chili*, p. 252.

university friends, who saw his service as a 'demonstration of ideological weakness'.[17] Others also wondered if he had joined in order to benefit from the romantic advantages of the uniform.[18] In fact, it was in Tacna that Allende first gained a reputation as a womaniser. In the male society of the time, this success brought Allende admiration and sometimes envy. No doubt Allende was influenced by his father — also a notorious womaniser. In the early twentieth century Chile and for a man of his class, this behaviour was normal; it was seen as confirmation of 'manliness' and of exalted social status. There is no doubt that it brought him no criticism at the time. According to his later press secretary, Carlos Jorquera, it was in Tacna that Allende also became accustomed to street fighting between Chilean soldiers and Peruvian youths — with the notable characteristic that the losers 'won' because the point of the fights was to show a handful of international arbiters that they were the victims of aggressions from the other side.[19]

Meanwhile, Allende argued that his time in the military had given him the opportunity to mix with men from other social classes and, therefore, to learn more about Chile's social reality firsthand. It is also likely that Allende wanted to follow in the footsteps of his family tradition in the military. At this stage of his life, Allende appears to have had a somewhat ambiguous attitude to the Chilean state, rebelling against its injustices but, as yet, without a revolutionary mission. His experiences in the army, where he was punished for articulating 'collective complaints', helped to convince him that the military was no place for someone with social concerns, and Allende definitively turned towards medicine.[20]

---

[17] M. Labarca, pp. 31, 35.

[18] Miguel's son, Eduardo, later wrote an excellent biography of Allende; see Eduardo Labarca, *Salvador Allende: Biografía Sentimental*, (Santiago: Catalonia, 2007).

[19] Carlos Jorquera Tolosa, *El Chicho Allende*, (Santiago: Ediciones BAT, 1990), p. 25

[20] Diana Veneros, *Allende: Un ensayo psicobiografico*, (Santiago: Señales, 2003),

In the 1920s, Chile was a country in economic and social turmoil. As the editors of *Accion* (the newspaper of national purification) put it, Chile was, 'a country that at only 100 years of age is old and rotten, full of tumours and suppurating cancers'.[21] The old oligarchic regime was weakening, and the state was incapable of answering social demands stimulated by the Mexican and Russian revolutions without making profound political and economic changes. Meanwhile, after the end of the First World War, the economy suffered from the collapse of Chile's nitrate export markets. Both workers and students were at the forefront of challenging the regime. In 1906, students had founded the FECH, which became an increasingly radical critic of the establishment and the status quo. In 1912, Luís Emilio Recabarren and others split from the Democratic Party and formed the POS, building on the vast growth in working-class organisations that occurred after 1890. With this event, as Neruda later wrote, the working class had:

Acquired a name, and it was called
People, Proletariat, Union
And it had a form and stature.[22]

This acquisition of demands, of a sense of itself, and the creation of its own political party, made the Chilean *pueblo* a conscious actor in national politics. The party led by Recabarren had a vision of socialism and of how to achieve that; it was similar to that which Allende espoused later. In 1912, the POS published a series in its paper called 'How will socialism be realised?', in which, it stated:

p. 44.

[21] *Accion*, Number 2-14, 6-21st of August 1925, see Chilean National Digital Library:
http://www.bibliotecanacionaldigital.gob.cl/visor/BND:317954

[22] Thanks to my father, Ricardo Figueroa Villegas, for his assistance with this translation.

> ... in order to realise itself, socialism will use the following weapons: moral and doctrinaire education of the people through the leaflet, the book, the newspaper, the tribune, the conference, the theatre, art and the organisation of all kinds of associations that concur in the same goal; political action to conquer all the public power, the organisation of cooperatives to help monopolise commerce ...

Although this programme was modified after the 1917 Revolution and Recabarren's visit to Soviet Russia in the early 1920s, the idea of using social, ideological, political, and economic action to achieve power remained. The origins of Allende's political thought can be clearly discerned in it:

> Socialism carries out all these actions, using the legal systems that exist in every country, whenever possible. [...] Socialism will be methodically created through the means described, bit by bit, with one measure being realised today, another tomorrow.[23]

In 1922, under the influence of his Russian Revolution experience, Recabarren led the POS into becoming the Communist Party of Chile (*Partido Comunista de Chile*, PCCh). This entailed some changes to the Party's internal structures, but it did not fundamentally alter the Party's political line.

At the same time, feminist groups were established across the country, many of them overlapping with workers' organisations. The elites unleashed a harsh anti-socialist campaign from the pulpit and from the pages of the elite-owned press, but neither these nor brutal repression were able to stifle the growth of socialist consciousness among the workers. In 1919, the trade

---

[23] Edited volume, *El pensamiento de Luis Emilio Recabarren*, Volume 1, (Santiago: Austral, 1971), pp. 49-61.

union — FOCH — declared the need to destroy capitalism. In the same year, anarchist trade unions were also set up under the IWW. Mass demonstrations became increasingly common. Inflation was making food expensive, and people began to starve. Fearful of revolution, some sectors within the elite supported putting forward a candidate they hoped would be able to modernise the country while maintaining their social position.

Liberal, Democratic, and Radical groups thus allied behind the incendiary rhetoric of the Allende's old family friend, Arturo Alessandri — the so-called 'Lion of Tarapacá' — who provided an attractive populist alternative for the middle classes. He also gathered working-class support with the talk of his 'beloved rabble' while spitting fire at the 'golden swine' who ruled the country. Alessandri was elected president in the mid-1920s, despite the opposition of the most conservative elite who feared that this 'Chilean Lenin' would end their predominance.[24]

Despite Alessandri's victory, no single political force dominated the scene. Alessandri had attracted the middle classes, but they lacked an effective political vehicle for their aspirations, and the elite maintained control of the political institutions and the levers of economic power. They resisted Alessandri's efforts to build a social security net, recognise trade unions, and provide a Labour Code by blocking his reforms in the Senate. When the masses tried to claim the promises made to them, Alessandri responded with repression. Nevertheless, the workers' movement did win some legal concessions. The government legislated an eight-hour day and a six-day week. Unfortunately, these measures, like those that followed it, were rarely applied, if ever, and so did little to reduce worker discontent. Alessandri's government was stalemated, which provoked the collapse of his government and its replacement by a military junta on 11 September 1924. This junta

---

[24] It should be remembered that only 4 per cent or 5 per cent of the population could vote at this time.

was backed by conservative forces but was forced to introduce progressive reforms such as mandatory worker insurance, arbitration panels, and the recognition of trade unions. As with Alessandri's reforms, these were not enforced. In January 1925, this junta also fell, and Alessandri was recalled. With military support, Alessandri proclaimed a new constitution in September 1925, but the structural issues remained the same.

This was the political situation when Allende finished his military service in November 1925. Allende had, by this time, already developed many of the traits that came to define his personality. He was a fashionable young man, an accomplished athlete, a practical joker, a womaniser, and a leader among his peers. In early 1926, he moved to Santiago to study medicine at the University of Chile, initially staying with an aunt. At university, he studied hard, and took up boxing and Greco-Roman wrestling, as well as continued playing chess. Allende even requested to sit exams for a law degree, but was turned down. A few months into his university life, Colonel Carlos Ibañez took power, and the struggle against this dictatorship defined Allende's early political activism.

Ibañez came to power amid the social instability that was accompanied by increasing competition between British and American interests in Chile. Britain had historically dominated Chile, but after the First World War, its influence began to wane while US economic interests grew ever more powerful. Each tried to win the elite over to its side in order to win beneficial terms for its business interests. Among the elites and in the armed forces, different views on dealing with the crisis emerged. Some believed in the need for political reforms, while others believed that repression was the answer. In such an unstable situation, the political space for a strongman who could preserve the system began to emerge. One military officer began to establish himself as the power in the shadows. By May 1927, Colonel Ibañez was able to have himself elected with 97 per cent support, calling for 'heat-cauterisation both above and below to eliminate gangrenous elements of society'.[25]

For much of the oligarchy, 'the Ibañez government represented a guarantee against communism and social agitation, but it also promised efficient solutions for the problems that affected the working of the political and economic system.'[26] The diffuse ideology that sustained his regime called for a 'new Chile' but one based on authoritarian concepts such as 'patriotism, authority, hierarchy, order, discipline and tradition'. One of Chile's leading historians wrote that the Ibañez regime 'was similar to that of Primo de Rivera in Spain, although also containing many features similar to those of Mussolini's early regime.' The regime was notably fascistic in its militarism, violence against the working class and in its economic policy — Ibañez opened Chile up to US investment, notably in the copper industry. The regime tried to create anti-Communist trade unions, established what today would be called the tripartite mechanisms to resolve labour conflicts and wrote a Labour Code — measures that even encouraged some confused Leftists to lend him their support. Ibañez had the left-wing opposition in Congress expelled, and Congress became completely secondary to the extraordinary powers given to Ibañez.[27] The army was purged of the few more socially minded officers.

Drawing upon Italian fascist inspiration, Ibañez set up 'Peoples' Houses' where workers could relax in a suitably anti-Communist atmosphere as well as an Italian-modelled police force known as the *Carabineros,* whose main job — supported by a large network of paid thugs and informers — was the efficient

[25] Julio César Jobet, *Historia del Partido Socialista de Chile* (Santiago: Ediciones Documentas, 1987), p. 30.

[26] Jorge Rojas Flores, *La dictadura de Ibáñez y los sindicatos (1927-1931),* (Santiago: Editorial Universitaria, 1993), pp. 15-19.

[27] Hernán Ramírez Necochea, *Origen y Formación del Partido Comunista de Chile,* (Moscow: Progreso, 1984), p. 190.

maintenance of social order. Ibañez also began to borrow large amounts from foreign banks in order to fund public works. In March 1928, Alessandri backed a coup against Ibañez, and the latter called it a 'Communist conspiracy' and used it as an excuse to exile Alessandri and his followers in the elite as well as to smash the workers' movement. Severe repression of the FOCH and the PC followed.[28]

The brutality of the Ibañez dictatorship, its closure of the FECH students' union and its incapacity to resolve any of Chile's growing social and economic problems stimulated student opposition. However, the bulk of the opposition to the dictatorship came from the organisations of the impoverished and repressed working class. Nevertheless, with a wide range of rather superficial reforms, Ibañez, with media support, was able to create the impression of a whirlwind of activity. As a result, Ibañismo developed a substantial support base among the middle-class and the centre-right political parties and even some popular support, becoming one of the pillars of Chilean centre-right ideology and particularly of the Chilean military for decades to come.[29]

When Allende moved to Santiago to study, he initially lived with a well-to-do aunt in the city. As soon as Allende could, he left his aunt's comfortable home and moved to the area near the Vega Central food market in Recoleta, one of Santiago's poorer neighbourhoods where the majority of medical students lived. The environment encouraged political activism since the students lived with poverty all around them, and in the hospitals, they encountered its effects. Allende's experiences at this time moved him to poetry, and in 1929, he published a poem titled 'Anguish', which vividly described a mother's loss:

In silence, the desolate mother
Devours her anguish

[28] Ibid., p. 196.
[29] Ibid., p. 192.

Feeling her poor heart broken into pieces
Seeing that the child of her love now sleeps
Forever in her arms[30]

It was the beginning of a lifelong concern for the well-being of mothers and children, which led Allende to put the 'mother-child binary' at the heart of his policies. This was a notable distinction from the emphasis on 'family', which many saw as the basic unit of society and that characterised much of the language around social issues at the time. For Allende, it was clear that the basic unit was often a mother and her children, with the father as a secondary figure.

Soon afterwards, Salvador's father became ill with diabetes and subsequently was unable to provide for all his children while they studied. Salvador was therefore forced to find work, becoming an assistant in the hospital morgue, as well as working in a psychiatric hospital and teaching at a night school. This everyday contact with the toll of misery and poverty became his second university and played an important part in converting Allende's political concerns into revolutionary ideas.[31]

It was while he was a student that Allende began his political life in opposition to Ibañez. In his second year at university, he was elected the President of the Medical Students' Association (1927) — historically one of the most combative of the University of Chile. Allende also joined a new organisation dedicated to democratising the university and achieving social justice. The Avance (Advance) group of students and intellectuals was one of the several organisations promoted by the illegal PC to connect with broader society. It was made up of radicalised students, united — in their opposition to Ibañez; by their concerns for a university with the freedom to determine its own curricula and develop a strong

---

[30] Salvador Allende, *Angustia*, cited in Veneros.
[31] Iosef Lavretsky, *Salvador Allende*, (Moscow: Molodaya Gvardiya, 1974), p. 28.

social commitment. Avance was dominated by two factions but witnesses recall that Allende did not become strongly associated with either of them. It was in Avance that Allende began to study and analyse political texts. Allende recalled members gathering at night for 'readings of *Das Kapital* and Lenin, and also Trotsky.'[32] Allende impressed his comrades with his capacity to remember verbatim quotes from these texts, having just heard them read. Through this, Allende was introduced to Marxist writings, but it seems that at this stage, Avance's leaders mostly valued Allende for his ability to garner them the numerous female votes of the School of Obstetrics.[33]

In August 1930, the students re-established the FECH in defiance of Ibañez. Fiery discussions on what actions to take against the dictatorship were held in packed meeting halls. The still-small Avance group had its speakers booed off stage by an audience packed with supporters of the Radical Party. In a somewhat desperate move, Avance leaders put Allende forward to speak because he looked like a 'toff' and was relatively unknown. Hundreds of students filled the hall, whistling and shouting. Allende walked onstage, put his left hand in his jacket pocket, raised his right hand and began: 'Gentlemen!' The crowd fell silent, with the Radicals thinking one of their own had taken the stage.

Meanwhile, the members of Avance were disconcerted. This supposed revolutionary had committed the heresy of not addressing the gathering as 'comrades'. Oscar Waiss was witness to this speech, and he recalls that, 'Salvador had a notable intelligence and extraordinary mental agility. So, he began to speak about liberty, a topic nobody dared to express disagreement with, and in the name of that re-conquered liberty, he asked for respect for

---

[32] Régis Debray, *Conversations with Allende: Socialism in Chile*, (London: NLB, 1971), p. 64.

[33] Óscar Waiss, *Chile vivo: memorias de un socialista*, (Madrid: CESA, 1986), p. 24.

his ideas. He achieved the miracle, and from that day on, he was converted into a university leader.'[34]

The way Allende approached that speech was evidence of how he came to his socialism. One of his socialist comrades later wrote that Allende had come to socialism from the 'rationalist Jacobin stream, with its consequent instrumentalist and pragmatic projection serving as the great ideals of Liberty, Equality and Fraternity … ' which this early speech certainly illustrates.[35] Soon afterwards, he was elected vice president of the FECH. Allende then became a regular presence at demonstrations against the dictatorship and was also known to the police.

As the Great Depression hit Chile and the Ibañez dictatorship continued, the social situation reached revolutionary proportions. Over 200,000 workers from a population of some 4 million were thrown into unemployment. As a known student leader, Allende was arrested and briefly imprisoned along with others accused of rabble-rousing. Despite this, Allende was also elected to the Council of the University of Chile. From April to July 1931, the students were at the forefront of social mobilisations against the dictatorship. In July, Ibañez was forced to assemble a civilian government of 'national salvation'. On 18 July, the Minister of the Economy admitted that the government was broke.

Meanwhile, mobilised by the Avance group, the students — including Allende — seized the buildings of the University of Chile, declaring a national strike to bring down the dictatorship. Ibañez's *Carabineros* tried to dislodge them but were armed with pistols provided by their wealthy families, and they fought to defend positions on the rooftops of the university and upon the castellated walls of the Santa Lucia hill in central Santiago. Workers' demonstrations also brought together tens of thousands

[34] Ibid., p. 21.
[35] Clodomiro Almeyda, *Reencuentro con mi vida*, (Santiago: Ornitorrinco: 1988), p. 169.

of people. Cavalry charges with lances and running battles took place across the city centre; hundreds of people were arrested, and over 20 were killed.[36] Funerals on 25 and 26 July drew over 100,000 people despite the repression. The unrest and the strikes made the country ungovernable. On 26 July, Ibañez stepped down and was forced to flee the country. The crowds turned on the *Carabineros*, and many were lynched.

The Ibañez dictatorship was replaced by the government of Juan Esteban Montero, Ibañez's former interior minister. To cope with the economic crisis, this government attempted to cut public spending. One measure was to slash the pay of naval ratings by 30 per cent, affecting some 14,000 sailors and their families. The cuts led to a mutiny in August 1931 by sailors in Valparaíso, Coquimbo, and Talcahuano. Officers were arrested and revolutionary committees got established. In Valparaíso, the Maipo regiment of the army went over to the mutineers. The sailors had broad social demands and they called for an agrarian reform, an end to foreign monopolies and the democratisation of the armed forces. In various towns and cities, Revolutionary Committees were established. The Chilean elite went into a frenzy. In the northern town of Vallenar — named after its founder's birthplace of Ballenary in Ireland — a small group attacked the police station. The press called it a 'Bolshevik uprising'; a state of siege was declared and ultra-right-wing groups set up a 'Citizen Guard'. Meanwhile, the *Carabineros* in Vallenar hunted down dozens of Communists, officially killing 37 people but possibly many more.[37] However, the sailors were acting in the absence of a strong and well-organised social and political movement. The unity of the struggle against the Ibañez regime had evaporated and the revolutionary groups were weakened. Communists argued for 'Soviet power' — the creation of soviets of 'workers, peasants, soldiers and students',

---

[36] Jorge Rojas Flores, *La dictadura de Ibañez y los sindicatos 1927-1931*, (Santiago: DIBAM, 1993), p. 170.

[37] Waiss, p. 20.

but few outside the Left understood what this meant. A general strike failed to generate enough support. The student movement was also disabled by sectarian arguments. Allende was expelled from Avance when he argued against a manifesto proposing the creation of soviets of workers, peasants, soldiers and students, which according to him was to copy foreign experiences and excluded the professionals that the students would later become. As he later recalled, 'I said it was crazy [...] that I, as a student, didn't want to sign something that tomorrow, as a professional I couldn't accept.'[38] He was expelled for being a 'reactionary'. It was a harsh blow and it helped instil in him a lifelong dislike of ideological dogmatism and political sectarianism. As if that were not enough, Allende was also thrown out of university and was not readmitted until early 1932.

The sailors' mutiny was put down by loyal army units and bombarded by the air force. Some 2,500 soldiers and sailors were killed in the fighting.[39] Ten of their leaders were sentenced to death, others to hard labour and some to internal exile on Easter Island or the cold islands of the far south. The mutiny was part of a revolutionary moment in a revolutionary time, but the Left was too disorganised, disunited and incapable of taking advantage of the chaos to unite with the sailors and take power. The government reversed the wage cut and began severe repression of trade unions and left-wing organisations. In October 1931, Montero won new elections, but like the captain of an immense sea vessel, he was unable to change the country's course because the economic system remained unchanged. The chaotic political situation and the repression of the Left continued. On Christmas Day, 29 Communists were hunted down and killed. In January 1932, workers called a general strike, which lasted two days before the armed forces and police put it down. Nor were the indigenous peoples of the south excluded from the ferment. In early 1932

[38] Speech at the University of Guadalajara, Mexico, 2 December 1972.
[39] Lavretsky, p. 34.

the Mapuche declared an 'indigenous republic', identifying the indigenous struggle with that of the proletariat and calling for an alliance of indigenous peoples, peasants and workers. Its leaders were arrested and imprisoned.[40]

Meanwhile, Salvador Allende returned to Valparaíso in order to complete his dissertation and to be near his ailing father. The political situation remained unstable, but some people exiled by Ibañez were able to return to Chile, among them the Italian anarchist of Allende's adolescence, Juan De Marchi, and the Allende family's friend, Marmaduke Grove. A charismatic and mercurial man, Grove had been a key figure in conspiracies against Ibañez. He had been exiled first to Europe and then to Easter Island after supporting the mutinying sailors. In an effort to assuage his supporters in the military, upon his return to the mainland, he was appointed Commander of the Chilean air force. From this position, he continued his plotting. The Montero government was incapable of resolving the deep structural crisis, or changing Chile's subordination to external interests that were in large part to blame for the economic situation, and the opposition that grew. Finally, in June 1932, Marmaduke Grove led a military coup that overthrew the Montero government and declared a Socialist Republic in order to give 'bread, roof, and clothing' to the people.

The revolutionary government's forty-point programme included controls on food distribution, the handover of uncultivated lands to peasants, the creation of state enterprises in key sectors, the nationalisation of banks, an amnesty of political prisoners, the creation of a cooperative sector of the economy, the opening of diplomatic relations with the Soviet Union and an end to foreign interference in Chilean affairs. One of the new government's most popular measures was to return property, often work tools, that had been confiscated from poor debtors. The Socialist Republic terrified the Chilean elite and shocked the

---

[40] José Bengoa, *Historia del Pueblo Mapuche*, (Santiago: LOM, 2000), p. 398.

United States and the UK, both of which refused to recognise the revolutionary government. The US also announced it was sending a naval squadron to the Chilean coast in order to 'protect private property'.[41] Chilean Communists did not quite know how to judge the new government, which called itself Socialist but rejected them. In turn, the PC, which was following a harder political line after Recabarren's death, also rejected alliances with 'bourgeois' organisations — including the new Socialist government.[42] They argued that socialism could not be created by bourgeoise leaders following a coup. Instead, the Party demanded that the government arm the people and create soviets of workers, soldiers and peasants. Some Socialists in the government also called for the creation of a 'Popular Militia', but Grove refused to do this, fearing the reaction of the armed forces. Years later, similar debates paralysed Allende's UP government.

The revolutionary government was also divided, with Carlos Davila — Ibañez's former ambassador to the United States — opposing many radical measures. Davila then led the military counter-revolution that deposed the Socialist Republic, although it claimed to be a continuation of the Socialist government. Marmaduke Grove was exiled once more to Easter Island, from where he would return to fight in the upcoming elections. In Valparaíso, Salvador Allende defended the Socialist Republic at a

---

[41] Arrate and Rojas, v1, p. 155.

[42] Recabarren committed suicide after internal party struggles, in which a group of young radicals attempted to take over the leadership in order to shift the Party towards what they saw as a more 'orthodox' revolutionary line. Recabarren and his allies in the Party eventually won the struggle, but it seems he was deeply demoralised by it. He was also exhausted and seems to have been suffering from a depression caused by his partner's infidelity. Some of these young leaders were subsequently expelled, some later identified with Trotskyism. Many of them subsequently joined the newly-founded Socialist Party. The harder political line was partly a response to these internal problems and a local adaptation of the Comintern's harder line which was in turn a response to war fears in the Soviet Union and social-democrat hostility to Communist Parties in the European context. It was soon abandoned by the PCCh.

public meeting in the Law Faculty of the University. His friendship with the Grove family was well known, and following the speech, Allende was arrested and imprisoned alongside Alfredo, his elder brother and Marmaduke's brother, Eduardo. After being released by one military tribunal, the two Allende brothers were re-arrested by another and court-martialled. While in prison, their father became seriously ill, and the brothers were allowed to visit him on his deathbed. Their father had had one leg amputated, and gangrene was affecting the other. Salvador could see his father was dying. Since Don Salvador had no material wealth, he told his sons that all he could leave them was a clean, honest upbringing. He died the next day. At his funeral, in a romantic gesture echoing Bolivar's liberation oath in Rome, Allende solemnly vowed to dedicate his life to the social struggle.

Reaching Political Maturity

> … the political alliance between the proletariat and the bourgeoisie, whose interests on basic questions in the present epoch diverge at an angle of 180 degrees, as a general rule is capable only of paralyzing the revolutionary force of the proletariat.
> — Trotsky

> The workers wage the *democratic* struggle together with a section of the bourgeoisie, especially the petty bourgeoisie. On the other hand, the workers wage the *socialist* struggle against the whole of the bourgeoisie.
> — Lenin [emphasis added]

In taking a vow at his father's graveside to dedicate his life to the social struggle, Allende took a step further than Ramón Allende Padín, his illustrious grandfather. Ramón Allende had been a liberal, a philanthropist and a social reformer, but not a socialist. His grandson, imbued with a Marxist critique of capitalism and influenced by the revolutionary times he was living, took the decision to struggle for a total transformation of the society, building upon and extending the ideas of his progressive ancestors. In a 1930 society, where the average lifespan was 35.4 years for a man and 37.7 years for a woman, many of his contemporaries did likewise.[1] At the same time, the Left organisations had learned

---

[1] Veneros, p. 138.

valuable lessons from the unrest of the late 1920s and early 1930s. The Socialist Republic had failed because it had not organised mass support, because the Left was divided, and too many people had thought that it was enough to hold executive power that socialism could be built by decree. In the PC, a fierce critique of the Party's role in the failure of the Republic led to a return to policies first used under the leadership of Luís Emilio Recabarren, policies of mass politics and alliance building. The failure of the Republic also led directly to the merger of many smaller socialist groups and the founding of the Socialist Party of Chile (*Partido Socialista de Chile*, PS) on 19 April 1933.

Although Salvador Allende was not present at the PS's foundational congress in Santiago, he participated in preparatory meetings and helped set the Party up in Valparaíso, and therefore counted himself a founding member. After his release from prison, shortly before the 1932 elections, he joined Marmaduke Grove's electoral campaign in Valparaíso, where Grove won the highest number of votes for any candidate. Although Arturo Alessandri won the national elections, Marmaduke Grove won the second-highest number of votes overall, and his party got eight seats in parliament. Alessandri's election gradually brought to an end the chaotic period that had lasted since 1920. After 1933, the Chilean elite was forced to accept the inclusion of the organisations of the working class in the political system, although it did not completely abandon using repression. Having helped Grove's electoral campaign, Allende was able to return to his studies in time to finish his dissertation by the end of the year.

Allende's dissertation was titled 'Mental Hygiene and Crime' and was based in part on his work in the Santiago psychiatric hospital. His subject was chosen with a practical purpose in mind, to contribute to the improvement of the treatment of these illnesses received in Chile. Using the plural, common at the time, he wrote, 'We read, and the scientific exposition and the exact accounts of what has already been achieved in favour of this cause in other countries comforted our spirit. We observed, compared and lived our reality and were overcome by disappointment. [...] We were moved to [write the thesis] in the desire for better days, and with the memory of long hours of conversation in which criminals and delinquents opened the doorway of their intimate lives to us, spilling around us the blood, pain and misery-spattered source of their feelings.'[2] The description of one of Allende's case studies brings these words to life:

> Name M.Z.C. 38 years of age. Father died of a cardiac seizure. He is a habitual alcoholic. Patient has been secluded in the insane asylum four times. Mother lives; she is ill and very nervous; she has had epileptic fits. Fourteen siblings, ten of whom died in early childhood. Another at the age of ten. The eldest was killed by M. The remaining brother is very weak. He cannot work and suffers from nervous afflictions.'[3]

Such traumatic upbringings were shockingly common, and here we can glimpse why Allende had such a concern with infant mortality and what he later called the 'mother-child binary'. The study showed Allende's deep concern and empathy for the fate of the poor and the most vulnerable in society, but also his passion for finding pragmatic and logical solutions to social problems. The thesis argued, 'Yesterday's charity is today's social assistance. The collective need has overwhelmed [the possibilities of] personal kindness.' It was an early indication of his search for the solution of concrete and urgent problems.

The solutions Allende proposed bore much in common with his later legislative agenda. To overcome widespread alcohol abuse, Allende recommended an education campaign and state control of distribution. With regard to tuberculosis, he proposed

---

[2] Salvador Allende, *Higiene mental y delincuencia*, (Santiago: Chileamerica-CESOC, 1933), p. 8.

[3] Ibid., pp. 31-32.

the creation of a comprehensive public health system that would tackle the symptoms and the causes of the disease by dealing with diet, housing and education, as well as providing hospitals, access to medicine and sanatoria. To deal with venereal diseases affecting 20 per cent of the working population, he recommended a public information campaign in cinemas, factories, and workplaces; and sexual education classes for both children and adults. With regard to the problem of drug use, he observed that an international approach was needed and that the production of drugs ought to be under state control. Allende also called for the creation of special establishments for the reclusion of drug addicts, recognising addiction as a form of illness since it was wrong that 'these ill people be treated and attended to in the insane asylum as is the case today.' Allende also argued for penal reform along scientific lines ('it has been our lot to have a close acquaintance of our country's prison organisation' he wrote, no doubt recalling his own time behind bars). Prisons should separate prisoners according to the severity of their crimes, he argued, and they should receive treatment in order to promote their social reintegration. His thesis was clear evidence of how advanced his thinking was for the time and of the dynamic relationship that existed between Allende's medical experiences, his political thinking and his practical mindset. It was the first expression of something that remained key to his thinking for the rest of his life — socialism was the solution to the poverty, disease, crime, and desperate insanity caused by 'over-exploitation' and deep structural socio-economic problems.

A few years later, Allende developed some of the ideas presented in this thesis in 'Chile's Social-Medical Reality' — published in 1940 — after he had served as the Health Minister in the Popular Front government. The book described the shocking state of healthcare in Chile, which he blamed on 'old economic methods ... based on free competition', and proposed a series of measures based on cooperation and planning which would restore the 'virility and health' of the working people to the benefit of the national economy, and which would provide 'a better disposition and spirit to live and appreciate life.'[4] In both texts, Allende developed his idea that the redistribution of wealth and the rational re-ordering of society would resolve the material, physical, psychological, and spiritual problems faced by the vast majority of Chileans.

Despite graduating with honours, Allende's entry into professional life was not easy. He specifically chose to go into public service, although it was not well paid, and it exposed him to political pressure. After graduating as a surgeon, Allende took part in four public job competitions. Four times he won the selection process, but had the job withdrawn at the last minute because of his political activity. He eventually got a job as an assistant in the morgue of the Van Buren Hospital in Valparaíso. Here, he did the work of three doctors — transferring, undressing, cleaning, and autopsying 1,500 bodies. Allende dealt with the bodies of young and old, men and women, and even abandoned newborn babies — all bearing the signs of poverty, violence, illness and misery. As he later said, 'I won my bread sticking my hands in pus, cancers and death.'[5] It gave Allende first-hand knowledge of poverty. He worked long days, beginning at 6 am and often ending at 10 pm. When possible, Allende continued his political activity, attending PS meetings or working in the free 'Socialist Assistance' polyclinic.

The PS that Allende helped establish in Valparaíso was founded by the fusion of several Socialist groupings, among them was the 'Socialist Revolutionary Action' — the group that included Allende's friends Marmaduke and Hugo Grove, as well as several other influential freemasons. The elected leadership of the new party included former anarchist Oscar Schnake as general secretary and Marmaduke Grove as 'leader'. The PS agreed to use a Marxism 'rectified and enriched by all the scientific contributions of social progress' to interpret reality and recognised the need for class-

---

[4] James D. Cockcroft (ed.), *Salvador Allende Reader: Chile's Voice of Democracy*, (New York: Ocean Press, 2000), p. 35.
[5] ASD, Session 65a, 12 March 1968.

based struggle. The Party envisioned the necessity of a 'workers' dictatorship' in the transition from capitalism to socialism, and it stated that an 'evolutionary transformation through the democratic system is not possible, because the dominant class has organised itself in corps of armed civilians and has established its own dictatorship in order to keep the workers in misery and in ignorance and impede their emancipation.' This was the origin of the Party's fickle and contradictory attitude towards electoral politics, which it was never able to resolve adequately.

The new PS had an internationalist outlook, and it proposed achieving the economic and political union of the peoples of Latin America in order to arrive at a 'Federation of Socialist Republics' and the creation of an 'anti-imperialist economy'.[6] This perspective showed the influence of Peru's APRA (Popular Revolutionary American Party) — an anti-imperialist and indigenist party — itself heavily influenced by the Mexican Revolution, many of whose leaders were exiled in Chile. This ideological influence was key in developing a more nationalist and 'eminently Americanist' focus among Chile's Socialists, who felt that Chile was part of a larger organic Latin American whole.[7]

Furthermore, many influential Socialists were former Communists who had been expelled or left because of their differences with the 'partyline' as it recovered from a radical turn shortly after Recabarren's death. Among them were some Trotskyists who strengthened the general perception in the PS that the Soviet Union was not the bulwark of the global working class and ought not to be defended. The Socialists, therefore, maintained a series of important differences with the Chilean Communist Party, which they accused of being too heavily influenced by the Soviet Union. Allende shared some of the critiques of Soviet socialism, although he was not critical of Stalin, recognising him as a great leader even many years later. However, Allende emphasised the need to

---

[6]   Jobet, pp. 79-80.
[7]   Interview in *Chile Hoy* No.43, April 1973.

find Chilean solutions to Chilean problems, and he recognised that the Chilean Communist Party largely sought the same. This recognition and his respect for its working-class composition formed the basis of Allende's long cooperation with the PC.

The first members of the PS were from a wide variety of backgrounds, unlike the PC, which remained overwhelmingly proletarian until the 1960s. Some of its members had anarchist, radical, democrat, or even Communist backgrounds or had been independent activists and agitators. Some were freemasons, others — former members of the military, trade unionists, professionals and intellectuals. It was what the Socialist historian, Julio César Jobet, called 'a motley mass, tumultuous and impatient.'[8] Some saw the Party as a 'true' PC, striving to make it a working-class vanguard, others as a platform for building a broad cross-class mass movement. The two visions would often come into conflict. In the late 1930s, another element was added to the Party when Trotskyites, expelled from the PC, joined it. The PS's heterogeneous composition was reflected in its politics and its structure and meant that the Party tended towards *caudillismo,* or the gravitation around popular chieftains within the Party. On the other hand, its lack of ideological discipline meant that it was a relatively broad church and was able to grow rapidly in its early years.

The union of these disparate socialist groupings was a big step forward for the Chilean Left, creating a scenario where all those Leftists that did not fit into the Communist mould could act within a political organisation that still acknowledged the need for a revolutionary transformation of society. The key to their success would lie in whether they would be able to cooperate effectively with the Communists in order to achieve their goals, and in this, Salvador Allende would play a key role.

In the 1930s, Latin America witnessed a repressive process in response to the unrest provoked by the global economic crisis.

---

[8] Jobet, p. 90.

As occurred later with the onset of the Cold War, in the 1930s, the repression was justified by ascribing local struggles to Soviet interference, and many governments cut diplomatic relations as a result. In Chile, for example, President Alessandri came to believe that the PC was taking orders from the Brazilian Communist leader, Luís Carlos Prestes, who was, in turn, receiving them from Moscow.[9] The supposedly foreign inspiration of social unrest also justified repression.

Membership of any of the popular parties or trade unions, in the Chile of the 1930s was a mark of real commitment to the popular struggle. Left-wing activists risked torture little different to that applied during Pinochet's dictatorship years later. One leader and later friend and political ally of Allende's, Elías Lafertte, described his 1936 arrest following a railway workers' strike.

Laferrte was interrogated by four agents who tried first to ascertain his address. He gave the address of a nearby trade union office. The agents swore and shouted, demanding a different answer. Lafferte recalled in his memoirs that:

> They began to hit me. They punched me in the stomach, the chest, on the back. They didn't hit my face, maybe so as not to leave visible marks. After beating me for some time, they went back to asking, 'Where do you live, you so-and-so?' 'San Antonio 58'. They went back to beating me. Later, after they realised that the beating was useless, they decided to make use of the electric machine. While two of them tried to electrocute me with it, two others held me down.

The agents were prevented from electrocuting his testicles by an elasticated truss Lafertte used to contain a hernia. But he was shocked several times in an interrogation that lasted until midnight. Afterwards, he was taken to see an officer who was

---

[9] Arturo Alessandri Palma, *Recuerdos de Gobierno*, Vol. 3, (Santiago: Nascimento, 1967), p. 62.

accompanied by a 'silent foreigner'. He complained about his torture, but the officer simply denied it had happened. Lafertte was then photographed from all angles and then sent back to the cells.[10]

Although such treatment was less likely for Leftists from wealthier backgrounds, such as Allende, it was a brutal reality for most Socialists or Communists. The threat of police, army or paramilitary militia violence was constant, as was the very real threat of losing a job and being blacklisted. At the same time, this ha rdship created a palpable sense of common struggle, solidarity, and comradeship.

The repression of the Left was a regional and global phenomenon. In Brazil, Getúlio Vargas established his dictatorship, and Venezuela, Peru and Argentina also came under authoritarian rule. In El Salvador, General Martinez destroyed a small PC and massacred over 30,000 — mostly indigenous peasants. In Nicaragua, Anastasio Somoza consolidated his dictatorship after assassinating the resistance leader Augusto Sandino in 1933, and in the Dominican Republic, Rafael Trujillo took power. Fearing 'Bolshevism', the US backed these regimes and, in the wake of the 1930 economic crash, built an economic system that used loans and bilateral agreements as indirect means of control. It was designed to create what Robert Freeman Smith called, 'an integrated hemisphere system.' A key feature of this international political system was the US practice of insisting on bilateral agreements.[11] This ensured that individually weak countries had no chance of effectively defending their interests. While it is true that the United States rejected the direct military interventions of earlier years, which was itself immensely popular across the region, it simply transferred coercive functions to local leaders and institutions,

---

[10] Elías Lafertte, *Vida de un comunista*, (Santiago: Horizonte, 1961), pp. 60-61.

[11] David F. Schmitz, *Thank God They're On Our Side: The United States and Right-Wing Dictatorships 1921-1965*, (London: University of North Carolina Press, 1999), p. 47.

who often relished the opportunity to crush dissent.

Europe underwent a similar process of repression during these years, with fascist regimes notoriously installed in Italy, Germany, and much of Southern and Eastern Europe. In response, to resist the fascist onslaught, the Soviet Union pushed Communist Parties to begin creating 'Popular Front' governments of democratic forces. In France and Spain, Popular Front governments came to power, but one was ineffective, and the other was overthrown in a brutal and bloody civil war. The spectre of the Second World War loomed large. In Chile, these global processes were reflected in Alessandri's increasingly repressive government; in the creation of a Spain-inspired 'National Falange', led by conservative students like Eduardo Frei; in the threat of a takeover by Chile's Nazi-inspired 'National Socialist Movement' and in the efforts by the PC to create a Popular Front coalition that would include Socialists, Radicals, and Democrats.

Five days after the PS was founded, Alessandri's government passed a law handing the president 'extraordinary powers' in order to deal with 'subversion'. Leaders of the new party were arrested, some forced into internal exile, others into hiding. As if the official repression was not enough, from 1935, Alessandri developed a 'Republican Militia' — a paramilitary group armed by the military — to repress left-wing organisations. It was largely funded by landowners and other wealthy Chileans. Fascist right-wingers, who had originally been leaders of the Republican Militia, also created Nazi-style 'assault groups'. With tacit support from Alessandri's government, the right grew in strength. In response, the PS created its own, albeit unarmed, militia. Mass street fights became common as the Left sought to prevent fascist groups from organising openly. The PS's young members fought, too, in battles that often involved the *corvo*, Chile's traditional knife with a viciously curved point. One of them recalled that they would attack Nazis and strip them of their uniforms and any weapons. They would also attack sellers of the Nazi paper, beating them and burning the newspapers. The intention was to intimidate and disorganise. One of the biggest battles took place in Valparaíso, with Allende fighting alongside one of his later ministers, Orlando Millas, as well as a Chilean boxing legend known as Tulio 'El Chicharra' Salinas.[12] El Chicharra was a colourful character who, through his socialist politics, was later able to spar with both Allende and the soon-to-be president of Venezuela, Rómulo Betancourt. The socialist anthem that became known as the 'socialist' Marseillaise was written at this time, and it reflects the nature of the period well:

> Socialists to the fight!
> Decided on victory
> Fervour, action!
> Until our revolution triumphs,
> We will seal history with blood,
> Our mark powerful and triumphant
> The Party will give those who fight
> A worthy example of action against evil

It was this tough environment, far removed from the rhetorical competition of parliamentary politics that defined his later life, that Allende was formed as a PS leader. Allende later emphasised the importance of this period in the development of the PS since this 'frontal struggle against Nazi fascism' was not just 'the era of uniformed marches, of batons and Nazi attacks against the workers'; it was also a period of ideological struggle that helped the Party develop.[13] It was also a notable period in his personal political development. Carlos Briones, Allende's then-flatmate, a socialist from the Trotskyist wing of the Party, recalled that the Allende he met in 1936 did not yet have much 'clarity in Marxist

[12] Orlando Millas, *La alborada democratica en Chile: Memorias*, (Santiago: CESOC, 1993), p. 109.

[13] Interview in *Chile Hoy* magazine, No. 43, April 1973, published in Eduardo Gutierrez and Vladimir Sierpe (eds.), *Salvador Allende. Entrevistas 1970-1973*, (Santiago: Editare Editores Asociados, 2009), p. 182.

thought'. Allende was 'living a process of theoretical definition' in which he sought to combine Marxism's scientific approach and its rationale for revolution with the anarchist ideas of his youth and the liberal and Masonic ideas of his revered ancestors in order to overcome them with more 'progressive social thinking.'[14] It was a process that took place in the midst of a heated and often violent social struggle and in close contact with the poor of Valparaíso. It was around this time, in 1935, that in recognition of his ability and leadership, Allende was elected Regional Secretary of the PS in Valparaíso.

It was also a period during which the basis for the Popular Front government was laid. In July 1935, Allende spoke for the PS at a public meeting held in Valparaíso in honour of a recently deceased Radical politician. Speaking alongside the radical, democrat, and Communist leaders, Allende discussed Chile's 'social ills', and after recalling the recent killings of two left-wing activists, he proposed that to combat these social problems with 'a formidable block made up of the workers of the whole country.'[15] Américo Zorrilla, who later became one of Allende's ministers and who was a member of the PC in Valparaíso, later recalled an example of Allende putting this attitude into practice:

A problem in the PS's printworks in the city had led to a worker being fired. The worker took his problem to his union, which was led by the Communist Party. The union nominated two representatives to resolve the issue, one anarchist and one Communist. They tried, but some local Socialists accused the Communists of stirring up trouble against their Party. The Regional Committee of the Communist Party decided that the matter needed to be resolved with the local leaders of the

[14] Carlos Briones in Francisco Flores (ed), *Allende Cercano*, (Zacatecas: UAZ, 1988), p. 164.

[15] From Consigna, 3 August 1935, cited in Mario Amoros, *Allende: La biografia*, (Santiago: Ediciones B, 2013), p. 63.

PS, one of whom was Salvador Allende. They went to Allende's surgery, which was located behind the city's old cathedral. Allende met them politely, 'but very seriously'. Allende called in his colleague, the Socialist senator Hugo Grove, brother of the Party's leader. Upon entering Allende's office, Grove recognised the visitors and stated flatly that he would not talk to them. Zorrilla later recalled that Allende stood up 'and spoke to him in a very severe tone, as a father scolding a son'. Allende asked Grove to stop being emotional, since the issue at hand was serious. To Zorrilla's surprise, Grove changed his attitude, and the problem was discussed 'harshly at first', but eventually, a solution was found.[16]

Meanwhile, the Alessandri government continued its barely concealed dictatorship, maintaining favourable policies for US companies and cracking down on the political opposition. An indigenous people's revolt in the south was crushed with great brutality, and over 300 people killed.[17] The massacre caused great upset as it followed the brutal crushing of a railway workers' strike earlier in the year. As a well-known Socialist leader in Valparaíso, Salvador Allende was sent into internal exile to the small fishing village of Caldera, some 600 miles north of the capital. Characteristically, Allende did not remain idle. During his six-month sentence, he provided free medical care to the locals and their families, vaccinating them, teaching the rudiments of maternal and infant healthcare, as well as giving political talks, and he also founded the area's first PS section. For a long time afterwards, the area remained a left-wing redoubt. The PS protested his exile, and in Santiago, Marmaduke Grove raised the

---

16 Communist Party of Chile (Italy), *Don Américo: un chileno comunista*, (Savona: Coop Tipograf, 1981), p. 35.

17 Thomas M. Klubock, 'Ranquil: Violence and Peasant Politics on Chile's Southern Frontier', *A Century of Revolution*, Greg Grandin and Gilbert M. Joséph (eds.), (London: Duke, 2010), p. 121.

issue in the Senate, putting Allende's name on the national agenda for the first time.

Shortly before his exile to Caldera, Allende was put forward for membership of the 4th 'Progress' Lodge of the Chilean Freemasons by its Venerable Master, his good friend Jorge Grove. Allende was attracted by its philosophy that aimed to 'sweep away ignorance, overcome obscurantism' and create 'a regime of equality of rights and expectations for all men' as well as by his family history of freemasonry. After his grandfather's death, the freemasons had bought the family two houses — one to house his widow and children, and the other for them to rent out for an income. Allende later told his wife that this reinforced his loyalty to the institution.[18] In a country, where many leading figures in business and politics were freemasons — among them was Marmaduke Grove, the leader of the PS — membership could also open doors to a politically minded and ambitious young man and in mid-1935, Allende indicated his willingness to join.[19] Despite his distinguished family background, Allende's politics were controversial and sparked an intense debate which was only resolved after an investigation. The Masonic report on Allende stated that he had 'a very superior intellect' and 'great character'. It noted that he had volunteered for military service and had a sober lifestyle 'correspondent with his age'. His honour was considered untainted. As a result, his candidacy was approved. He was initiated on the evening of 18 November 1935, shortly after his return from Caldera. As part of his initiation, Allende had to respond in writing to three questions. The surviving record of the questions and his answers shows the maturity that Allende's thought had already achieved despite his relative youth:

[18] Hortensia Bussi, *Revista Analisis, numero especial con motive del decimo aniversario del golpe de estado*, September 1983.

[19] Juan Gonzalo Rocha, 'Salvador Allende, un mason consecuente', *Salvador Allende. Fragmentos para una historia*, (ed.) Fundacion Salvador Allende, (Santiago: Fundacion Salvador Allende, 2008), p. 204.

1. What duties does a man have towards his fellow men?
   Man is only a part of the social whole; therefore, his life should be at its service, that is, at the service of his fellow men.
2. What duties does he have towards himself?
   That of organising his existence in accordance with a clear conception of his obligations, duties, and rights, which are subject to the duties and rights of everyone else.
3. What memory of yourself would you like to leave for posterity?
   That of having fulfilled the obligation I gave myself of having been useful to society, pushing each day for the spiritual, moral, and material perfection of society. [20]

Although initially, being a Freemason may have assisted in Allende's rapid rise to prominence, it soon caused him problems when a rightward turn in the PS leadership sparked a debate on whether the freemasonry was causing the party to deviate from its revolutionary politics, and again when the party became more doctrinaire during the 1960s. In the wake of the Cuban revolution, many freemasons also found it increasingly difficult to sympathise with Allende's political project. Allende wrote a resignation letter in 1965, in which he asked, 'Can anyone with intellectual honesty imagine that [our Order's] composition reflects that of Chilean society today? The Order only takes in elements of the bourgeoisie', and he contrasted this with other periods in its history when its workshops were decorated by many 'artisanal extraction'.[21] Nevertheless, his resignation was rejected unanimously by the Lodge's officers, and he remained a Freemason to the end of his life.

Apart from its practical appeal, for Allende, freemasonry had 'a great and sublime mission' to promote among its members the

[20] Ibid., p. 199.
[21] Ibid., p. 204.

need for them to define, 'using modern standards', the principles of Liberty, Equality and Fraternity, in order to create a society free of 'alienation, unemployment, low wages and preventable diseases' through the creation of a 'well-functioning and efficient social security system' that would open 'the broad roads of culture' to all.[22] Allende, constantly, albeit unsuccessfully, encouraged the Freemasons to adopt this vision of their mission and to include more working-class members as well as young intellectuals and to become more democratic. Juan Gonzalo Rocha sees Freemasonry as the third pillar of Allende's existence, alongside his medical profession and his membership of the PS. While this may be an exaggeration, it is likely that masonic beliefs did provide a connection between his personal, perhaps spiritual world and that of the broader social struggle. For Allende, a man who saw his activism as part of a historic struggle for Chilean sovereignty, freemasonry was a living connection to past struggles. As he said in a speech to the Great Lodge of Chile in 1970:

Here we are, undisputedly, men who have a way of thinking that was held for years and years by other men who passed through the Order and the Temples but who acted and spoke a language that we do not speak today. We are the same, but we are different, and being different, we are the same in relation to the principles of the Order that we have made our own. And from here, the importance of masonic philosophy, which I wouldn't say adapts — because that would be to belittle it — but rather that it makes possible for man, in reaction to different social realities and facts, to apply in the profane world the concepts and principles that in different ways and epochs, were loyally applied by our Brother Masons.[23]

Allende, the newly-initiated Freemason, dived straight back

[22] Ibid., p. 205.
[23] Ibid., p. 208.

into his political activity. He founded the Chilean College of Medicine and began editing its bulletin in 1936. In recognition of his work in organising the PS in Valparaíso and Caldera, the Party put him forward as a congressional candidate for Quillota and Valparaíso in 1936. He was also elected Deputy General Secretary of the PS in 1937.

Allende won his seat in Valparaíso, as well as contributed to the victory of three other Socialists in the city. It was part of an impressive showing — in four short years, the Party had established a national presence with just over 11 per cent of the national vote. Allende soon developed a reputation as a pugnacious parliamentarian, who, as a Peruvian friend later recalled, tended to 'unequivocal and sharp responses to impertinence'.[24] It was part of a harsher side of his character, an intolerance of what he perceived as mediocrity or dishonourable behaviour. Yet, Allende was not otherwise intolerant, and his friends and collaborators recall a man who distinguished between adversaries and enemies and who once said, 'I am passionate and violent in the defence of my ideas, my principles, of the party doctrine that I sustain, but I have never made it personal.'[25]

In one of his early speeches in Congress, Allende critiqued a government healthcare bill arguing that only socialism could adequately resolve Chile's problems. Allende argued that poverty and lack of healthcare caused Chile's horrific mortality and infant mortality rates of 26.8 per thousand inhabitants, and 238 per thousand births, respectively. Allende described how 53 per cent of hospitals had no children's wards, and none had central heating. Furthermore, social insurance only covered 13 per cent of the population. Allende described how 87 per cent of working people's salaries went on food, clothing, and heating. He described how Chileans ate only 30 per cent of what was then considered normal. 'It isn't possible to allow an entire people to continue to

---

[24] Luis Alberto Sánchez, 'Siluetas Latinoamericanas', Nuevo Zig Zag, p. 17.
[25] Veneros, p. 122.

be starved', he exclaimed. Starvation was exacerbated by lack of clothing and shelter; 'there are innumerable sick people that arrive at hospitals who only need warmth and shelter', he said. In order to remedy the chronic shortage of decent housing, he argued for the construction of 300,000 new homes. Allende criticised the government's proposed legislation since it showed 'no leadership, no systematisation' and was underfunded. The legislation did not provide for an integrated system and did not contemplate tackling the fundamental cause of ill health — poverty — which could only be tackled in a 'controlled, planned, socialised economy, in which the anarchy of today, which allows the few to live at the expense of the many, can be overcome.'[26] In his four-year career as a parliamentary deputy, Allende presented bills on the education of workers and peasants, the prohibition of monopolies, reforms to the Labour Code, and the creation of the Supreme Council for the Protection of Children and Adolescents demonstrating his consistent concern with the practical needs of working people.

Shortly after Allende's election, the Radicals and the Socialists agreed, with Communist encouragement, to present a unitary Popular Front candidate in the 1938 presidential elections. The candidate chosen was the radical Pedro Aguirre Cerda, whose slogan was 'to govern is to educate'. The road to the Popular Front was not easy. The Left was divided. Street fights between Communists, Trotskyists, and Socialists were common. Many Socialists opposed an alliance with sectors they considered bourgeois and potentially treacherous. They, therefore, had a policy of a United Workers' Front, excluding any bourgeois party. In the vigorous internal debate on the Popular Front, Allende supported Grove and Oscar Schnake in backing an alliance with the Communists and Radicals — a posture that eventually won out. Allende and those like him thought that bringing the Radicals into government would mean an advance since it would bring 'the petit-bourgeoisie into the

---

[26] ASD, Monday, 26 July 1937.

exercise of power'. However, Allende was also aware that despite being a big step forward, the Popular Front was also a coalition dominated by the Radicals, who would therefore dominate economic policy. According to Allende, 'the Popular Front did not imply and could not imply political liberation and full sovereignty' and therefore, 'we consciously acted within the Popular Front as a stage [of political development]'.[27]

Even within the PC, there were those who mistrusted Aguirre Cerda, who had been a minister under Alessandri. However, with their policy, now officially supported by the Third International, the Communists vigorously built the Popular Front with allies in the Radical and Socialist parties. Meanwhile, the Radicals, who had spent much of the 1920s and 1930s see-sawing between opposition and government, were feeling pressure on the Left by the energetic and popular PS but were also incensed by the brutal repression of civil liberties under Alessandri. For all three groupings, the alliance had its advantages, and the Popular Front began to take shape with Socialist and Communist support for a victorious Radical candidate in an April 1936 by-election showing how effective the new coalition could be. Then the Socialist, anarcho-syndicalist, and Communist trade union federations united in December 1936 in the Confederation of Workers of Chile (*Confederacion de Trabajadores de Chile*, CTCH), proclaiming their support for the Popular Front. This historic unity soon brought them the reward of electoral victory, but the parties that came to form the Popular Front still contested the 1937 parliamentary elections separately.

Aguirre Cerda asked Allende to lead the electoral campaign in Valparaíso. Allende agreed but on the condition that he be in complete control. Aguirre Cerda agreed, and Allende ran a successful campaign in the region. Allende got to know Aguirre Cerda, who he later recalled 'had a very human attitude' with a notable ability to listen. Shortly before the election, Allende had

[27] Debray, p. 70.

a narrow escape. He was on a train from Quillota to Valparaíso when he was accosted by a gang of Chilean Nazis. However, before Allende could be hurt, one of them drew a pistol on his fellows, yelling, 'Nobody touches Dr Allende!'. The man had been severely injured in a clash in Valparaíso some months before, and Allende had treated him in hospital until he recovered. The youth was killed in Santiago shortly afterwards when a Nazi coup attempt was put down by the army, killing sixty-three youths. Allende recalled that the Popular Front marched in homage to the dead. 'They had been our adversaries', he said, 'but they had been concerned about Chile. They had a patriotic zeal we didn't share, but that perhaps was honest from their point of view'.[28]

The October 1938 presidential election was the first to be fought in Chile, on an explicit left-right split, much influenced by distant events in Spain. The Left campaigned on the slogan 'Bread, Roof, and Clothing', the right on 'Order and Work'. The limitations of Chile's democracy were a significant challenge to the aspirations of the Popular Front. Of the population of five million people, only 500,000 could legally vote — a circumstance that clearly benefitted the right. Furthermore, the right habitually used underhand tactics to get votes — from bribery and blackmail to *encerrona* — the practice of locking people that might vote for the Left in their workplaces until the polling stations closed. The parties of the Left used a variety of methods to counter this. Socialist students went out to rural areas to invigilate the voting process. Others even used home-made tear gas grenades while fighting the thugs protecting the *encerronas* where working people were corralled.[29] This combative stance was key in allowing a democratic electoral result; despite widespread fraud, a weighted electoral system and a propaganda campaign mounted by the right, the Popular Front

[28] Mario Amoros, *Allende: La biografia*, (Santiago: Ediciones B, 2013), pp. 74-76.

[29] Arturo Olavarria, a Radical Party member quoted in Arrate and Rojas v1, pp. 192-193.

candidate, Pedro Aguirre Cerda, won. As in Allende's victory 32 years later, Aguirre Cerda's was statistically narrow, and some elements of the right tried to claim that the result was illegitimate. As in 1970, the distortions of the electoral system hid a much broader level of support.

On the evening of the elections, Allende was having dinner in a Valparaíso restaurant in the company of a Communist deputy. On their way in, they greeted some liberal and conservative politicians at other tables. At eleven thirty, the radio announced the official result, and these politicians approached to congratulate Allende and his companion. For Allende, 'It was an unforgettable democratic expression because it was the recognition of a victory that had been marked by a harsh and difficult struggle.'[30] It was regular interactions such as these that strengthened Allende's belief in the flexibility of the Chilean political system.

Nevertheless, the Popular Front's victory was just the beginning. As Allende had stated at the end of the Valparaíso campaign, 'The Popular Front government cannot be confused with a Socialist government. The 'Frontist' government has been created to defend the democratic guarantees against the shadowy threat of fascism.'[31] There was no question of profoundly changing the existing socio-economic order. Accordingly, the Communists did not claim any ministerial posts so as to maintain support for the government among right-wing sectors in the Radical Party and to avoid provoking a coup, as had occurred in Spain, but the new cabinet did include several Socialist ministers, including a youthful Salvador Allende as Health Minister.

Soon after the Popular Front took power, Chile was shaken by a ferocious earthquake, which struck the city of Chillán on 25 January 1939. The city was completely destroyed. Tens of thousands of people perished. In the aftermath of the earthquake, Allende rushed to the scene in order to help organise the relief

---

[30] Allende quoted in *El Siglo*, cited by Amoros, p. 77.
[31] Arrate and Rojas, v.1., p. 196.

effort. Chile did not have a public emergency service, so it was down to the public, political parties, and other civil society organisations, together with the army and police, to organise the emergency relief. The Socialist Militia were mobilised and provided immediate assistance, rescuing survivors and clearing rubble. The PC did the same, and the joint efforts amid the ruins provided some of the first experiences of a common struggle for militants of both parties.[32]

Allende himself provided medical care to some victims. To help rebuild after the earthquake, the Popular Front government created the National Corporation for the Promotion of Production (*Corporación de Fomento de la Producción de Chile*, CORFO). This organisation played an important role in Chile's subsequent economic development, substituting for non-existent national private investment in industry and strategic sectors of the economy. It was initially led by the Minister of Finance alongside some members of Congress and representatives of Chile's business sector and trade unions. The CORFO created a steel industry, a plan for the electrification of the country, and a system of loans for agricultural producers — all with the intention of creating the basis for development. As one Chilean economist later put it, 'the industrialisation and modernisation of the country were owed almost exclusively to the state intervention, since the state had to take on the role of the entrepreneur as a result of the weakness or lack of interest of the private sector.'[33] The government also pushed hard to improve and expand the education system under the slogan — 'to govern is to educate'. The state founded vocational schools designed to create a qualified workforce, and 385,000 children were brought into primary education. Together, they were the Popular Front's most lasting legacy.

At the time of the earthquake, Allende was attending a

---

[32] Millas, *La alborada democratica en Chile*, p. 178.
[33] Max Nolff, *Salvador Allende: El politico. El Estadista*, (Santiago: Ediciones Documentas, 1993). p. 32.

Masonic meeting in central Santiago. While out on the street, after having fled the building, Allende bumped into a friend who was accompanied by Hortensia Bussi. Despite her criticising Allende's masonic membership, the two began their romance shortly afterwards. One of the things she recalled attracting her was the way he described the tragedies of the disaster zone with deep empathy for its victims.[34] Within a few months, 'Tencha', as she was known, fell pregnant. Under some pressure from friends and relatives, the couple married in a civil ceremony in Santiago on 17 September 1939. Tencha herself later recalled the wedding occurred without a party or invitations, partly because of Salvador's ministerial workload but also because 'we weren't a traditional couple.'[35] The newlyweds moved into a building just by the Santa Lucia hill, sharing the residence with a number of notable political figures, including Rómulo Betancourt, the later president of Venezuela who was exiled to Chile in October 1939. Betancourt shared a love of boxing with Allende and soon became a regular sparring partner, alongside Tulio 'El Chicharra' Salinas, who had known Allende since the street battles of the early 1930s. Years later, when Betancourt was the freshly inaugurated president of Venezuela, residing at the Miraflores Palace in Caracas, one of his uniformed aides informed him that a poorly dressed man was at the gates demanding to see him. Betancourt asked for details and was given the name Tulio Salinas Castillo. 'El Chicharra!' he shouted and ran to embrace his old friend. Chicharra did the same with Allende in November 1970.[36]

The central location in a distinguished neighbourhood allowed Allende to mix his work and social life. Each morning, Allende rose and did exercises before heading to work. After work, Allende attended meetings or conversed for long hours in cafés or

[34] Hortensia Bussi in Francisco Flores (ed), *Allende Cercano*, (Zacatecas: UAZ, 1988), pp. 143-145.

[35] Ibid., p. 122.

[36] Jorquera, p. 25.

friends' homes, mixing with politicians, Peruvian exiles, and with the young Socialists that he grouped around himself.

In August 1939, General Ariosto Herrera launched an attempt to overthrow the Popular Front government. At the time of General Herrera's ultimatum, Allende was with Aguirre Cerda and in 1970, he recalled, 'I heard and learned, and will never forget the serene firmness of dignity made flesh.' According to Allende, Aguirre Cerda told General Herrera's envoy, 'I am a man of the Law. I will leave here feet first [dead], but I will never abandon the post that the people entrusted me.'[37] Some 200,000 people marched through central Santiago in support of the Popular Front, and the coup attempt failed. Years later, Allende must have recalled these moments as he himself faced military opposition, and there is a clear echo of Aguirre Cerda's words in Allende's own in 1973.

In September 1939, thanks to his work on Aguirre Cerda's campaign, Allende was appointed as Health Minister. Allende developed the project of a National Plan for the Defence of Public Health, which became the social and human development arm of the government's programme. As Allende later explained, measures to improve public health would only work if supported by economic and financial measures that increased the overall standard of living. The Plan called for the allocation of USD 20 million to fund new hospitals, polyclinics, psychiatric institutions, a cancer institute, the construction of waste burning facilities, sewerage works, increased funding for laboratories at the University of Chile, improved facilities for mothers and children, and a raft of measures designed to improve the supply of drugs (which were mostly imported from Europe and therefore in short supply thanks to the war). Peasants were to be given small loans in order to help boost milk production, and each province was to receive a pasteurisation facility to process it. Together with the measures envisioned for the CORFO, Allende said that the National Health

---

[37] Speech to the Great Temple of the Chilean Lodge, 14 April 1970.

Plan represented 'the most serious steps yet taken in defence of the human economy, in defence of human capital, that we consider the source of all wealth and the base of all progress.'[38] The legislation was approved, albeit with serious modifications, which changed the substance of the reforms, but it was still a big advance.

Chile's Popular Front government was a direct precursor of the later UP. It was, along with the Spanish Civil War, the experience that all the actors in the later drama looked back upon for lessons. It was one of the major features in the mental maps of subsequent politicians. The parties of the Popular Front had a programme pivoting around economic development. It envisaged the creation of an international nitrates cartel (similar to OPEC, the oil exporters' cartel that Betancourt helped establish in 1960), and the introduction of tariffs to protect domestic industry, as well as progressive tax reform, stronger regulation of working conditions, anti-monopoly legislation, and a programme of home, hospital and school construction. Apart from the healthcare measures described above, the government also sought to introduce political reforms that would revoke anti-socialist legislation. These reforms brought the government immense popular support.

During this period, Allende proposed many other bills that showed his and the PS's interest in gaining sovereignty over Chile's natural resources and improving the lives of Chile's people. One concern was with the poor state of Chile's housing. In 1940, he demonstrated his flair for publicity by organising a National Housing Conference, where he had examples of poor people's huts erected in front of the Union Club, where the Chilean oligarchy met. During the same week, a team of six workers built a decent, fully equipped home right next to them, showing that it was possible to resolve Chile's housing problems.

As was to be expected, the Popular Front's programme provoked serious hostility from vested interests. The conservative

---

[38] ASD, Session 31a, 30 July 1941.

opposition-dominated Congress, and it blocked the passage of legislation, even that of creating the CORFO after the earthquake. It also vetoed the appointment of Communists within government institutions. Outside Congress, Ibañez renewed his habitual conspiratorial activity, as did the newly-pardoned leaders of the Nazi party, now known as the Socialist Popular Vanguard. It was with their backing that General Herrera launched his coup attempt in August 1939.

But the Popular Front's biggest weaknesses were internal. The Radical Party was deeply divided over whether it should cooperate with Socialists and Communists. After the election, one Radical sector immediately said that the alliance had merely been an electoral one. They began to backpedal on the more progressive elements of the Front's development programme. The Communists did little to prevent this in their efforts not to rock the boat for Aguirre Cerda's government.

Within the PS, too, participation in the Popular Front government had been controversial from the beginning. One wing pushed an anti-Communist line that preferred an alliance with the Radicals to one with the Communists. For its left-wing, being in government meant too many compromises. They preferred a 'Socialist front' without the Radicals. Led by César Godoy Urrutia, they became known as the 'non-conformists'. Their views are well captured by this extract from the Socialist Youth newsletter, *Lucha Obrera* (Workers' Struggle):

The class of owners only accept collaboration when they are convinced of the loyalty and servility of those who offer it; it is the 'representation' they concede to the people. This is the representation that the so-called 'Socialist ministers' of the current Popular Front government show off. They are there to serve their masters, and they do it while maintaining the resignation and hope of the workers that they will be able to 'do something'. But the people have seen what they can do:

while Allende has his great housing project, the tenements remain filthy, allowing the easy spread of epidemics.[39]

Allende criticised the non-conformists saying, 'All socialists are probably non-conformists. I am a non-conformist, but my non-conformism doesn't consist of demagogic shouting or personal attacks that lead to division. No. My non-conformism has been displayed in getting the Chilean people to understand the reality of its miserable sanitation while proposing measures to resolve it.'[40] In May 1940, they were expelled from the Party, setting up their own Socialist Workers' Party (*Partido Socialista de Trabajadores*, PST).

In his 21 May speech to Congress, where Chilean presidents traditionally addressed the nation, Aguirre Cerda called for 'patriotic cooperation', but the opposition demanded that in return, he must purge Communists from his government and civil society. In June 1940, the Conservatives called for the PC to be banned, while the Liberals called for a 'centrist coalition' to be formed.[41] These problems led to the weakening of Aguirre Cerda's government, and he was forced to appoint a series of more right-wing ministers, including some leading landowners.

The right was emboldened, and in the run-up to the 1941 elections, it established a National Council to coordinate its activities. This Council established secret armed groups that included members of the National Socialist (Nazi) Party.

Neither was the economic situation favourable. With the beginning of the Second World War, Chile lost access to European production, and prices began to rocket. The United States became the only source of available credit and machinery, forcing the government to alter its National Development Plan to benefit the

---

[39] From *Lucha Obrera* No. 1, June 1940, cited in Amoros, *Allende: La biografía*, p. 89.

[40] Interview in *Ercilla*, 15 May 1940, cited in Amoros, p. 89.

[41] N.M. Lavrov et al., *Ocherki Istorii Chili*, p. 358.

private sector, including US corporations. Nor was the government able to push through land reforms. Prices rose, and real incomes fell throughout the period. Washington insisted that Chile provide it with cheap metals and other raw materials. So, while Chile was forced to buy imports at high prices and invest in light industry instead of heavy industry, it was also forced to sell cheap in the interests of supporting the democratic struggle against fascism.

In this polarised atmosphere, the government called for demonstrations of its supporters, which were particularly massive in the mining regions of the north. Government supporters set up Vigilance Committees and began guarding party and trade union offices. The government also used the police to arrest members of the Nazi Party and other right-wingers. The opposition was scandalised, and in Congress, the Minister of the Interior was accused of violating the constitution in what it called the 'persecution of social activists'.[42] Nevertheless, the scale of the pro-government mobilisation was such that the right was forced to retreat. They soon signed what they called a 'political ceasefire' with the Radical Party, which acted without the knowledge of the Socialists and Communists.

Towards the end of 1940, the PC held a Plenum at which it called for the creation of a Popular Militia to defend the government from future coup attempts. This provoked hysteria among the Conservative opposition, but the Communists organised a 100-thousand-strong demonstration in Santiago that amply demonstrated their level of support. The opposition declared it would boycott the upcoming March 1941 parliamentary elections.

This political instability was exacerbated by problems within the PS. In August 1940, socialist leader Oscar Schnake travelled to the US to negotiate loan conditions and returned in December, pushing for the Communists to be expelled from the Popular Front, going against the will of the majority of the membership.[43]

---

[42] Ibid., p. 357.

[43] Millas, *La alborada democratica en Chile*, p. 207.

This worsened the already serious problems between Socialists and Communists — thanks to the assassination of Trotsky in Mexico earlier that year and the Communist position supporting neutrality in the war. Schnake insisted on his position with the result that the PS left the Popular Front in early January 1941, to be shortly followed by the Radical Party. Allende and the other Socialist ministers offered their resignation to President Aguirre Cerda, but he refused, asking them to remain in their posts in the public interest.

The Popular Front fell apart in the run-up to the March 1941 elections, which led the opposition, sensing victory, to abandon their electoral boycott. Meanwhile, the PC and various left-wing groups presented a joint list of candidates and eventually managed to convince the Radical Party to join a new electoral alliance. The Left campaigned to re-establish the Popular Front, but this time without the PS.

The elections were held in March 1941, and the PS polled 17 per cent of the vote and the PC 12 per cent. Both parties were now undoubtedly major players in Chilean politics. However, the conflict between them sharpened, and just a month after the elections, the Socialist Interior Minister closed the Communist newspaper, *El Siglo*, because of its 'anti-Americanism'. Along with internal debates in the Radical Party, this infighting weakened the government and contributed to the dilution of its economic and social programmes. However, Nazi Germany's surprise attack on the Soviet Union on 22 June 1941 changed the political dynamic at a stroke. The Communists immediately abandoned their policy of neutrality, removing a key bone of contention. The inclusion of the USSR in the war split the right and united the Left to the advantage of the Popular Front. In a sign of the new reality, the Socialist Workers' Party re-joined the Popular Front.

The respite was brief. Pedro Aguirre Cerda died of tuberculosis in November 1941, forcing fresh elections to be held. The PS put forward its own candidate, Oscar Schnake, but he was soundly beaten by Juan Antonio Rios, the candidate of a fresh alliance of Radicals, the PST, and Communists. Although Rios pledged to continue the process of reforms, the PS again fell victim to bitter infighting, officially leaving the government although its ministers, including Allende, remained in post. In power, Rios began to retreat on many issues, and he even began to repress the Left. Shortly afterwards, in February 1942, Salvador Allende resigned from the government. With his Party in crisis, Allende decided to stand for the leadership, competing with his old friend and mentor, Marmaduke Grove, who wanted the Socialists to support the Rios government. In January 1943, Allende was the elected General Secretary of the PS. Grove resigned and formed a breakaway party. The Party was disintegrating under pressure.

Allende was seen as the candidate who could put the PS back on course, popular among the leadership and the membership of the party.[44] In August 1943, he presided over an extraordinary congress that was held in his hometown, Valparaíso. Allende sought to clarify and resolve the Party's internal problems while identifying lessons to be learned from its first experience of government. In his opening speech, Allende described the political situation and then commenced an extraordinary critique of the PS itself, 'Perhaps I do not faithfully interpret the thought of my comrades, I take personal responsibility for this', he began. He accused the Party of failing to understand its past, criticising its lack of political understanding. 'The Party', he said, 'has not been a school by socialists for socialists'; it lacked 'philosophical and social preparation', and the lack of a uniform doctrine meant 'the militants do not separate doctrine from tactics or political line.' This made it extremely difficult to adopt a coherent political line because it was always thought to be in violation of the Party's doctrine. Allende also identified organisational failures and a culture of individualism, gossip, and slander within the Party.

---

[44] Ibid., p. 287.

In the past, we had incorporated the old anarchist principle 'an offence against one is an offence against all', echoing Bakunin's rules for his secret association, which stated, 'Equality of rights for all members, and unconditional and absolute solidarity — one for all and all for one — with the obligation of every single member to help, support and succour each member to the utmost, within what is possible without damaging the association.' Bakunin also demanded 'absolute sincerity'.[45] Yet, now, Allende said, 'insults were the subject of gossip'. Allende also criticised the 'exaggerated internal democracy' that had led to disciplinary chaos. Local and regional leaders were able to distort internal elections and then do what they wanted, even if it violated Party policy. This *caudillismo* needed to be overcome: 'We don't ask or demand respect for the man, but for the role he carries out', Allende remarked.

Allende identified the lack of a programme as the Party's greatest fault saying, 'Our philosophy is Marxism enriched by experience, but we have no programme.' He continued, 'We need to give the Party a uniform, homogenous, and compact orientation.' Such a programme had to take into account that 'tactics change according to reality and this demands that the political line, or the tactics, be changed to fit that reality.' It was a criticism of what he saw as the Party's dogmatism, its inability to agree on the compromises necessary to ensure they could preserve a progressive government. 'This Congress,' Allende continued, 'could be the starting point of a new life. Let's take advantage of our past experiences; let's keep making stark and hard criticisms of ourselves'. The Party had to move from standing together to having a flexible ideological unity that he called 'unity of thought'. Almost as if he knew that his speech would be badly received, he ended by saying, 'Comrade delegates, you will decide'.[46]

---

45   See Bakunin, Letter to Nechayev,
     https://usa.anarchistlibraries.net/library/mikhail-bakunin-letter-to-sergey-
     nechayev
46   Speech to the Valparaíso Extraordinary Congress, 15 August 1943.

Unfortunately, the debate in the PS over whether to support reformist measures was never resolved. The Socialists were never able to rally around a coherent vision of what their political method was — did they want an immediate socialist revolution? If so, then reforms and participation in government were of questionable utility — and even threatened to strengthen the political centre. However, if the struggle was a process, then — as long as they were in line with the long-term goal — elections and other gains could be building blocks contributing towards an eventual victory. This was closer to Allende's vision, which echoed Recabarren's original vision that socialist action in politics should, 'in the creation of laws, Socialists will make every effort to introduce measures that will help to defend the people from bourgeoise rapacity' and as part of this, the movement makes gains that it can build on.[47]

However, Allende did not attempt to formulate a theory for his political vision, at least not beyond his speeches and the example of his political practice. This could be because Allende considered theory 'a cold maze', as he later defined it, or it could be because he felt the theory being developed by his fellow Socialist, Raúl Ampuero, was entirely adequate. This theory left open the issue of 'how' to make the revolution, stating that 'The revolutionary condition of socialism resides in the historical impulse it represents. It does not depend on the means it uses to achieve its ends. [...] It is the objective and subjective conditions that will determine in each country the character of the revolutionary process.'[48] It was a nice way of avoiding a strong commitment, but unfortunately, it also meant that the PS consistently failed to develop a unified position on this, arguably its greatest failure.

Allende did not give up trying to get his comrades to be less dogmatic. In a courageous move, a few months after the Valparaíso congress, Allende organised a demonstration to pay homage to

---

[47] Edited volume, *El pensamiento de Luis Emilio Recabarren*, p. 62.
[48] From the 1947 Programme of the Socialist Party of Chile, which was written by Raúl Ampuero.

the Popular Front government that the Socialists had recently left. Allende emphasised the successful measures undertaken by the Popular Front and claimed them for the PS. In effect, he was trying to make its members understand that while the Popular Front had indeed become a 'left-wing government with a right-wing economic system', it had also fought and won many battles against the elite.[49] Therefore, it could not be disowned or denigrated. Allende praised the Popular Front for beginning a new stage in Chilean history that had brought the Left into power and showed that it could make a real difference to the lives of ordinary people.

In 1943, while Allende was General Secretary of the PS, the leadership of the PC, caught up in the enthusiasm for Browderism, proposed that the two parties should merge in order to unite the parties of the working class. The dissolution of the Comintern in May of that year seemed to eliminate one of the major problems between the two organisations. However, Allende, while agreeing to the idea in principle, had strong reservations. In a meeting between Socialist and Communist leaders, he expressed his strong conviction that both parties had shown that they were deeply rooted in Chile's social reality. Rather than fuse the two parties, he believed that they should simply commit to united action, as Orlando Millas recalled:

… he emphasised this so as to argue that it was realistic to defend the full independence and autonomy of both collectives. Then, he enthusiastically proposed what he emphatically called the Socialist-Communist unity, a new term that became fashionable a decade later. According to Allende, this unity should mean that the parties formulate a joint programme with regard to the other democratic forces and set up liaison committees at the level of the central, mid-level and grassroots organs.[50]

---

[49] Speech in Homage to the Triumph of the Popular Front, October 1943.
[50] Millas, *La alborada democratica en Chile*, p. 288.

In a subsequent official letter to the PCCh leadership, Allende argued that unification had to be the end of a process and not the beginning. There were still many knotty issues of difference.

For example, Allende highlighted that the Second World War had broken the old 'imperialist mould', which made dictatorship unnecessary in the construction of socialism (a criticism of the Communist belief in the need for a 'dictatorship of the proletariat'), and he predicted that there would be new relations between great powers and 'small countries'. The PS also asked the Communists to define their position on the unification of Latin America since, as Allende wrote, 'only a united and firm Latin America will be heard in the future peace.' Then, expressing the views of many in the PS, Allende wrote that 'the Communist Party has proposed the 'National Unity' (alliance with the Radicals) as the solution to Chile's problems. We cannot accept a policy of this type. The great problems of today demand more than ever a clear definition that allows people to have an orientation, to act within its postulates and in accordance with the economic solutions that these determine.' Thus, the two parties continued to have differences too deep to unite, but the PS did 'esteem it convenient that the country knows that Socialists and Communists are ready to join a common electoral struggle.'[51] For Allende, it seemed, the Socialists had to become a little more like the Communists and the Communists a little more like the Socialists.

In 1944, Allende was put forward as a senatorial candidate for the south of Chile, from the Lakes Region down to Tierra del Fuego. Recognising that much of the nearer reaches of the region were dominated by right-wing landowners, he concentrated on the far south, on Tierra del Fuego, where the PS had identified a large working class of shepherds, meat packers as well as port and agricultural labourers. The region also had a history of strong leftist activism that went back to the arrival of Communards fleeing

---

[51] Letter from the Socialist Party Central Committee to the Communist Party, 1 December 1943.

France in the 1870s.[52] Allende travelled the length and breadth of the isolated and undeveloped region, spending much of the time on horseback, reaching out to rural communities. He won the election, and in March 1945, he became one of two PS Senators.

The situation in the Popular Front remained fractious. It was beset by heavy opposition from the right and undermined by the difficult economic situation experienced by the masses. It could not rectify this because its Radical leadership consistently channelled the proclaimed structural reforms away from challenging the basis of elite power. The Popular Front's reforms had reinforced the national industrial elite and had created substantial growth in the working class. The government's international orientation became more aligned with the US demands, and Chile eventually declared war on Germany and Japan. Chile ended the war with a budget surplus that was soon spent on US imports. At the same time, US demand for Chilean raw materials plummeted at the war's end.[53] By 1946, Chile's budget was in deficit by 6.7 billion pesos.

Meanwhile, Allende's party was exhausted by its internal struggles and disputes with the Communists. These struggles also confused the voters. In the March 1945 elections, it polled 12.7 per cent — down from over 17 per cent in 1941. Meanwhile, the PC maintained its showing (despite remaining illegal and having to campaign under another name), gaining over 10 per cent. Shortly after this election and thanks to his unpopular criticisms, Allende was voted off the PS leadership, and he was never again to hold Party office.

The following year, Chile held presidential elections. The social and political situation remained conflictive, with a general strike of more than 300,000 workers in January 1946. The strike was called in protest at the repression of a previous demonstration at which

52 Arrate and Rojas, p. 106.

53 Andrew Barnard, 'Chile' in Leslie Bethell, Ian Roxborough (eds), *Latin America between the Second World War and the Cold War Crisis and Containment, 1944-1948*, (Cambridge: Cambridge University Press, 1993), p. 70.

troops opened fire on demonstrators, killing six and wounding hundreds. The growth of the PC from 10,000 members to 50,000 during the course of the war and the consequent increase in the strength of working-class militancy alarmed the elite.[54] In the run-up to the presidential elections, each party put forward its own candidate, and among the parties of the Popular Front, the internal struggle between left and right was, as usual intense, exacerbated by US interference, which sought to deepen the contradictions between Socialists and Communists.

The PS candidate polled 2.53 per cent. The Communists supported the Radical candidate Gabriel González Videla, who won, promising to implement the programme of political and economic reforms that had been diluted by his predecessors. In the April 1947 municipal elections, the Communists polled nearly 17 per cent — with more voting for Communists standing on a Radical ticket — confirming them as the biggest single political party in Chile. The Socialists remained hostile to the government and to their erstwhile allies. However, while the electoral pact with the Radicals succeeded for the third time, the Communists' faith in González Videla could not take into account changes in the international situation. In Europe, with the Second World War over, the chills of the Cold War began to replace the warmth of wartime cooperation. In Greece, Communist partisans were crushed with US and UK support. In Italy, France, and Belgium, the main concern of the Western allies became preventing Communists from dominating the post-war situation.

In Latin America, under US pressure, Communists became the target of renewed repression in order to 'protect' democracy.[55] In fact, while Videla was promising his commitment to the Popular Front programme and his friendship to the PC, famously stating

---

[54] N.M. Lavrov et al., p. 379.

[55] Before Videla made the Communist Party illegal, his predecessor, president Rios, told his allies that he was coming under heavy international pressure to do so, Arrate and Rojas, p. 245.

that 'there was no human or divine force' that would 'tear him away' from it, he was simultaneously promising US representatives that he would soon ditch them.[56] Videla's nomination of three Communist ministers was met with open hostility by the United States. In his memoirs, Ambassador Bowers wrote euphemistically that 'the reaction abroad was naturally bad and for a few months the effect on his [Videla's] administration was not good.'[57] Bowers' boss in Washington, the copper magnate Spruille Braden, wrote to him after the election to say, 'It would certainly be the better part of discretion for González to take a firm hand in dealing with them [the Communists] as a trouble-making group. I am inclined to suspect that he is a good enough politician to do this.'[58] Meanwhile, Braden ensured that the US starved Videla's government of credits made essential by the difficult economic situation.

Unlike the over-optimistic Communists, Allende and the PS thought that although the Second World War had changed the world, competition between the victors was inevitable. While the war had destroyed fascism and created an alliance between the Anglo-Saxon powers and the USSR, and had forced immense socio-economic changes on the UK and the United States, Allende foresaw that potential Soviet domination of Europe would lead the western Allies to seek to neutralise it by looking to their own areas of domination. In a 1944 speech, Allende argued that for Britain, the situation in Europe meant strengthening the Empire; for the United States, it meant 'seeking the support of its satellites in Latin America'.[59] Latin American support was not just necessary in the new United Nations but also to allow continued cheap access to

[56] US National Archives and Records Administration (NARA), RG59, State, 1945-49, Gabriel González Videla, Box 5358, Telegram to Acheson and Braden, 13 September 1946.

[57] Claude Bowers, *My Life*, (New York: Simon and Schuster, 1962), p. 310.

[58] US National Archives and Records Administration (NARA), RG59, State, 1945-9, Gabriel González Videla, Box 5358, Letter Braden to Bowers, 31 October 1946.

[59] Speech in the Caupolican Theatre, 1944.

vital raw materials. In effect, the nations of Latin America were to provide the materials that financed the Marshall Plan for Europe. Therefore, the renewed repression of the Communists was not entirely surprising. As Guatemala's Democratic president, Juan José Arevalo, later observed the impact of the ensuing violence, the United States had gone from 'an alliance against Hitler alive, to an alliance with Hitler dead.' Across Latin America, 'the anti-Kommunist [sic] breeze became a hurricane.'[60] In Chile, González Videla also changed his tone. In one anti-Communist speech to the women of Valparaíso that the US ambassador described as 'gratifying', he responded to catcalls and jeers by shouting 'in the vehemence of his anger' that he would 'rule by the sword if necessary'.[61] The virulent anti-Communist fears of the Chilean oligarchy were now allied to that of the US government and US corporations. The three would, from now on, fight together to contain what they saw as the Communist menace.

In Chile, the immediate effect was that the Communists began to be pushed out of the government they had helped elect. The three Communist ministers were expelled from the Cabinet, and in September 1948, the Party was proscribed. Its members were erased from the electoral rolls, sacked from government jobs, and its leaders sent to concentration camps in the northern desert. Some high-profile members sought exile — among them was Pablo Neruda — Chile's future Nobel Prize winner. For Salvador Allende and for the Chilean Socialists, it was now time to decide whose side they would stand on. With government and US encouragement, some leading Socialists opposed any alliance with the Communists.[62] Throughout the war, the FBI had collected information on the membership and activities of

---

[60] Juan José Arevalo, *Anti-Kommunism in Latin America*, (New York: Lyle & Stuart, 1963), pp. 77-78.

[61] US NARA, RG59, State, 1945-49, Gabriel González Videla, Box 5398, Confidential Report to James E. Wright, 26 September 1947.

[62] Some of these even joined a paramilitary group known as ACHA (axe) or the Chilean Anti-Communist Alliance which also included far-right elements.

the Chilean Left, particularly the PC. In 1947, it was replaced by the newly established Central Intelligence Agency (CIA), but it continued to sow discord between Socialists and Communists — for example, by funding Socialists in the trade union movement so as to undermine Communist influence.[63] Allende and the Socialist majority that believed in the unity of the working class, were forced to set up a new party called the Popular Socialist Party (*Partido Socialista Popular*, PSP) which was to be the cradle of most of the Socialist leaders of the UP.

There were immense pressures on Chilean Socialists to join the anti-Communist bandwagon, and some did. Socialist parties across the world were breaking the anti-fascist unity of the war years and joining forces with liberals and other conservative forces. Why did most of Chile's Socialists not do this? Why did Allende, a man who felt deeply that democracy was an essential element of humanity's spiritual progress, choose to defend Communists at this most difficult point in time?

Part of the reason was the fact that the two parties had arisen independently, whereas, in many countries, Communist parties had arisen from a split in pre-existing socialist parties. Part of it was due to their pre-war cooperation in the Popular Front, but the Socialists' traditional independence from international groupings, alongside the Party's Marxist philosophy, also helped ensure that at this crucial point, most of them refused to abandon their fellow revolutionaries.

Allende tried to explain his view on this in one of his most important speeches, in opposition to the Videla government's anti-Communist 'Law for the Permanent Defence of Democracy'. This speech lacked the finesse, the turns of phrase of his later orations, but its greatness resided in the way that it laid out the basis of his political thought and connected it to universal themes. It also showed Allende's taste for taking the battle over to his opponents

---

[63] Andrew Barnard in Bethell and Roxborough (eds), p. 86.

— he went through the positions of the other parties one by one and highlighted their hypocrisy.

It was not devoid of hyperbole, either. In a sign of the recently-initiated atomic age, Allende denounced this law as a 'veritable atomic bomb fallen in the midst of our social coexistence'. The reason was that the issue had divided every single political party and had affected their 'ideas, principles and doctrines'. For Allende, that division was an indication of the catastrophic potential of the banning of the PC for Chilean society as a whole.

Allende must have had in mind the recent events in other parts of Latin America. In Bogota, in the midst of the 9th Pan-American Conference[64], the leader of the Colombian Liberal Party, Jorge Eliécer Gaitán, had been assassinated. Gaitán had transformed the Liberal Party into a force for social change and had developed a cooperative relationship with the Colombian PC, and his assassination provoked massive riots (witnessed by Fidel Castro) and began a civil conflict that has yet to end. In Costa Rica, earlier in the year, a Communist-backed government was overthrown in the aftermath of a contested election and a short civil war that killed thousands. The year before, Paraguay had experienced the same. This is why Allende expressed his concerns that the anti-Communist law could provoke 'serious convulsions' in Chile and that the law could, 'tomorrow, easily be applied to us, who are [also] doctrinally Marxists and revolutionaries'. For Allende, the law put Chile's entire political system at risk and was potentially the first step on the slippery slope to dictatorship or chaos.

Allende responded to criticisms of communism's materialist ideology by describing the origins and development of materialist philosophy and its influence on Liberalism. He thus implied that Socialists, Communists, Radicals, Liberals, and Democrats shared

---

[64] This conference re-established the Organisation of American States (OAS) and passed a resolution condemning 'international communism and any other totalitarian doctrine'.

a philosophical ancestry and a concern with democracy.

He explained that while the dominant class sought to give its institutions a 'permanent character', they could not be eternal because they themselves created 'cultural impulses that create revolutionary changes in the structure and functions of society'. In materialist ideology, there were 'no definitive institutions or eternal values', only endless transformation. From this perspective, Allende argued, it was obvious that capitalism was no longer useful to social development. 'The World', he said, 'has entered a period of social revolution'. Capitalism limited both the physical and 'moral life' of humanity. The effort to overcome this, he argued, made socialism 'in essence' humanism.

Allende moved on to describe the PS's differences with the Communists. It is one of the few existing references to the way he saw these differences and is worth discussing. Allende emphasised that the Socialists did not believe in the dictatorship of the proletariat, although they did believe that an 'economic dictatorship' would be necessary during the transition towards socialism. It was arguably ideological salami slicing, but it served his argument that the dictatorship of the proletariat was 'an issue of tactics, of strategy, not one of doctrine' and that Marxism was not a recipe — there were, therefore, differing interpretations.[65]

The greatest differences between the two parties, Allende said, were in the international sphere. While Chile's Socialists were 'deeply interested in what happens in Soviet Russia', this interest did not make them forget their 'critical spirit' and 'it does not make us unconditional supporters of its policies'. He added that

---

[65] The issue was and remains a bone of contention among Marxists since Lenin argued that to be a true socialist one had to recognise both the class struggle and the dictatorship of the proletariat (otherwise one would fall into social democracy). In the nineteenth century 'dictatorship' had different connotations more similar to what would be called a 'state of emergency' today. Marx and Engels in several places wrote about the role of 'dictatorship' or 'despotism' in building socialism, for example, writing in Neue Rheinische Zeitung, Marx stated, 'Every provisional state set up after a revolution requires a dictatorship, and an energetic dictatorship at that'.

for Chile's Socialists, Latin American unity was a more important concern.

Allende discussed the various issues that had separated the two parties at length, perhaps exaggerating when he concluded that 'we can say, without fear of contradiction, that we have been the most tenacious and permanent adversaries.' However, he developed the point in order to argue that 'no-one can accuse us of being "crypto", "philo", or "para" Communists for opposing this law.'

Allende then highlighted that because the socialist idea of revolution was of 'profound and creative transformation', Socialists believed that they could 'loyally, within existing laws', improve the democratic regime and keep making material gains for the people. But this did not imply an uncritical view of Chile's existing democracy. Those who defend capitalism and economic liberalism, he argued, 'ignore that there is no effective liberty if there is no economic base that can guarantee the human being the possibility of their integral development'. 'The majority of our fellow citizens,' he said, 'all those whose only tool for earning a living is their hands and their intelligence, are not free.'

Moreover, Chileans were not free because of economic imperialism — a theme that was to become a constant in his speeches for the next two decades. 'The Honourable Senators rudely attack "Soviet imperialism" and "political imperialism"', Allende said, but were silent on economic imperialism. 'Is that because it doesn't exist?' he asked. 'Are we the owners of our natural resources? Do Chileans own the copper, the nitrates and the iodine?', he asked. Allende then outlined the structure of the global economy, highlighting the way the US Metal Reserve had fixed prices, amounting to a loss of some USD 500 million, for Chile and the way that the US was generally able to buy cheap while Latin America had to buy at elevated prices.[66] 'Is the relationship

---

[66] Nolff, p. 101. About USD 6 billion today.

between powerful countries and poor countries fair?', he asked. He quoted extensively from a recent UN Economic Commission on Latin America and the Caribbean (ECLAC in English, CEPAL in Spanish and Portuguese)), which highlighted the many distortions Latin American economies suffered, such that Allende argued, 'speak to us clearly of the tragedy of the peoples of Latin America.'

Allende then turned to analyse the positions of the various political parties. The Conservatives had forgotten that they, too, had almost been banned in the nineteenth century for being 'sectarian', 'intolerant', and ultramóntane (recognising the authority of the Pope over that of secular governments). Moreover, he argued, some Catholics supported social struggle and justified solidarity strikes by workers. He discussed the emergence of Social-Christianism and said that if this concern with social problems, evolved into concrete actions, then he would be 'at your side in the trade unions, in the schools and factories, in order to struggle for the trampled rights of the vast majority of Chileans.'

Allende then discussed the position of the Radical Party and quoted from his own Radical grandfather's letters, in which Ramón Allende Padín had written, 'the struggle of [political] parties [...] is great and beautiful', whereas sectarianism was 'small-minded and worthy of damnation.' At the same time, Allende reminded them that his grandfather, now a respectable member of the Radical pantheon, had in his own time been condemned for being 'red'.

Allende then moved back to the international sphere to discuss the emerging Cold War. 'The World', he said, 'oscillates between Soviet Russia on the one hand, and North American capitalism on the other'. Chile's Socialists recognised the many advances made in the Soviet Union but rejected its form of political organisation. They also rejected US imperialism. Allende feared for Chile's future. 'Are we slowly accentuating personalist government?' he asked. 'Democracy had a right to defend itself', true, 'but within its own norms and principles'. Any laws to protect it had to be clear and could not generalise or be arbitrarily imposed.

Allende argued that those who sought to proscribe the PC misunderstood democracy, which, 'well understood, is the possibility of rebellion against injustice, the chance of fulfilment, it is a spiritual attitude of constant improvement. Democracy, Mr President, is a conscious result arrived at, through principles, ideas, and doctrines and not with police measures.' It was also perhaps a distant echo of Bakunin, refracted through Allende's adolescent discussions with De Marchi, who had written the following at around the same time that Allende's grandfather was politically active:

> Examine the whole of history, and you will be persuaded that at all times and in all countries, when there has been development and exuberance of life, of thought, of creative and free action, there has been dissension, intellectual and social struggle, the struggle of political parties — and that it is precisely in the midst of these struggles and thanks to them that the nations have been happiest and most powerful in the human sense of that word.[67]

Allende, in his first public expression of his later political practice, then described how, in his view, a democratic transformation would be truly revolutionary. 'He who manages to achieve power temporarily by force is not revolutionary. On the other hand, a governor, who manages to transform society, social coexistence, and the economic basis of the country [after] arriving to power legally, can be revolutionary. That is the sense that we give to the concept of revolution — profound and creative transformation.' For Allende, the socialist revolution was thus something that other political groups could share in, something that also belonged to them.

[67] Bakunin, Letter to Celso Ceretti, March 1872, available at https://www.libertarian-labyrinth.org/bakunin-library/bakunin-on-life-harmony-and-struggle-1872/

In light of his experiences, it may seem bewildering that Allende maintained such a strong faith in Chilean democracy. As is clear from this speech, Allende did not idealise democracy. He saw its limitations. His socialism was a direct result of him having internalised a fundamental critique of the system he had grown up in. In his youth, he had witnessed how this democracy had descended into Ibañez's tyranny. He had been imprisoned and seen the movements of workers, peasants, students and indigenous people crushed with great brutality. He knew the corruption and violence that characterised Chilean elections. He had literally fought hand-to-hand against the armed militias that the elite had established to defend itself during the 1930s. So, why did he maintain this faith even as Videla and others turned their backs on the Popular Front?

This speech shows us that it was because Allende saw democracy as essential to the development of socialism. For Allende, socialism — economic democracy — was the means to achieve a true political democracy that would allow the full physical, spiritual, cultural and intellectual development of every human being. Moreover, as is clear from the extract cited above, for Allende, democracy was a social structure that enabled people and society to strive for continual self-improvement — a sort of political 'jihad' in the sense of the constant struggle for self-perfection. From this perspective, democracy enabled the exercise of true sovereignty over Chile's collective 'self'. Yet, from other speeches from around this time, we can also glean another, more practical reason. Chile was, he repeated, 'a democratic island' in a sea of Latin American dictatorships. By the late 1940s, Allende was talking of Chile being surrounded by 'an international of swords', led by Argentina and the United States.[68] For Allende, the Popular Front government had shown the potential of the 'peaceful road' to socialism because it had created the incipient

---

[68] From a senate speech on 30 August 1949, reproduced in a CIA Information Report on 'Realidad Argentina' from 1 November 1949.

basis for the development he sought for the people of Chile. The Popular Front had shown that Chilean institutions were flexible enough to change their purpose and sustain a process of radical change, and the experience of the political twists and turns of this period formed the reference point Allende later used to navigate the complexities of the UP government. It was a vision to which he held firm for the rest of his life.

In this speech, we can also see why Allende maintained a lifelong commitment to an alliance with the PC. For him, the main difference between the PS and the PCCh was international, yet their sphere of activism was national. They could afford to disagree on the Soviet Union as long as they worked together in Chile. Allende had witnessed the activity of the Communists in the Popular Front; he had engaged with them over the creation of a united party. He had seen how their ministers had pushed through measures such as the creation of a national wheat company and had fought for several foreign-owned railways to be nationalised. They also abolished the system of permits that limited the rights of Chilean citizens to access the property of US mining companies. They had also helped achieve the increased taxation of US companies. In their own ministries, the Communists held admirably transparent fortnightly meetings of all staff where they gave a full account of their activity. They also tried to involve the ministry workers in problem-solving.[69] How far was this different to what Allende wanted for Chile? Their interests and their methods clearly had a lot in common.

This long, and to modern eyes, ungainly speech was historic in that it laid out the basis of Allende's subsequent political thought — democracy as a popular gain that had to be defended and expanded upon socialism, as economic democracy, anti-imperialism and Latin Americanism in foreign policy, all intended to create the opportunity for material and spiritual fulfilment. The

---

[69] N.M. Lavrov et al., *Ocherki Istorii Chili*, pp. 383-384.

method was a broad political alliance with Communists as fellow Marxists, who shared a goal, if not always tactics, but also with other groups who valued democracy and had social concerns.

Despite Allende's arguments, the Law was passed, and the PC was made illegal. The passing of what the Communists called the 'Damned Law' marked the end of the Popular Front governments and the internationalisation of the Cold War logic that would increasingly dominate Chilean politics and society. For Allende, it marked the completion of a process of ideological development, in which he came to envision a peaceful revolution, a 'Chilean road to socialism' in alliance with the PC, as well as the moment that foreign intervention became a fundamental enemy of Chilean independence.

Becoming the Leader of the Left

A reformist change is one which leaves intact the foundations of the power of the ruling class and is merely a concession leaving its power unimpaired. A revolutionary change undermines the foundations of power.

— V.I. Lenin

At the moment of the death of the Popular Front, there came a slight pause in Allende's political life. The PC was banned, the PS divided, and their erstwhile Radical allies in government teamed with the enemy. The unity of the trade union movement was also in tatters. The Left's immediate task was to rebuild unity and their mass movement. It was a task that Allende would contribute greatly to. Freed from the pressures of government, it was also a period when Allende was perhaps more able to devote time to his family and to the development of networks and working habits that would characterise his later years.

Allende was now the father of three daughters — Isabel, Carmen Paz, and Beatriz. He had a small circle of close collaborators, to which a new and important addition arrived in 1950. His name was Miguel Labarca, a fellow student activist of the 1920s who had been in exile in Europe and Argentina since the early 1940s. A fellow freemason, Labarca was an irascible intellectual on whom Allende came to rely for political advice. Upon his return to Chile, Labarca found what he considered a far more developed proletariat and an Allende who had achieved 'full maturity of thought, faith in himself and a definitive aplomb.' Allende was giving a speech at a copper workers' strike, and Labarca heard him speak about the impossibility of social development under capitalism for the peoples of the Third World. 'There is underdevelopment because there is imperialism, and there is imperialism because there is underdevelopment', Allende said. Labarca agreed.

Labarca, according to several contemporaries, was an important influence on Allende during the 1950s and 60s. Ozren Agnic, Allende's secretary at the time, has even written that Labarca was the 'ideologue' behind Allende's speeches, and Labarca has left a memoir where he details many aspects of Allende's political thinking alongside political anecdotes. The two men had a curious relationship, characterised by profound respect, although, as Agnic recalled, also by 'heated discussions and even verbal fights'. These must have been pretty severe because Agnic worried that 'these fights would mean the definitive breakdown of the relationship.' However, a few minutes later, the two 'would carry on talking as if nothing had happened.'[1]

Labarca joined the group of Leftists that worked alongside Allende. Such group work had characterised Allende since the mid-1930s, perhaps, as Diana Veneros argues, a habit picked up from his medical work. Throughout his mature life, Allende gathered groups of Leftists around him, mostly young, politically independent men with a commitment to his vision of the road to socialism. Unafraid of the brilliance of others, each decade furnished him with a new group of collaborators who joined previous generations and assisted him in his research, in his fundraising and with whatever needed doing. Labarca was soon helping Allende improve his oratory by learning from the nineteenth-century British Prime Minister, Benjamin Disraeli, who adapted his tone and style to his audience.

This effort to improve was a constant feature of Allende's life. Back in 1939, when he became the Health Minister, Allende had

---

[1] Ozren Agnic, *Allende: El hombre y el politico: Memorias de un secretario privado*, (Santiago: RIL editores, 2008), p. 44.

sought to learn to control his temper, 'the irresistible compulsion to react with violence to impertinence', which had been a necessary characteristic on the combative streets of the 1930s — an effort he largely succeeded in, possibly by learning to meditate.[2] It was demonstrative of Allende's belief in 'mind over matter', for as he told Osvaldo Puccio, one of his young collaborators, in 1951, 'The body obeys the instructions of the brain, one can order the body to do whatever the brain wants. It is a question of having the will to do so.' This attitude meant Allende was capable of immense hard work, and by the 1950s, Allende was squeezing '30 hours into a 24-hour day', waking early, exercising and waking friends and colleagues with 6 am phone calls.[3] Allende did not neglect the body, exercising daily and reputedly eating an apple a day, which he peeled with a pocketknife, leaving a single coil of peel.

During the early 1950s, Senator Allende had a small office in the Congress building in Central Santiago, equipped with leather armchairs, a desk each for Allende and his secretary and a small table for a typewriter.[4] Like other politicians, Allende had a constant stream of petitioners and visitors, and he eventually had the room divided by a wooden partition screen. Allende requested that the Senate press office send him press cuttings on issues that interested him, and together with his team, he used these to develop ideas and illustrate his speeches. His constant need for data also led him to promote the work of the Library of Congress, eventually enabling it to become one of the most important social science collections in Latin America. The office was in no way secure, but Allende laughed off adopting any security measures, arguing that they would be too much bother and their absence would keep them honest.[5]

An established politician, Allende now lived a comfortable

[2] Orlando Millas, *Memorias: la alborada democratica en Chile en tiempos del frente popular 1932-1947*, (Santiago: CESOC, 1993), p. 206.

[3] Siluetas Latinoamericanas, 'Salvador Allende', p. 17.

[4] Agnic, p. 39.

[5] M. Labarca, p. 114.

middle-class existence with his wife, three daughters and a dog called 'Chagual'. The couple were given a loan, and they bought a small house in Providencia, a well-to-do but accessible area of Santiago. He returned home for lunch most days, usually with guests. During mealtimes, he sought to avoid discussing politics. In the evenings, his collaborators often gathered in his red and gold-carpeted study to work on speeches or proposals. Well-equipped with books and a comfortable sofa and seats, Allende's study was watched over by a large portrait of his grandfather, Ramón Allende Padín and was notable in that it lacked a desk. People wrote with pads or typewriters perched on their laps, or brought in what the Allende's called a 'bridge table'. Work would proceed overseen by the signed photographs of revolutionary leaders and cultural figures from across the world on the shelves of a floor-to-ceiling bookcase on one wall.[6]

However, with the Left and its unions in disarray, money was short. Allende was forced to undertake business ventures that might help finance his political campaigns. One involved bringing US-style milk bars to Chile, and another a factory to make fish powder. Both were quite successful and were later sold off. Allende also bought a small house in the seaside village of Algarrobo, which soon developed into a highly fashionable beach resort. Here, he would often take his daughters and friends sailing in a small dinghy.

In early 1951, with presidential elections looming, the PSP leadership agreed to conversations with Carlos Ibañez, the former dictator, who had been elected senator in 1945 and who was in the process of a 'democratic cleansing' of his name. Allende firmly opposed any alliance with a man he characterised as a kind of fascist and who had brutally repressed the Left during his 1927-1931 dictatorship. Despite his opposition, the PSP continued to work with Ibañez, and Allende resigned from the Party. Shortly

---

[6] Ibid., p. 87.

afterwards, he joined the Socialist Party of Chile. This faction, led by a small group of anti-Communist Socialists, had progressively lost influence since 1947. Allende was undoubtedly a heavyweight political figure in comparison to its leaders, and he soon turned it on its head, allying it with the PC.

Meanwhile, the PC was operating underground, but it still had a national organisation and was capable of backing a nationwide electoral campaign. It was a marriage of both convenience and ideology. For the Communists, Allende was a man who could be trusted with his consistent defence of a strategic alliance with their Party and his eloquent rejection of the 'Damned Law'. For Allende, the Communists represented both an electoral base and an essential component of any revolutionary process, 'they are the party of the working class'; he told Osvaldo Puccio in early 1950, 'whoever wants to form a socialist government without the Communists isn't a Marxist'.[7]

The new alliance was dubbed the People's Front (*Frente del Pueblo*), and Allende became its candidate in November 1951. This was his first presidential campaign. It was under-resourced, and much of the Left's support had been repressed into silence or had leached away to Carlos Ibañez's populist campaign. Volodia Teitelboim, Allende's election secretary, later recalled, 'We felt a feeling of loneliness. The repression had taken its toll. The people were in retreat. The old organisation had been dispersed. We had to start again, and that's what we began.'[8]

With scant financial resources, the campaign consisted of a small group of companions, usually Allende, the aged Communist leader Elías Lafferte and a few others travelling in Allende's personal car, if close enough to Santiago or in a small Cessna piloted by a friend of Allende's, if further away. Standing on

<hr>

[7] Osvaldo Puccio, *Un cuarto de siglo con Allende: recuerdos de su secretario privado*, [Santiago]: Emisión, 1985, p. 24.

[8] Volodia Teitelboim, *Un hombre de edad media*, 2nd ed., (Santiago: Editorial sudamericana, 2000), p. 343.

soapboxes, Allende's comrades would gather a small crowd before Allende addressed them. His speeches, as Miguel Labarca recalled, were didactic and 'not distinguished by brevity'.[9]

We can get a flavour of what these meetings were like from the description of a young witness — Ozren Agnic — the son of Yugoslav immigrants, who later became Allende's personal secretary. Recalling a meeting in the northern city of Antofagasta, Agnic described how the crowd first sang the national anthem with left fists clenched in the air; then, 'The Internationale' and the socialist 'Marseillaise'. After warm-up speeches, Allende rose to speak. 'The man captivated me from his first words,' Agnic wrote. Allende spoke a little about his life, and then, 'He spoke of things I had lived in my own flesh during my time in Chuquicamata [the famous copper mine].'[10] Allende then explained how these socio-economic inequalities were caused by Chile's international situation and how elites acted to protect its interests through the political right. In other speeches, Allende would explain Chile's history and insist that the people had to unite in order to take a leading role in politics. 'It was like listening to a professor give a masterclass', Agnic recalled.

Allende's first campaign lasted 283 days, using the slogan — 'The people to victory with Allende!'. A close atmosphere characterised the campaign. Despite the difficulties and the small crowds, Allende never lost his enthusiasm or sense of humour. He insisted that the speakers had to include irrelevant words or phrases in the midst of their speeches, with failure punished by donation to the campaign fund. Carmen Lazo, a companion on the 1952 campaign trial, also recalled Allende tying knots in the sleeves of her nightdress. 'He would shriek with laughter when I chased him', she remembered.[11] On their car journeys, Allende, while driving at breakneck speed, would share sips of whisky and

[9] M. Labarca, p. 47.
[10] Agnic, p. 28.
[11] Carmen Lazo quoted in Veneros, p. 186.

the travellers would recite poetry and sing songs. The campaign was punctuated by events that underlined the seriousness of their task. On one journey in the north, the car was signalled to halt by a waving torchlight. A woman's voice came out of the darkness, 'we want to speak to Dr Allende'. It was a group of nitrate workers who had been hounded out of their jobs and who had scrabbled together some money for Allende's campaign. On another trip, Allende's group met with undercover trade union leaders, who were being illegally persecuted by bosses in an American-owned mining company. It must have made clear the complete absence of Chilean sovereignty in the foreign-owned enclaves and the tremendous responsibility that Allende had to defend those with no voice.

It was during the 1952 campaign that one of the picaresque episodes of Allende's life occurred. Allende was challenged to a duel by a fellow senator and old schoolfriend, Raúl Rettig. For many years, it was thought the duel was over an insult that took place during a heated parliamentary discussion, but shortly before his death, Rettig explained that it was over a woman — Leonor Benavides — a former adolescent sweetheart of Allende's and his then passion.[12] Allende's comrades were aghast at what they considered his frivolity. His Communist allies despaired at what they considered a 'bourgeois affectation'. Allende responded by saying that he had to act in a society of bourgeois values and that if he allowed an insult to pass, his image would be fatally undermined.[13] Given the cause, this was doubtful, but the duel duly took place at a farm in the Santiago suburb of Macul early on 6 August. The two men took a few steps apart and fired; luckily for them, both shots missed, with Allende claiming that he felt the bullet pass his face.[14] It was a testament to Allende's old-

---

[12] E. Labarca, pp. 79-80.

[13] M. Labarca, p. 54

[14] The duel is described by Jorquera and also Amoros.

fashioned sense of honour and his political nous. In 1952, he was the candidate of a small, underfunded campaign facing an uphill battle. He needed to seize some limelight, and the duel briefly brought him some attention.

The 1952 elections were the first in which Chilean women could vote. Allende's politics had always been marked by a concern for women and children as the most vulnerable sectors of society, and Allende, therefore, formed a women's committee in his campaign. Other committees considered the economy, foreign affairs and Chile's various social problems. In this organisation, Allende was ahead of his time. Nobody had previously sought to examine the full spectrum of problems facing the nation using scientific data and internationally recognised indices. Along with providing him with the information that he needed, over the years, these teams helped to create a corps of social scientists with the knowledge and experience to administer the key sectors of the economy in the future. Allende's campaign was the antithesis of Ibañez's populist simplicity. It mattered little. Ibañez won the elections, and an Ibañista mob attacked Allende's campaign offices. Allende returned to his duties in the Senate. He had polled only 5.6 per cent of the vote, but the campaign had placed Allende on the national stage for the first time. The 1952 elections marked the beginning of the long road to the unity of the Left and marked Allende out as a future contender.

During the early 50s, Allende was heavily involved in pushing for more state control over Chile's US-dominated copper industry. Despite providing 65 per cent of the national income, the industry was in the hands of three US companies. To make matters worse, the State had no expertise in the copper industry or the world copper market. He demanded that the government take action by forcing copper companies to register in Chile and create a National Copper Commission that would authorise imports and exports. Chile would be given a percentage of copper production to sell freely on the market, and the Commission would support studies of production costs and the diversification of the copper industry. Allende protested that the situation was 'a crime against the nation'.[15] Allende was also offended by the way in which US companies were allowed to control parts of Chile as 'sovereign owners', 'where they impose their will despotically and their laws arbitrarily over workers and employees'.[16]

Allende was also indignant that the copper companies could make immense profits while Chile was forced to beg for loans, and he was outraged that nobody in the government appeared to know whether a copper agreement had been signed between the two governments or even whether one had been signed with the copper companies. The confusion belied a cavalier attitude to Chile's main income and was an affront to Chile's national dignity. That the world copper market, and therefore Chile, depended on the whims of six US copper magnates made the situation a 'typical example of imperialism'.[17] Allende therefore, pushed for the creation of a National Copper Corporation that would oversee copper production and that would sell Chilean-produced copper on the world market so that the State would know what costs were involved and would be able to control an important part of the economy effectively.

Chile's experience in the Second World War was an example of this unjust situation. During the war, the Roosevelt administration had fixed the price it would pay for copper (and other strategic materials) through the Metal Reserve, while Chile agreed to sell its entire production to the US. It cost Chile some USD 500 million (over USD 5 billion today). 'Imagine, honourable colleagues, what could have been done with this extraordinary amount,' Allende asked.[18] He also reminded the Senate that after the war, the value

---

[15]　ASD, Session 19a, 16 January 1951.
[16]　ASD, Session 9a, 21 June 1951.
[17]　ASD, Session 19a, 16 January 1951.
[18]　ASD, Session 22a, 7 August 1951.

of Chile's currency reserves had fallen by 25 per cent — thanks to the rise in the price of imports from the US. This could not be allowed to happen again. Allende repeated his demand for a National Copper Corporation.

Radomiro Tomic, a later leader of the Christian Democrat Party, tried to explain why Chile could not do as Allende asked. Tomic admitted that a copper agreement had in fact, been signed with the US government, but another one was still being negotiated with the US copper companies. The agreement with the US government agency had led to an increase in the amount Chile would receive from sales of copper in the US and had allowed Chile to sell 80 thousand tonnes of copper on the global market. Tomic had helped negotiate the agreement, and he explained the situation using the same arguments given by the US negotiators. Tomic explained that the US negotiators did not think an increase beyond that agreed was fair — 'they thought it would produce serious effects on the general structure of prices in the US metal market and would make US rearmament and industrial mobilisation more expensive.' The US side reminded the Chileans that their agency also fixed the prices of US exports to Chile, and 'they didn't wish for US producers or exporters to take advantage of the scarcity caused by the emergency.'[19] Thus, Tomic explained, 'they had an effective economic reprisal within reach.' Here was the brutal reality of the imperialism Allende talked about — the US could increase the price of 60 per cent of Chile's imports, cancelling out any benefit from the increased price of copper. Nor could Chile have got more copper to sell freely on the market. He explained that the US bought 80 per cent of copper and Europe 20 per cent, but that Europe paid for its copper with money provided by the US through the Marshall Plan and that the Marshall Plan's European Administration needed to agree any payments made

---

[19] The emergency being referred to is the National Emergency declared by US President Truman in December 1950, after which he established the Office of Defense Mobilization to coordinate the US economy.

with its money. 'The truth is, Mister Senators, that there aren't many buyers of Chilean copper; there is only one', said Tomic. 'It is,' he said, 'a dangerous illusion to think that we were in conditions to demand that the US accept European prices.'[20]

Allende responded that, in his view, the government had reached, at most, a partial agreement, one that ignored Chile's real needs and one that had not been reached transparently. Allende complained that most Senators showed little interest in the issue. When the copper price was discussed, the Chamber was full, 'but when the drama of Chile is expressed, the lack of policy, when the anguished situation of national dignity is exposed when the conscience of the Senate is hit with the tragedy of the copper workers, then here we feel the cold echo of silence, the absence of those Senators, who for so many years have impassively heard these things. I, Mr President, rebel against this coldness, this hardness, this refusal to learn what the real and essential national problems are.'[21]

Thanks to Allende's work, a Department of Copper was created, which was able to buy copper from US-owned copper companies and then sell it on the global market, diversifying Chile's export destinations. Although this was far short of the nationalisation that Allende sought, it was an improvement, albeit short-lived. With the end of the Korean War, the US released its copper stocks onto the world market, pushing the price down. Chile initially held onto its stocks to avoid pushing the price lower, but these stocks were then discovered to have been 'lent' to the US-owned Anaconda copper company, which promptly sold them on the world market. Prices fell further. Then, in 1955, a new law was passed which gave the copper companies tax breaks and allowed them to take over the sale of copper again. When the Vietnam War began, the US again forced Chile to sell its copper at just over half of its market value.

[20] ASD, Session 9a, 21 June 1951.
[21] Ibid.

Allende denounced the injustice, but nevertheless, Chile, one of the world's poorer countries, in effect, subsidised the US war effort by USD 52 million.[22]

Allende was not just interested in copper's economic potential but also in the fate of the people who worked in the industry. He noted that many workers contracted silicosis and that even as copper was being debated in the Senate, they were engaged in a strike in protest at the arbitrary treatment meted out by the copper companies. The strike had even involved US workers, paid in dollars, who had subsequently been repatriated. If the welfare of the copper workers was poor, it was dire in the rest of the economy. As always, Allende demonstrated a deep concern for ordinary people, and he worked hard to push through healthcare reforms that would benefit them. As a Senator and the Chairman of the Senate's Health Committee (1950-1952), Allende was behind a law that regulated the working conditions of public doctors as well as the bill on the creation of a National Health Service, which amalgamated Chile's existing healthcare bodies. These reforms brought much improvement to the working conditions of Chile's public doctors and made the public health service more efficient. It was still not a comprehensive healthcare system, but it was a step in the right direction.

In 1954, Allende was elected vice-president of the Senate, a testament to the respect that his fellow parliamentarians held him in. In June of that year, Guatemala's progressive government was overthrown, and its president, Jacobo Árbenz, was sent into exile in an event that reverberated around Latin America. The Árbenz government had attempted a land reform that would affect US fruit companies. Allende protested the US intervention in his speeches. He condemned the Tenth Inter-American Conference that had been recently held in Caracas as being designed to

---

[22] Chilean economists later estimated that in total these 'loans' had amounted to over USD 800 million.

attack Guatemala under the pretext of attacking international communism. 'How is it possible that [the US] wants to fool us in front of the entire world by calling the few Democrats there are in the Caribbean 'Communists' while it considers the most abject governments and dictatorships that have flogged and subjugated their peoples with such unusual violence, that they are the disrepute of America, democracies?'

He also condemned the role of the United Fruit Company and its dramatic exploitation of Guatemala and other Central American countries, saying that it was 'indispensable to underline what the imperialist businesses are and how they 'control' the political and economic life of peoples'. This control created dire poverty for the majority of Guatemalans. Guatemala's drama was that of a country that had 'rebelled in dignity in the search for a better destiny'. If in the future, Chile was to take similar measures, it too would 'surely feel over us the threat of foreign arrogance.'[23] For Allende, as for many Latin Americans, Guatemala was an outrage and a clear example of US imperialism. The episode demonstrated US hostility towards any Latin American government seeking greater sovereignty. While some have argued that Allende was naïve in his belief in the 'Chilean road' to socialism, Guatemala clearly showed that Allende knew the risks and considered his strategy strong enough to deal with them. Allende's speeches from the 1940s and 1950s show that he was far from underestimating the challenge posed by US imperialism.

According to Miguel Labarca, Allende's growing success could be measured in the number of people who wrote to him or visited his offices in the Senate. Many were poor people requesting his help in getting medical treatment for themselves or a loved one or some miscarriage of justice that they needed assistance with rectifying. It was a necessary area of work that had to be covered in and around the Senate sessions and other political meetings.

---

[23] ASD, Session 4a, 2 June 1954.

Often the letters were dealt by one of his assistants, who would refer the matter to some contact of Allende's in the relevant field. Sometimes, too, the mentally ill would visit to warn Allende of some conspiracy or complain of some injustice. One former civil servant unveiled a bolas, heavy lead weights attached to lengths of cord a couple of metres long. As he recalled his misfortunes, he began twirling the bolas around his head, forcing Allende to step in. Allende, ducking the weights and swooshing around in the air, approached the man and talked to him in a friendly and understanding tone until the man calmed down and put away the bolas.[24] Not for the first time, Allende's experience of working in Santiago's psychiatric hospital had stood him in good stead.

Shortly after the 1954 election, Allende was invited to join a tour of the Soviet Union, which he did with Tencha, his wife, despite strong criticism from some within the PS who felt that this was tantamount to accepting some sort of bribe. The Chilean delegation spent a month visiting the USSR. Freed from the restrictions of public life in Chile, Allende felt relaxed and enjoyed himself. He was asked to write an article for *Pravda*, which was published in August 1954. He was soon excoriated in the Chilean press as an anti-patriot for having outlined Chile's economic reality to Pravda's Soviet readers — that 83 per cent of Chile's income came from the export of minerals and US companies took 88 per cent of the profits, thanks to bilateral agreements that Chile was forbidden from selling minerals to socialist countries and that 87 per cent of the land was owned by less than 2,000 people.[25] While in the USSR, the Chileans decided to extend their visit to China. The group travelled onwards to Beijing, where they spent another three months. They attended the celebrations of the fifth anniversary of the Chinese Revolution and briefly met Mao Tse Tung and Chou En Lai. Allende, therefore, had the chance to experience something of the world's foremost socialist countries and meet their leaders. The

[24] M. Labarca, p. 78.
[25] Lavretsky, pp. 72-74.

tour was testament to Allende's willingness to take political risks in order to learn from different revolutionary processes and show international solidarity. To his own supporters, this reinforced his revolutionary credentials, strengthened his relationship with the PC and helped to make him far better informed than most other Chilean politicians, which helped him in his political debates and added to his reputation.

Following his return home, Allende plunged himself back into his political work. The Ibañez government was failing to live up to people's expectations, and the economy was suffering from high inflation. Seeking ways to remedy the situation, on the initiative of the owners of the right-wing *El Mercurio* newspaper, the government invited a group of foreign economists to Chile. This team advocated wage freezes, reducing tariff barriers, cutting public spending and encouraging foreign investment — a precursor of the modern neoliberal austerity programme. The measures succeeded in cutting inflation but inflicted significant suffering on ordinary Chileans. The cuts also coincided with a fall in the price of copper. In April 1957, popular protests erupted, and Santiago was rocked by mass rioting. The government declared a state of emergency, but it was the end of Ibañez's political life. The PSP abandoned his government, and in February 1956, it joined the People's Front. The new alliance was dubbed the Popular Action Front (*Frente de Acción Popular*, FRAP), and shortly afterwards, in July 1957, the two socialist parties reunited, recreating the PS of Chile.

Two months later, Salvador Allende was nominated the FRAP's presidential candidate for the 1958 elections in a popular convention that included two thousand delegates from social organisations across the country. The night of his nomination, Allende went to visit his then-lover. He later told Miguel Labarca that, feeling elated by the convention, he had decided to climb over the gate instead of ringing the doorbell. Unfortunately, at the top of the gate, his trousers got caught, and Allende was forced to undo them and take them off before escaping from his predicament. According to Allende, this was complicated by his unstoppable paroxysms of laughter as he imagined being caught by a wandering Carabinero.[26]

The anecdote is from 1958, but it could have been from any year of Allende's life. Labarca recalled that — 'at each twist of his route, Allende needed a woman, fascinated above normal limits' to 'resonate with'. Allende's loves, Labarca argued, cannot be separated from his political career because each woman complemented some aspect of his life, helping him to develop artistic or cultural tastes and new interests and because Allende's affairs helped him to overcome the pressures of an intense life in which he was increasingly targeted by a hostile media. Allende needed to share the drama of his life, and he chose to do so at each stage of his life with different, often married women.[27] However, Allende was not careless of those he seduced by all accounts. Witnesses describe him as an attentive partner, and he was honest in that he made clear he would never leave Tencha, with whom it seems like he had something of an open relationship. He gave himself to his lovers fully for a time, allowing a mutual seduction of minds and hearts. Nor did Allende completely abandon them once the passion had evaporated. Many became or remained friends, and he helped them resolve problems even many years later. As one biographer has noted, they became stars in a 'constellation' that rotated around him throughout his life, staying in touch through letters and birthday flowers.[28] Nevertheless, to modern eyes, this is perhaps Allende's most controversial characteristic and one that betrays him as a man of his time, class and culture.

Allende and the Communists sought to broaden the FRAP coalition further. In 1957, the National Falange (who later became the Christian Democrats) and the Radical Party had allied with

---

[26] M. Labarca, p. 137.

[27] M. Labarca, pp. 133-135.

[28] For a more detailed description of Allende's love life, see E. Labarca, *Allende: Biografia Sentimental.*

the Left to overturn the proscription of the PC, and Allende hoped the alliance could be extended into the presidential elections. However, within the PS, there was significant opposition to this, and the coalition remained more narrowly 'working class'.

The 1958 FRAP campaign was full of hope and enthusiasm. The country seemed ready for change; the Left was united and vibrant, and over the years, people had become increasingly receptive to its message. The PC was legal again, and new regulations made the voting process more transparent. The campaign was funded by numerous concerts and plays, by trade union collections, a percentage of the wages of the FRAP's parliamentarians, workers giving a days' wages and small contributions of businessmen hedging their bets.[29] It was a relatively shoe-string operation, and on one occasion, Allende's car ran out of petrol between Valparaíso and Santiago. In the heat of the day, Allende and his companions pushed the car half a mile to the nearest petrol station. As they sweated and pushed, Allende joked, 'Look what you guys have the future President of Chile doing!'[30]

Allende's campaign was supported by many of the leading left-wing journalists of the day, such as Augusto Olivares, who was later made the editor of National Television; the editor of *El Clarin*, Alberto Gamboa; the radio journalist, Mireya Latorre; José Tohá, who later became Allende's Minister of Interior; Frida Modak and later, the winner of the National Prize for Literature, José Miguel Varas.[31] Yet, despite the backing of journalists of this quality, the campaign had no way of reaching its voters in the more isolated areas of the country. People often had to walk for hours to reach the nearest town. Salomón Corbalán, the PS general secretary, had an idea. The campaign could use its links with the railway workers' trade union to hire and man a train to take Allende's message

---

[29] Puccio, pp. 66-67
[30] Puccio, p. 58
[31] Agnic, p. 43-44.

directly to the people.[32] At the time, trains connected nearly the entire country, and it allowed them to reach towns and villages that would have otherwise remained out of reach. The workers chose to use an old steam locomotive, painted it black and fixed the national coat of arms to the front. The destination was given as Santiago-Puerto Montt-La Moneda.[33]

Allende was accompanied by musicians, artists, intellectuals, and political figures from the FRAP coalition. The campaign developed to the soundtrack of the theme tune from the recent cinema hit 'Bridge Over the River Kwai', which left-wing musicians had adapted to a song supporting Allende. In a time before TV, and when many Chileans did not even have radios, the arrival of the 'Train of Victory' was a real event — a chance to hear popular songs and poetry and to meet the stars of the day. The train stopped at 136 places on the route, up to ten stops a day. At each one, crowds of thousands gathered to listen to Allende.[34] Allende was developing into a popular national figure.

However, having such a profile brought its own challenges. In one village, a peasant woman bent to kiss the hem of his trousers. Allende reacted angrily, lifting her to her feet. Back on the train, he sank his face into his hands and said, '*Compañeros*, I am not a messiah, and I don't want to be. I want to appear before my *pueblo*, before my people, as a political option. I want to be like a bridge towards socialism.' However, as with Monty Python's Brian, it was not up to Allende to determine how ordinary people saw him.

Allende also foresaw a political problem if the people carried unrealistic expectations, 'We can't change this country in a matter of hours. A woman who kisses trousers or tries to kiss one's feet is expecting miracles that I cannot provide because the miracle has to be made by the people.'[35] For Allende, as a Marxist, it

---

[32] Agnic p. 44; Puccio, p. 68.

[33] Palacio de La Monedais Chile's Presidential Palace in central Santiago.

[34] Agnic, p. 45.

[35] Puccio, p. 72; Arrate and Rojas, p. 330.

was mobilised masses of ordinary people that made history, not charismatic leaders, but history has shown time and again that charismatic leaders can and do make history if they can both articulate and channel popular demands. Arguably, in fact, such figures are necessary to successful revolutions.

Allende may not have liked it, but the peasant woman's action demonstrated that he had become a real symbol of hope for many ordinary people who thirsted for change. Like many political leaders before him, Allende had the hopes and aspirations of the downtrodden projected onto him. For them, he *embodied* the hopes of those accustomed to being victims, not protagonists of history. Many peasants asked Allende to be godfather to their children, and others, emulating peasant practice with their landlords, offered him their sisters or daughters. It was a contradiction that Allende wanted to be a hero for the people, and at the same time, he also wanted the people to become the master of their own destiny. It was not a contradiction that affected his growing popularity. The contrast with the poorly attended meetings of 1952 was stark, and confidence boomed through Allende's supporters. The X-shaped graffiti of a V superimposed over an A began to appear across Chile, its message simple and clear even in a society with high rates of illiteracy — Vote for Allende.

The optimism made for a relaxed campaign. A documentary maker filmed the campaign. For one clip, the crew asked Allende to re-enact a speech he had given earlier that day, and the recording would be added later. For the amusement of his collaborators, Allende used the opportunity to swear and curse while making all the right expressions and gestures. The pre-recorded sound was added later, and nobody was wiser until a letter was received from the Director of a deaf school in Valparaíso complaining at the Senator's market-stall-language, despite his 'being a doctor and coming from a good family'.[36]

[36] Jesus Manuel Martinez, *Salvador Allende*, (Santiago: Catalonia, 2009), pp. 236-237.

Allende's companions on the 1958 campaign were astonished at their candidate's energy. He would go from door to door for hours, introducing himself and asking residents if they would listen to what he had to say. Often, a whole family lived in one room, 'filled with the smells of food, cheap perfume and poverty.' Allende felt it was necessary to explain to people face-to-face what leaders like himself proposed.[37] Despite constant activity, speaking at public meetings at least ten times a day and sleeping little, he never seemed to tire. Allende himself found his follower's amazement amusing. He could sleep like Napoleon, he explained; wherever he was, he could relax and sleep for 5 minutes and wake up fresh. Others recall him practising yogic breathing techniques to rest.[38] His collaborators also marvelled at his iron constitution, with Allende rarely succumbing to colds or other ailments. Allende himself used to jokingly recall a poem recited by another Socialist Deputy to explain his energy:

They say that the giant Antaeus used to embrace the ground to gather strength … I am no giant and no Antaeus … but I, as this mythical titan, embrace my people, and from them, I obtain the strength I need to struggle for you and for my *patria*.[39]

Nevertheless, Allende did need to relax, and he did so often by playing chess with whoever was around him at the time. He was a good player and often had to convince his companions to play by sacrificing a piece or two to give them a chance. One exception was Ozren Agnic, who had declined to tell Allende that he had been the national chess champion of the University of Chile. Agnic challenged him to play again, but Allende, who didn't enjoy losing,

[37] Puccio, pp. 108-109.

[38] Luis Corvalán, 'Salvador Allende, Presidente del Pueblo', in *Salvador Allende: Presencia en la ausencia*, ed. Miguel Lawner, Hernan Soto, and Jacobo Schatan (Santiago: LOM, 2008), p. 41.

[39] Agnic, p. 46.

'always avoided the rematch'. When in Santiago, Allende would walk his dog around the neighbourhood, stopping to chat with the local children who played in the street. On occasion, he would join in a game of football and trigger an old injury in his foot, leaving the pitch with a limp. Allende would also read favouring detective novels and science fiction, particularly Isaac Asimov. He wasn't a keen reader of Marxist theory, although he would sometimes 'give one a leaf through'. He read the Bible quite often, perhaps the better to manage the rising challenge of Social Christianism. But Allende's real passion was books on economics, international politics, and current affairs.[40] Allende had a library in a shed at the bottom of the garden where he stored economic reports, particularly CEPAL documents, letters and documents belonging to his father and grandfather and documents and campaign materials.[41]

Frightened by the gathering strength of Allende's campaign, his opponents tried to accuse him of demagoguery. As a provincial youth in the metropolitan Santiago, Allende had cultivated a unique dress sense that had led to him being labelled a 'toff'. He also enjoyed good food, especially traditionally prepared seafood and red wine, but Allende was far from being the frivolous snob that the media portrayed. In one attack, the wealthy right-wing newspaper owners accused Allende of owning a yacht, something clearly beyond the reach of most Chileans. In response, Allende organised for his sailing dinghy to be transported to Santiago, where he had it floated in a fountain on Bulnes Square. That afternoon, a demonstration of 300,000 people assembled in the square to hear him speak, and he pointed out his floating 'yacht'. As with Allende's housing exhibition outside the Union Club in 1938, the evidence before people's eyes spoke more than a thousand words.

Nevertheless, Allende's opponents tried to make it stick. During his electoral tour of the provinces of Malleco and Cautín, Allende

---

[40] Puccio, p. 121.
[41] See M. Labarca, pp. 84-86 and Agnic, pp. 67-68.

was giving an evening speech in some small village, which, like most Chilean villages, had no electricity. The crowd stood listening in the dark as Allende spoke through a megaphone. Allende was underlining his honest behaviour when someone in the crowd shouted out, 'What about your yacht?!' Allende was infuriated. 'Who said that?!' he demanded to know. The crowd parted and left a smartly dressed man standing alone. Allende jumped down from the wooden podium and rapidly closed on him. 'Say it to my face, if you are man enough.' The man apologised. Allende returned to the podium and finished his speech, highlighting the negative propaganda that was spread about him and the way that it influenced people's views.[42]

Despite Allende's efforts, many people still distrusted politicians. Standing behind a thin wooden partition wall, Allende and Carlos Jorquera, one of Allende's collaborators and later press secretary, overheard a conversation between two peasants after a stop on the 'Train of Victory'. One of the peasants doubted that Allende would fulfil his promises. After some debate, the two made a deal: they would vote for Allende and work towards his victory, but if he betrayed them, they would travel to Santiago and kill him 'so that nobody ever laughs at us peasants again.' Allende initially wanted to interrupt the two men but thought the better of it. He, however, swore to Jorquera, 'these *compañeros* won't need to go to Santiago to kill me … you know why? Because I really will honour my word to them. I'd rather the right kills me for honouring my word to the peasants than that they consider me a traitor.'[43] It was one of the many encounters with the people of Chile that shaped Allende's political commitment. From the hilltop shacks of Valparaíso's port workers to the shepherd's huts of Tierra del Fuego, Allende knew how Chileans lived. He drank their tea and maté, slept on their straw mattresses and was sometimes bitten by

---

[42] Agnic, p. 118.
[43] Jorquera, p. 32.

their fleas. He also remembered how they often died — starved, abused, addicted or broken. He knew the gap tooth grins of those aged by hard lives, the limping gaits and the acrid smell of poverty, but he did not flinch from them. He may have been middle class, but there was no sense of separation between himself and these 'others'. The *frapista pueblo* sensed this, and they loved him for it.

While the Left was united around Allende's candidacy, the right united behind Jorge Alessandri. Two centrist candidates, Allende's friend Eduardo Frei, who stood for the newly formed Christian Democrats and a Radical candidate, were also in contention. A final candidate joined the fray in the last weeks of the campaign, Antonio Zamorano — the 'priest of Catapilco'— whom many suspected of having his campaign financed by the right.[44] He would have a profound impact on the election results. The first two official counts gave Allende a narrow victory. However, the news coming from the voting tables changed. While Allende was winning on the men's tables, women were voting for Alessandri.[45] At 11.30 pm, Allende headed home, where a small group of his comrades gathered to wait for the official result. The third official count also gave Allende victory, but some radio stations picked up on Alessandri winning on women's tables by a margin strong enough to give him victory. The Ministry of Interior, which usually kept the nation informed, maintained a strange silence.

The reason for the silence became clear at 1 am when the doorbell rang at Allende's Providencia home. Ozren Agnic, Allende's assistant, went to answer the door. Five senior military officers stood in the doorway. The officers explained that they had a personal message for Allende from the President, General Carlos

[44] Despite campaigning as a Leftist, Zamorano disappeared from politics until he was found supporting Pinochet's 'yes' campaign during the 1988 referendum, Agnic, p. 53.

[45] In Chile, voters are registered to vote at particular numbered 'tables' within the polling station. Men and women vote at different tables. The votes are counted up and declared at each table, allowing a relatively accurate ongoing tally of votes.

Ibañez. Allende and Agnic listened as the officers told Allende that President Ibañez was holding back the final result to give Allende time to consider the offer of the Presidency 'in the interests of the nation' — in other words, Ibañez was proposing to subvert the election result. Allende replied with contained anger, 'General, I have never heard such stupidity and monstrosity. I am extremely surprised that a General of the Republic should lend himself to be the messenger of this infamous manoeuvre.' 'Go back to where you came from and tell Mr Ibañez that I will be the first person to respect the verdict of the ballot boxes, as I will be the first to fight any seditious attempt in Chile.'[46] Allende's distrust of Ibañez was well founded, and his commitment to democracy total. Moreover, if he had taken up the offer, he would have been beholden to Ibañez as well as the legitimacy of Allende's government and the Left as a whole would have been mortgaged to his political whims. It would have seemed an unnecessary risk to take at a time when the popular movement was surging.

When the results came in, it became clear that Alessandri had won by a scant 33,000 votes. Zamorano received just over 41,000. Allende missed out on the Presidency by 3 per cent. With such a close margin, Allende's relatively poorer showing amongst women had been key and in a 1970 interview, Allende wryly commented that in 1958 he had been 'defeated by the women'.

In the same 1970 interview, Allende indicated the contradiction that existed in his attitudes towards women. When asked about whether absolute equality between men and women was desirable, Allende answered 'a complete and absolute equality, with a complete and absolute difference', which indicates his understanding that power, that society, should consider men and women as equals, but treat and remedy the inequalities between them. It should be noted that his government was the first opportunity the Left had to try to put its ideas into practice, and it did so according to this

---

[46] This episode is recounted by Agnic, pp. 59-62 and M. Labarca, p. 67. Allende swore them to secrecy and it only came to light in 2008.

framework. In response to a question as to what kind of president Chilean women wanted, Allende responded, 'clearly defined, virile, but at the same time, understanding, gentle and empathetic (*sentido humano*)', a response that clearly shows how he saw himself at the time. Then, in a subsequent suggestive question about which contemporary women he would like to dine with, Allende answered, 'None. After dinner, with many. I'm discrete; I won't name names.' Who was this answer aimed at? Perhaps it is a provocative answer to an impertinent question. Perhaps it is a demonstration of machismo and Allende's understanding of 'virility'.

Despite recognising gender equality and the need for a distinct status for women, Allende seems to have understood that Chilean women wanted a president as some kind of idealised partner, yet at the same time, he was known for his womanising. Although this reputation probably won him some admiration among male voters, it may well have alienated women across Chile who often suffered emotionally and materially from men's infidelity. Yet, womanising was a common feature of Chilean male society and the extent to which it alienated women is hard to know. The effect was perhaps, as his lover Gloria Gaitán told him, that 'you address us, you praise us, but you don't interpret us'.[47]

Allende's was not the feminism of the twenty-first century, but the question is not whether Allende displayed contradictory attitudes towards women, for he was, like we are today, a product of his times and, inevitably, in capitalism, of a strongly patriarchal society. The political question is how his attitude differed from that of the dominant elite, whether he treated women as equals, whether his project aimed at emancipating and including them in decision-making, to provide them with the organisations to express their needs and gave them a leading role in the revolution he envisaged. One of Allende's personal secretaries has noted that 'Allende was a

---

[47] Gaitán , p. 16.

feminist for his time. He had immense respect for all of us [women collaborators]; furthermore, Allende named women as ministers, and in 1972, he created the National Women's Secretariat, which he tried to transform into a Ministry just before the coup.[48] In fact, the UP saw the highest number of women in parliament in Chilean history. Yes, Allende could be criticised for seeing women as mothers, but he also saw them as workers, as the equals of men, and he did not want them to remain mere housewives.

In a society where the middle and upper classes all employed *nanas* to look after children and do much of the cooking and housework and where the politicisation of women's issues had not yet become a widespread phenomenon, the importance of a distinct feminist debate was still limited. Furthermore, in a society where the working class and, especially, peasant women, were the *nanas*, the issue of domestic drudgery inevitably took on class characteristics. Allende's constant emphasis on improving material and social conditions for women as workers and as mothers, and particularly in getting them involved in politics, is a testament that for him, the economic and social emancipation of women was a key part of the revolution, not a separate and contradictory struggle.

Since Allende was well known for pushing legislation that favoured women and children, it seems probable that Chile's very social structure affected Allende's ability to reach women voters in 1958 and into the 1960s. In the late 50s, women were far less likely to work outside the home, live-in *nanas* were dominated by their employers, and women's social networks were, in turn, more likely to be dominated by the neighbourhood and the church. As the social movements of Christian Democracy developed through the 1960s, women found spaces there, too. Allende consistently asked his supporters to convert their wives and girlfriends to the cause, but the issue of Allende's female vote was not properly

---

[48] Patrica Espejo, '*Allende Inedito*', Kindle Edition, (Santiago: Random House, 2020), p. 48.

resolved until the 1970 campaign when the UP began to organise community-based committees that could reach women in their homes.

Many of Allende's supporters also suspected that in 1958, the various forms of vote buying used by the right had also played their part, and some were willing to question the results officially. Nonetheless, Allende's commitment to democracy, even a highly imperfect democracy, was total. It also showed that for Allende, the path to socialism mattered as much as socialism itself. The means determined the end. In Allende's view, if democracy was to be preserved in the socialist future, it had to be cherished in the capitalist present.

Whatever the causes of defeat in 1958, it is interesting to consider what might have happened had Allende taken up Ibañez's offer, given what happened in Chile later. Yes, Allende would have been beholden to Ibañez to a degree. Still, he would have enjoyed the immense advantage of beginning the transformation of Chile before the US had really had the opportunity to influence the social and political situation, before it had built up the training programmes for the Chilean military, before the construction of Christian Democrat social movements and above all, before the polarising impact of the Sino-Soviet split and the Cuban revolution. He would have been able to offer the nascent Christian Democracy a role in government, potentially harnessing them to the project for change. The divisions within the Left over the method of achieving the revolution would have been much reduced. Of course, the FRAP would eventually have had to confront US imperialism, but arguably on much better terms since the regime-change machinery would have been less developed than in the 1970s. Could not Allende, with his notorious political skill and understanding of Chilean institutions, have managed the risks that taking up Ibañez's offer entailed? Was this a lost opportunity? We will never know, but the decision taken shows Allende's profound and utterly inflexible commitment to democracy, no matter how limited and disfigured.

The 1958 campaign was a harsh defeat for the Chilean Left, but paradoxically, it was also a great victory. For the first time, the Left had been within touching distance of victory in a coalition of its own. The Left's message had reached the entire country, and Allende was now a truly national figure and the standard bearer of the Left's unity.

The Chilean Left and the Paths to Revolution

> Better take
> A state
> Intact
> Than destroy it.
> — Sun Tzu

> If you crave speed, then you will never arrive...
> — Confucius

Shortly after Allende's defeat in the 1958 elections, thousands of miles to the north, an anti-dictatorial rebellion matured into an outright revolution. On 1 January 1959, the Cuban Rebel Army entered Havana, overthrowing the Batista dictatorship. While initially, the revolution's political direction was unclear, it soon became apparent that its leaders were aspiring to build socialism. The revolution and its growing conflict with the US-inspired a generation of Latin Americans anxious for social change and brought the Cold War straight into 'America's backyard'. In the US, the revolution sparked fears that other countries might follow, and it thus defined US policy towards Latin America for a generation. In Chile, the revolution was to prove both an inspiration and a challenge for Allende and the Left in general.

The Cuban revolution overshadowed Venezuela's return to

democracy at the end of 1958, where elections brought Allende's old friend and Santiago neighbour, Rómulo Betancourt, to power. Allende was invited to Betancourt's inauguration in Caracas alongside fellow Chilean politician Eduardo Frei. While in Venezuela, Allende decided to visit Cuba to see what was happen ing for himself. Allende's first impressions were not favourable. From his hotel window, Allende saw the Miami and Havana police bands marching, preceded by young women doing gymnastics. Allende was leaving the city when he bumped into Carlos Rafael Rodríguez, the leader of the Cuban Communist Party, who asked him what he was doing in Cuba. Allende told him, 'I came to see the Revolution, but since there is no such revolution, I'm going.' Rodriquez told him not to be taken in by appearances and arranged for him to meet the revolution's leaders.

Che Guevara soon sent a car, and Allende met him in the eighteenth-century *La Cabaña* fortress above Havana harbour. In a room lined with books, Guevara lay on a camp bed, inhaler in hand, recovering from an asthma attack. 'Come in *compañero*, you're a medic, and you understand. Wait a minute, and we can talk', he said.[1] They then had a discussion about the situation in Latin America and the differences between the situations in Chile and Cuba.[2] Allende was then taken to meet Raúl Castro, complete with plaited hair, who took him to see Fidel, who was presiding over a cabinet meeting. Allende was surprised by the informality of the set up. Fidel spoke, standing up, 'There were peasants playing chess and cards, lying on the floor, machine guns and all' — a situation far removed from the parliamentary politics Allende was used to.[3] The two men had a discussion that laid the basis for a personal friendship that was to last until Allende's death. Castro wanted to know what Allende's position on the PC was and was satisfied to hear that he considered them his allies.

[1] Gaitán, p. 11.
[2] Agnic, p. 71; ASD, Session 7a, 18 October 1967.
[3] Debray, p. 73.

They discussed the situation in Chile and the region, and although Allende disagreed 'fundamentally and violently' with some of the Cuban leader's positions, there was an overall understanding between them. A few months later, at the July 26 celebration of the revolution, before introducing Allende to Gloria Gaitán, who was standing alongside, Fidel said, 'I know the man that will make the next revolution in Latin America.'[4] Years later, she travelled to Chile, where she and Allende began a relationship, and she witnessed the last months of his government.

Allende returned to Chile shortly after this first visit to Cuba, with his enthusiasm renewed. His early and direct contact with the revolution gave him a clear idea of where it was going, what the likely US response would be and, therefore, what its impact would be upon Latin America and Chile. Later, when his own road to socialism began to be criticised as 'reformist', the contacts Allende had made in Cuba would be vital in shoring up his revolutionary credentials.

Following his return to Chile in late 1959, Allende set up the Popular Institute, which was meant to act as a think tank for the Left and which managed to bring together a variety of left-wing social scientists to investigate Chile's social and economic reality and provide data and proposals. The Institute was the latest in a long line of efforts by Allende to systematise the data available to him and the Left in general, partly in order to train left-wing social scientists in the real details of national problems and partly so as to provide the basis for future policies. Allende also hoped that the Institute might serve to provide a space for discussion and debate for left-wing activists in order to foster a broader identity and plant the seed of a FRAP movement. Once more, it was largely his own party that let him down. The Socialists feared that the Communists would soon take over any new organisation, funding for the Institute soon dried up, and although it helped to train

[4] The daughter of the Colombian presidential candidate, assassinated in 1948, Gaitán, p. 9.

some specialists who later served the UP, it was unable to foster a broader left-wing identity.

Meanwhile, the radicalising effects of the Cuban revolution reached Chile. Washington's efforts to 'contain' communism in Latin America had a new urgency. In March 1960, Eisenhower gave the nod to the development of an invasion force of Cuban exiles in an action reminiscent of the overthrow of Árbenz in Guatemala. In May 1960, the Cubans established diplomatic relations with the USSR, and in August, the US responded with the Declaration of San José, which obliquely threatened Cuba. In April 1961, under Kennedy, US-backed exiles invaded Cuba and were defeated. Castro declared the revolution to be socialist and nationalised US companies in Cuba. In Chile, the Left was invigorated by the revolution and membership of its parties surged. The right responded with fear. The class struggle evoked class solidarities across the region, and Allende once again nailed his colours to the mast of the underdog.

In the Senate, Allende declared the Cuban revolution to be the next stage in Latin America's struggle for full sovereignty. Revolutions in Mexico (1910) and Bolivia (1952) had shown the way in their times, but the Cuban revolution was destined to better them. He underlined the revolution's legitimacy while highlighting that while the goals of the revolution in Chile were similar, 'We have repeatedly expressed that with differing strategy and tactics, such a process ought to flower in the various countries of Latin America, in order to end the stage of political vassalage, economic exploitation, the anguish, the hunger and the misery of thousands …'. In Cuba, Allende said he had witnessed a people spiritually and materially mobilised and fully interpreted by their government. He underlined that he had seen nothing like this in Moscow, Beijing, or the US. He also condemned the media campaign demonising the revolution saying, 'It seems unnecessary to me to underline how UPI, AP, and the information agencies controlled by the North American capital have deformed and continue to deform what has happened in Cuba. This kind of information is only comparable to the kind that existed when that great international robbery was perpetrated years ago against Guatemala.'[5] Not only did this media campaign distort what was happening in Cuba, but it also began to change the political environment in Chile and the rest of Latin America. Uncle Sam's baleful glare turned on the region, and nobody could escape its effects.

In 1960, three days after the Cubans celebrated the 26 of July and announced the nationalisation of US companies on the island, Allende and other senators denounced an 'organised and planned' slanderous media campaign against them in a Mayoral election in San Miguel. The aggressive tone of this campaign became characteristic. The FRAP leadership was accused of corruption and even murder. Allende responded with a harsh denunciation of the coordinated campaign by the media and government. The way victory was won foreshadowed the victory of the UP in 1970. In San Miguel, Communists had developed a 'popular university' which, together with the hard work of FRAP councillors, had mobilised the population. However, the new timbre of the attacks against the Left forced Allende's tone to change too. While he had never idealised Chile's democracy, he had always honoured it. Now, 'the unmeasured use of public power' in the service of an unworthy cause had further disfigured 'the putrefied channel of a democracy' that had already been warped by vote-buying.[6] While Allende always retained his faith in the possibility of a revolution that would overflow that 'putrefied channel', others would soon begin to question the wisdom of playing the democratic game. They would cause Allende more than one headache in the future.

The first electoral campaign after the Cuban revolution took place in March 1961. To the horror of Allende's team of supporters, he accepted the PS Central Committee's nomination for the

[5] ASD, Session 32a, 24 July 1960.
[6] ASD, Session 24, 10 August 1960.

constituency of Valparaíso and Aconcagua. The socialist vote was negligible in the region, and the other parties all had good candidates. However, Allende was thinking one step ahead. If he was able to win, his chances of being the presidential candidate in the 1964 elections would be strengthened. This was not just optimism: the FRAP's showing on women's tables had much improved in the municipal elections, and in the 1958 presidential campaign, he had developed a strong support base in the peasantry. If they worked hard enough, Allende was sure that they would be able to win over the peasants in Aconcagua. Over the objections of his team, Allende asked them to prepare a new campaign by convincing friends and collaborators to donate money, hold fundraising dinners or provide useful equipment.

Key to the success of the campaign was the 'Victory Bus', a large if rickety bus hired from an Allende supporter. A generator, a large canvas screen, a film projector, and a sound system were mounted on it. Wherever the bus went, it took a small team of painters and local singers and the bus was fitted with a portable stage on the roof. Inside, it carried beds for the team, paints and printing materials. Like the 1958 train, it was a mobile campaign centre. The bus would be driven around a selected area, loudspeakers advertising the evening's event, then the bus would make a stop, and the projector, screen, generator and stage would be set up. Short cartoons would be shown, followed by a longer political film. The crowd would be asked to bring newspapers that would then have Allende's image printed on them, and the people would then paste them up in public places. Teams of painters would go out to paint rocks and walls with pro-Allende slogans. Often, they would be arrested by police or beaten up by thugs hired by landowners — guards at one landowner's gates shot up the bus itself. The problem was particularly bad in rural areas. Peasants still lived in nineteenth-century conditions and were often illiterate. Laws were seldom applied, and children rarely went to school. People lived without electricity or clean drinking water and subsisted in terrible poverty. Landowners even forced *droit du seigneur* upon the daughters of their workers.[7] In such conditions, it was not easy to exercise the right to a free vote. Despite these difficulties, Allende's campaign was a great success, and he won his senatorial seat with enough votes for the two other FRAP candidates to get seats.[8] It amply demonstrated that Allende's appeal went beyond the parties of the Left, and it was the miracle he needed to set himself up for 1964.

While Allende was winning yet another electoral battle, events in Latin America and the world were creating new difficulties for the Left. The Cuban revolution and the guerrilla groups it inspired exacerbated fears of revolutionary change, leading Latin American elites to welcome US counter-revolutionary initiatives. Alongside a counter-revolutionary campaign against Cuba, the US launched an economic and diplomatic offensive to isolate Cuba. Then, in 1961, Kennedy proposed a set of economic, political and military measures to the rest of Latin America, an 'Alliance for Progress', ostensibly to tackle the socio-economic roots of revolution by seeding economic growth. At the same time, the US moved to transform and extend training programmes for Latin American militaries.

Intelligence agencies were set up or improved. The training was guided by a doctrine that emphasised an international Communist threat through subversion, shifting the focus of Latin American militaries from external to internal threats. Soon, the Latin Americans began to develop and adapt this doctrine, spawning a virulent right-wing ideology that built on earlier anti-Communist and conservative ideas. When the promised economic growth failed to materialise, the legacy of the Alliance was over-

---

[7] Agnic, p. 97.

[8] The Chilean electoral system used the D'Hondt method. Allende's vote was enough to get himself elected but also contributed enough votes to the FRAP total to ensure the election of the Communist candidate.

muscled and paranoid militaries with close links to the US defence establishment. It was no coincidence that country after country fell to right-wing dictatorships during the 1960s.

In Chile, this regional process of change had a series of repercussions. The first was the beginning of direct and sustained US interference in Chilean politics and the expansion of US military-ideological training for the military. The former was heavily based on the modernization theories espoused by scholars such as Walt Rostow, which assumed that Latin American societies needed help modernising (westernising) socially as well as economically. This modernisation would, in turn, prevent revolutionary change. The interference in Chilean politics took many forms, one of which was material support for the creation of 'social movements' linked to the Christian Democrats. The emphasis on these was new, a product of European and US scholarly analysis of unrest in the West during the 1950s and early 1960s. The new social movements supported by the US were, in essence, those that disconnected their demands from any structural change, from a coherent and holistic revolutionary worldview.[9] This is why they created a direct challenge to the 'social movement' of the Left in Chile, which had since their foundation fought to integrate the demands of the many groups across society, including women, *campesinos*, and the indigenous, into political programmes for the transformation of Chile. The result of the new 'social movements' was to limit the growth potential of the Chilean Left, at least while the kind words and good intentions of the new movements remained untested.

The expansion of military-ideological training for the Chilean military led the Chilean army to set up an intelligence branch as well as the sustained growth in the number of officers being sent

---

[9] The focus on social movements has continued today. It has become a label that creates an arbitrary division between the political and the social world. The term, as used in Chile, today reflects an anarchistic deification of the 'grassroots' and overt hostility to hierarchy and structure, where the ideal social movements are held up to be non-hierarchical, democratic and fluid, supposedly the opposite of political movements or parties.

for training to the US and to US bases in Panama. US military aid also enabled growth in the capacity of armed forces across the region. For example, in Chile, the armed forces grew in size from just under 37 thousand men in 1960 to 70 thousand in 1970.[10] The number of Chilean officers trained by the US was second only to Brazil, with almost 200 of them being trained each year.[11] The US also provided a Military Assistance Advisory Group (MAAG), which took up residence in the Ministry of Defence and Mobile Training Teams that trained troops in Chile. The officers trained by the US, in turn, taught others back in Chile. Through the 1960s, this training, alongside the increased resources available to them, began to transform the mentality of the Chilean officer class, marrying a militant anti-communism to its traditional conservatism. It was a venomous cocktail that played an immense role in the later overthrow of Allende.

The second major repercussion was the radicalisation of some sectors of the Chilean Left inspired by the Cuban Revolution. Castro's Second Declaration of Havana in February 1962 was, for many, a call to arms: 'In many countries throughout Latin America, revolution is today inevitable. [...] what does the Cuban Revolution teach? That revolution is possible, that the people can make it, that in the contemporary world, there are no forces capable of halting the peoples' liberation movement ... The duty of every revolutionary is to make the revolution.'[12] To those who saw revolution as an armed triumph, this seemed to contradict the gradual, more evolutionary position of the traditional Chilean Left embodied by Allende. The effects of the Cuban Revolution were compounded by the Sino-Soviet split and Chinese accusations of Soviet capitulation to imperialism because of the policy of peaceful coexistence. The polarisation of politics challenged the traditional

---

[10]   Brian Loveman, *For la Patria*, (Delaware: Scholarly Resources, 1999), p. 183.
[11]   Veronica Valdivia Ortiz de Zarate, *El golpe despues del golpe*, (Santiago: LOM, 2003), p. 28.
[12]   Castro Second Declaration of Havana, 4 February 1962.

parties of the Latin American Left from within, and in Chile, it resulted in the creation of an organisation that embodied the new revolutionary impatience, the Revolutionary Left Movement (*Movimiento de Izquierda Revolucionaria*, MIR).

This created an important problem for those like Allende, who believed in a 'peaceful road' to socialism in Chile. At an individual level, Allende was largely able to neutralise this challenge through his development of close relations with the leaders of the Cuban revolution, including Ernesto 'Che' Guevara, as well as his visits through the decade to Vietnam and other socialist and non-aligned countries. But at this stage, Allende did not attempt much of a theoretical defence of the 'peaceful road' in general. This he largely left to Raúl Ampuero (from the PS) and the PC.

Raúl Ampuero had been developing the unique Marxist theory of the Chilean Socialist Party since the late 1940s, one which successfully marked out an independent path that was similar to that of the PCCh in many general ways but which differed from it in some key areas. Under Ampuero's direction, the Party expressed its scepticism of the Chilean bourgeoisie's capacity to act as a catalyst of progress and, therefore, of the possibility of the 'bourgeoise democratic revolution' pursued by the PC. Nevertheless, this was largely an issue of alliances because Ampuero's theory still saw the electoral and trade union struggles as being essential in the social process leading to revolution. In his 1961 speech — 'Reflections on the Revolution and on Socialism' — Ampuero noted that in Latin America, the material conditions made for a revolutionary situation that 'tended to challenge the legal order' and that socialists had to play a role in the violent contradictions that this created or become irrelevant. However, while he admitted the importance of violence, it is clear that Ampuero did not limit the concept to the taking up of arms.

Ampuero highlighted that many social processes, such as the 1952 revolution in Bolivia, had passed through a democratic or electoral phase but that the structural issues had forced a violent resolution to the crisis. Yet, he emphasised the social nature of these victories and criticised those who saw the revolution 'as an exaltation of individual violence' or as 'a mere explosion of revolutionary anxiety'. Ampuero underlined that even the Cuban revolution had been a long social process and that Castro's Sierra Maestra campaign had 'brilliantly crowned' what was, after all, 'a heroic social cause'. For Ampuero, as for many other Leftists, violence had a broad definition that could include forms of social or political action. This did not preclude electoral activism, which in view of the Latin American context, acquired 'much more substantive, profound and transcendental' importance than in other regions. Ampuero, therefore, built the theoretical foundations within the PS for Allende's 'Chilean road to socialism'. Nevertheless, Ampuero also noted that Chile's socialists needed to overcome a theoretical vacuum around what their policy of the Workers' Front meant in relation to the forms of struggle, and he argued that they had to undertake a serious study of the role of violence in the Chilean process, a role that seemed 'unavoidable.'[13]

It was this conclusion that proved the Party's ideological Achilles heel, for the admission of the inevitability of a violent resolution, when combined with the ideological diversity of the Party's membership, the lack of precision over the definition of violence and the failure to impose a doctrine upon its members Left the Party exposed to what he called 'the victims of infantilism' as the decade wore on, eventually leading to his own expulsion in 1967.[14]

Meanwhile, the Communist response came in the wake of the Sino-Soviet split and within the framework ('that we have contributed to developing') elaborated by the international movement of Communist parties, which underlined the potential

---

[13] Raúl Ampuero, *Reflexiones sobre la revolución y el socialismo*, Revista Arauco, No. 18, July 1961.

[14] *Ampuero Ahora: 50 preguntas y 50 respuestas de la actualidad*, (Santiago: Prensa Latinoamericana, 1968), p. 11.

of the 'peaceful road' to socialism.[15] The Communist defence of the 'peaceful road' was, therefore, not just a defence of their national policy but also a defence of the international Communist movement and the Soviet Union in the face of Chinese accusations of 'revisionism'. Their response was further hindered by the reality that so far, no other revolution had succeeded using 'peaceful' means, which led to the widespread understanding that revolutions were, of necessity, violent and meant that they could not condemn this 'traditional' form of revolution outright. Therefore, they began by arguing that Marxist thought had always emphasised that the 'forms of struggle are determined by the resistance to change of the reactionaries'. In other words, violent repression could beget violent resistance, but in its absence, non-violent forms were possible.[16] But while this could legitimate the choice of unarmed struggle, it did not do much to defend the 'peaceful road' in the eyes of those who had their hearts set on rapid, violent, dramatic, and heroic change.

Therefore, the Chilean Communists began to argue that whichever form of struggle was adopted, it had to be a form of mass struggle. In other words, it had to be a form of struggle that the masses accepted and which the masses participated in. It could not be the role of small armed groups of adventurers to initiate violence. In this, they were in agreement with Ampuero. At the same time, they argued, the 'peaceful road' was still revolutionary because it mobilised the masses and sought a revolutionary transformation. The peaceful road did not reject all violence; it just rejected armed insurrection or civil war, which it began to categorise as forms of 'acute violence'. It still made use of many lesser forms of violence, such as the general strike, illegal strikes, street fights, and particularly illegal factory occupations and land

---

¹⁵ Response of the Communist Party to a letter from the Socialist Party, 24 June 1966, in Corvalán, *Camino de Victoria*, p. 149.

¹⁶ Moscow Declaration of 81 Communist parties 1960, in Corvalán, *Camino de Victoria*, p. 27.

seizures. These methods also ensured that the 'peaceful road' was not defined by legalism or by parliamentarianism and class conciliation. But the criticisms continued, and the Party was forced to further develop the defence of its road, gradually moving away from calling it the peaceful road ('which smacks of passivity') and towards it being 'non-armed' instead.[17] The advantage the Communists had was that they were more disciplined than the Socialists and prepared to expel those who would not work within the 'Party line'. For the Communists, the debate over the 'roads' was not of immense importance internally, but it did create difficulties between them and the newly mobilised sectors of society and with other political groups inspired by the Cuban example. While they might agree on the desirability of socialism, they did not agree on how to get there.

While a new challenge was gestating on the Left, the forces behind Salvador Allende also faced a newcomer to their right. In 1957, the youth wing of the Conservative Party split, admitting the need for social change and seeking to claim a space between the revolutionary Left and a traditional right, whose only response to calls for social justice was electoral fraud and repression. In 1958, now called the Christian Democrat Party (*Partido Demócrata Cristiano*, PDC), they put Allende's friend Eduardo Frei forward as presidential candidate. Frei, unflatteringly described by Pablo Neruda as a 'curious' and 'extremely calculating man' prone to 'parsimonious and frostily cordial' behaviour, was a tall, aristocratic figure of Swiss descent, a conservative with a social conscience.[18] He was confident that he could emulate the success of European Christian Democracy. In 1958, Frei took nearly 21 per cent of the vote. It was an impressive debut, but in the wake of the Cuban Revolution, in the 1961 parliamentary elections, PDC

---

[17] See 'La via pacifica y la alternativa de la via violenta' and 'La via pacifica es una forma de la revolución' in Corvalán, *Camino de Victoria*.

[18] Pablo Neruda, *Confieso que he vivido*, (Barcelona: Editorial Seix Barral, c1974), p. 155.

support fell to just over 15 per cent, showing how the radicalising effect of the Cuban Revolution had benefitted the Left. However, the PDC remained a national force and it had one key advantage — support from European Christian Democrats, the Catholic Church and most importantly, from the US.[19] It soon began to tell. By the 1963 municipal elections, it was the largest single party in Chile. The full-scale US intervention in Chilean politics after the Cuban revolution changed the political panorama and became one of Allende's and the Left's main challenges during the decade.

In 1964, the FRAP had no realistic alternative candidate to Salvador Allende. His victory in Valparaíso and Aconcagua, his name recognition among the people, and their familiarity with his programme meant that there was no real debate this time. While the mechanics of the campaign followed a similar pattern to the previous two, with a 'Train of Victory' heading south and a tour of the entire country, this campaign applied lessons learned in the past. Allende tried to remedy his weakness among women voters by setting up the Independent Committee of Allendista Women (*Comité Independiente de Mujeres Allendistas*, CIMA) under the leadership of his then-Catholic and rather conservative sister, Laura. She would help to convince the middle- and upper-class Chilean women that they had nothing to fear from Allende. An Allendista Catholic Movement was set up under Allende's old professor, Cruz Coke, to counteract the Christian Democrats. The campaign even counted on support from retired military officers in a Civic-Military Front. Allende campaigned with his customary energy. It went well initially, but Allende's campaign soon began to feel the effects of what the Church Committee later called 'a massive anti-Communist propaganda campaign' funded by the CIA.

The propaganda campaign in the Chilean media aimed at demonising Allende and was complemented by US support

---

[19] The 1975 Church Committee Report details CIA support for the PDC going back to the 1961 elections.

for Allende's political opponents. It was a campaign that spared no expense and broke the mould of previous Chilean elections, although the US had been influencing media in Chile for years. The CIA station in Chile had begun supporting news wire services, right-wing intellectual magazines and a weekly newspaper in 1953. In 1961, the CIA established relationships with key political parties and created the mechanisms by which it would spread its propaganda. 'Electoral committees' were set up in Washington and Santiago to coordinate US efforts to subvert the democratic process in Chile. From 1962 to 1964, nearly USD 4 million was spent on 15 'covert action projects'. The CIA involvement was such that it even covered over half the costs of the Christian Democrat campaign (over USD 2.6 million), helping the PDC to run a US-style election campaign supported by opinion polls, voting drives, and so on.[20] The CIA also initially provided funding to the Radical Party. The CIA effort was complemented by US multinationals who also provided funds, in particular to the right-wing National Party (*Partido Nacional*, PN).

While the material support for the PDC enabled it to win an unprecedented outright majority in the 1964 elections, the propaganda campaign against Allende was judged to be more cost-effective. This involved paying for street posters, leafleters, loudspeakers, broadcasting from helicopters, graffiti painters, radio news slots, and the cultivation of 'assets' in the Chilean media, notably in *El Mercurio* as well as letter campaigns. 'Black propaganda' — false materials attributed to left-wing organisations designed to promote arguments within the Left were also published. Many elements of the campaign sound primitive today, but they were effective enough. Radio programmes would be interrupted by machine gun fire, followed by screams as a woman shouted, 'The Communists have killed my son!', followed by more machine gun fire. This propaganda dominated the airwaves across Chile,

---

[20] This is the equivalent of nearly USD 20 million today.

with dozens of broadcasts a day.[21] Allende protested against this campaign in the Senate, saying that the FRAP was being victimised in the same way as Balmaceda, Alessandri, the Popular Front, and Ibañez had been victimised when they had tried to attack the privileges of the wealthy. He condemned this propaganda as dishonest because it did not focus on the concrete activity of any party but on a 'disfigured image of communism', which was used to gain political advantage by creating a climate of panic and terror.[22] That Frei did not speak out against this campaign was the main reason that Allende's friendship with Frei came to an end.

Allende did not limit himself to protests in Parliament. Allende had always been a combative personality, and when he could, he would confront attacks on his political or personal dignity in the way that he felt the context merited. The Senate was the place to denounce attacks in national media. Yet, on the streets, he responded to insults or threats with his fists. There are many testimonies of this — from the upper-class youths who insulted him in Viña del Mar (and who ended up on their backsides in a flower bed) to the Mexican photographer who was knocked out by Allende when the latter was travelling to Cuba. Allende may have worked hard to control his temper, but he let it loose on those who he felt had disrespected him as a representative of the Chilean people or the Chilean Left. This was not just a matter of temperament. Allende understood that letting opponents insult him freely would simply degrade his image without decreasing the intensity or number of attacks. After one fight, he told his companions, 'Note it well, boys, you have to confront the Chilean bourgeoisie directly.'[23] On a personal level, this meant that everybody knew that there would be a price for insulting Allende, whether in the media or in parliament or on the street. On a social level, this combativeness gave people confidence in Allende as their champion.

[21]   All these statistics are taken from the Church Committee Report 1975.
[22]   ASD, Session 52a, 6 May 1964.
[23]   Puccio, p. 55.

The tipping point in right-wing support for the PDC ironically came with a FRAP victory. In Curico, a FRAP deputy died, forcing a by-election to take place. The right proposed an alliance with the Radical Party since their combined vote was 46 per cent and promised easy victory. The by-election became a rehearsal for the main event because Curico reproduced the national electorate on a smaller scale.[24] The FRAP put forward Oscar Naranjo, the son of the deceased, who surprised everyone by winning the election. Some within the FRAP were jubilant. Victory seemed assured, but Allende was not so sure. 'We'll see that the right and everything that is behind it will not sit back now; they'll intensify the campaign against us, and I fear that we'll see important changes to the electoral picture over the next few days,' he said to his collaborators. Salomón Corbalán was just as astute, 'We've won a deputy and lost a president', he said.[25] Defeat was sealed after the FRAP held a mass meeting of 300,000 supporters in Santiago. Allende knew the right would not fail to understand that to avoid him winning; they would have to back Frei.

As Allende predicted, after the 'Naranjazo' victory in Curico, the CIA put its entire weight behind the Frei campaign while continuing to fund the Radical Party candidate 'in order to enhance the Christian Democrat's image as a moderate progressive party being attacked from the right as well as the Left.'[26] It wasn't all roses for the opposition to Allende. The increasing polarisation, and resistance to US interference forced a split in the Radical Party, and some of them declared their support for Allende. A Liberal Party senator, protesting at US interference in the elections, also switched allegiances. However, the FRAP's victory had forced the opposition to unite, and this did not bode well for Allende.

On election day, Allende voted in Viña del Mar and then returned to Santiago. He had lunch with friends and was

---

[24] Agnic, p. 140.
[25] Puccio, p. 135; Agnic, p. 141.
[26] Church Committee Report 1975, p. 15.

unsurprised when the results began to give Frei the victory. He then walked over to his campaign offices, where before giving his loser's speech, he patted Osvaldo Puccio on the shoulder saying, 'Don't worry, we'll win in 1970'. While those around him were devastated, Allende remained optimistic, but the defeat was a heavy blow nonetheless. Allende resorted to humour, joking that on his gravestone, it would read: 'Here lies Salvador Allende, future President of Chile.'[27] Some Socialists took the defeat with less humour. One leader said that the PS would deny the new government 'bread and salt' but Allende, in an interview in *Ercilla* magazine on the day of Frei's inauguration, marked a different tone when he said, 'As a Chilean and as a man of the Left, I sincerely hope that Frei will be able to fulfil his promises to the people, but in the same way as he has a deep commitment to them, he also has tremendous commitments to the historic enemies of the people. Because of this, his government will be an obstacle course and six years of contradictory pressures.'[28] Many ordinary Socialists and Communists were unable to take the defeat as philosophically. One Communist recalled a comrade furiously exclaiming, 'And now what? How long are we going to continue with these elections?!'

If such opinions were becoming more commonplace among Communists, among Socialists, who had always had more serious problems justifying the 'electoral road', the effects would be devastating. Just before the elections, the PS, led by Ampuero, had held a Congress in the city of Concepción, where it underlined its support of the 'electoral road' by stating that 'we confront the elections because there are favourable conditions for winning them and because by winning them, we can open a new stage in the development of the Chilean Revolution, and because objectively, no other option exists.'[29] This Congress was

---

[27] Jorquera, p. 59.
[28] Cited in Martinez, p. 277.
[29] Socialist Party Report of the Central Committee, XX Congress, Concepción February 1964.

also notable for Ampuero's efforts to expel leading members of the Trotskyist wing of the Party, who opposed his interpretation of the Workers' Front. However, after the elections, the Party held a new Congress at which Ampuero announced that he would not run for re-election to the leadership, perhaps preparing his future presidential candidacy.

Ampuero's political position was one that highlighted the need for Chilean responses to the Chilean situation and was, therefore, critical of both the Communists and the ultra-left for their adoption of what he saw as 'foreign dogmas' — one biased towards electoralism and class conciliation in the interests of the USSR, the other towards pointless armed struggle. He was a jealous guardian of the Party's autonomous Marxism. Ampuero was replaced as General Secretary by his close friend Aniceto Rodriguez, which would have seemed to guarantee the continuity of his political line in the PS, if not for the simultaneous election to the Central Committee of new, much more radical faces. At this Congress, the Party adopted a much more strident tone, a line more sceptical of the 'electoral road' which the unfortunate Rodriguez was forced to implement. Allende's role in these debates is not clear. Carlos Altamirano, one of the radical leaders elected in 1965, has written that Allende did not take part in ideological struggles at this time because he saw them as too 'metaphysical' and he was too grounded in practical politics.[30] But he also had practical political reasons for either standing back, or 'leading from behind', because his career had been marked by a rivalry with Ampuero. Ampuero had unseated him as Party General Secretary in 1946, and like Allende, he was a historic leader in the Party, with one Socialist leader saying that Ampuero was its 'internal' leader, while Allende represented it to the masses.[31] Though they shared a belief in the importance of the electoral road, they often disagreed on practical

[30] Gabriel Salazar, *Altamirano*, p. 187

[31] Luis Jerez, *Ilusiones y quebrantos (desde la memoria de un militante socialista)*, (Santiago: Forja, 2007), p. 115.

political matters. They had taken different sides in relation to the Popular Front and the later election of Ibañez. Ampuero himself believed that Allende had conspired with the radical Left to out-manoeuvre Ampuero so as to facilitate the broadening out of the FRAP towards the centre. Whether we see them as 'metaphysical' or not, the outcome of these debates would lay the basis for the later paralysis of Allende's government.

Developments in the PS were evidence that many were feeling that the electoral road was a chimaera. A growing sector of the PS became more dogmatic in its understanding of revolution and less nuanced in its understanding of violence, edging away from the 'Ampuerista' or 'Allendista' vision and towards a more 'orthodox' idea of the armed seizure of power. Stimulated by the appearance of guerrilla movements across much of Latin America and by the influence of the Cuban revolution in particular, these socialists wanted to stop wasting time with elections and start making the revolution.

Meanwhile, Frei had won a victory large enough to govern without a coalition. In March 1965, again, with US assistance, the PDC was able to win a majority in Congress. The Christian Democrats began to implement what they called the 'Revolution in Liberty', aggressively developing mass organisations, especially in unionising the countryside and building the legislative framework for a large network of social organisations that went from neighbourhood organisations to women's organisations. As was the intention behind them, these well funded organisations competed with the older shoestring networks linked to the PC and the PS. They articulated similar material demands but were shorn of their revolutionary framework. Nevertheless, these organisations brought large numbers of Chileans into the political process for the first time. Frei's 'Revolution in Liberty' promised much — an agrarian reform, banking reform, economic growth, and the 'Chileanisation' of the copper industry (buying majority stakes in the copper industry) but the question was whether it would be able to deliver without alienating its paymasters.[32]

Allende's words in *Ercilla* proved visionary. Frei and the PDC were unable to push through a large-scale agrarian reform against the vigorous resistance of the landed elites; their 'Chileanisation' of the copper industry was a blatant injustice in a poor country with severe economic problems. The failure to resolve Chile's many structural problems, despite high expectations, led to increasing popular pressures. Strikes, demonstrations, and land occupations took place increasingly, which the government responded to with repression. In April 1966, troops were called to put down a strike in the El Salvador mine, killing eight workers. In 1967, a strike in Santiago led to the killings of several people. In 1969, police opened fire on shantytown dwellers in the city of Puerto Montt, killing ten people and wounding dozens. The political effect of these brutal killings was severe, and the songwriter Victor Jara sang that 'not all the rain of the south would be able to clean the hands of the perpetrators'. The government was unable to stabilise the economy, and inflation topped 30 per cent in 1967. Repression and economic instability encouraged more and more people to think of a more far-reaching process of change. This was also reflected within the Christian Democrats, with some members moving Leftwards, eventually splitting from the Party in early 1969, arguing for an anti-imperialist and Socialist solution to Chile's problems.

A year after Frei was elected, Allende made a harsh judgement of his government. Allende was embittered by the violence of the election campaign, which had viciously slandered his person as well as the movement he represented. Allende had always valued his friendships, and he always had friends from across the political

---

[32] The 'Chileanisation' of the copper industry was thought up by US executives at Kennecott, who needed investment in the El Teniente copper mine in order to increase production. Unwilling to take the money out of their own profits, they envisioned a 'partnership' with Chilean investors. Since the Chilean private sector was too weak to take on this investment, they approached the government. See Nolff, pp. 210-212. US companies also pursued a similar policy in relation to nitrates.

spectrum, but the 1964 election campaign had breached the limits of the 'most basic political and human consideration'. This was disloyal to their friendship and to Chile because, in Allende's eyes, by allowing the PDC to benefit from such a campaign, Frei had put it at the service of US interests. 'It was a dirty victory', Allende later said.[33] Allende, therefore, pulled no punches as he analysed the first year of Frei's government.

Allende denied that Frei's government was carrying out a revolution. According to him, it was acting to prevent revolution by preserving capitalism, as had Christian Democrat governments in Italy and Germany. In the Chilean context, this meant that the PDC had subordinated Chile's national interests to those of imperialism. As Allende said, 'the party that governs today has the strange privilege of having, at a crucial moment for Chile, silenced the yearning for self-determination of our people through foreign pressure — both in inspiration and massive execution, which distorted and confused national patriotic feeling.'[34] He accused the PDC of allowing Chile to become 'psychologically colonised'.

The Chilean Left as a whole shared these criticisms of the PDC, although they were most pronounced in the PS. The tone of the US psyops campaign had poisoned the political atmosphere, and the high-handedness of PDC appointees in government rankled deeply. For those on the Left, the PDC had become an instrument of imperialist manipulation. The words of a 1963 Violeta Parra song took on fresh meaning in this context:

Look how they talk to us of liberty,
while they deny it to us in reality,
Look how they preach tranquillity,
While we are tormented by authority.

---

[33] *Discursos: Salvador Allende*, (Havana: Editorial Ciencias Sociales, 1975). 'La Democracia Cristiana no es Revolucionaria', p. 12.

[34] Ibid., p. 17.

Christian Democrat policies and leaders were marked by hypocrisy — talking of revolution but preventing it, talking of sovereignty but paying out immense sums to US copper companies and talking of liberty, while gunning down demonstrators. These perceptions were the basis of hostility towards the PDC among supporters of the Left.

Allende became increasingly concerned with imperialism in the late 1960s since the PDC had taken on, nominally at least, many of the projects first proposed by the Left, including agrarian reform, democratisation, educational reform, control of copper and other natural resources. Few now debated the need for these measures. The battleground had shifted to the purpose and manner of their execution. A focus on imperialism also allowed Allende to limit the growing attacks coming from more extreme groupings within the PS and outside it, which accused him of being a social democrat and not a 'true revolutionary'. The US interference in the Chilean political system through the 1960s made imperialism an economic and political reality for Chile — the Left's main enemy along with the Chilean oligarchy, particularly since the decade saw a progressive weakening of the latter, which did not even field its own candidate in the 1964 elections.

Internationally too, imperialism was an issue of massive importance. In 1964, the US had supported, if not instigated, the overthrow of João Goulart in Brazil and in 1965, US troops invaded Santo Domingo in the Caribbean. The US intervention in Vietnam escalated sharply the same year, deploying hundreds of thousands of troops and beginning a massive bombing campaign against North Vietnam. In response, in January 1966, the first Trilateral Conference was held in Havana, ostensibly to create a global alliance of revolutionary forces fighting imperialism. Allende was present. In a world full of national liberation movements waging war against colonialism, Allende represented a quiet and arguably unsuccessful Left in Chile. However, he was the elected leader of the Organisation of Latin American Solidarity (OLAS), the regional information section of the Tricontinental. In June 1966, Allende was back in Cuba, participating in the founding of the OLAS, but this time, without the moderating influence of the USSR, the tone was openly one of armed revolution. One participant recalled, 'Among greetings, winks, and backslapping, the Cuban commanders came and went from the Hotel Havana Libre, mixing with the Latin Americans that dreamed of emulating them. Salvador Allende circulated solemnly, wearing a *guayabera* shirt. The pressure in favour of the armed struggle was immense. The hosts freely offered courses in guerrilla warfare. The talk was of FAL and M-1 rifles, and whoever didn't know the slang was called a "softie".[35] Yet the reality of the various countries soon imposed itself. Each country's revolutionary process took its own path, often into obliteration. The OLAS never met again.

The same year, Allende was elected President of the Chilean Senate after convincing the Radical Party to support his candidacy. It was Chile's most important political post after the president, and Allende's election highlighted the respect that his parliamentary peers held him and his skill at manipulating inter-party rivalries to achieve his goals. Meanwhile, Allende's association with the leading lights of armed struggle helped him to maintain his revolutionary credentials in the eyes of those Chileans who dreamed of an armed revolution.

A year later, in Uruguay, Allende spoke at a meeting at Montevideo University, parallel to the second meeting of the Alliance for Progress being held in the same city. In this speech, he condemned the Alliance for Progress as the latest machination of US domination, in particular for the way in which it had led to dictatorships across the region and pulled Latin America even further into debt. The region was now obliged to pay off the interest on the acquired debts, forcing it into an even more subordinate position with regard to the US. For Allende, the solution to Latin

[35] E. Labarca, pp. 169-170.

America's problems had to be sought through integration, internally and through structural changes to the mechanisms of trade and the prices of Latin American exports. Allende condemned the new forms that US imperialism was taking in promoting regional integration through free trade and establishing mixed ownership companies, where Latin American governments held shares. These, Allende argued, did not alter US economic domination and would not improve life for the masses of Latin Americans. US policies had 'changed in their form, but not their content. The "Big Stick" was followed by Dollar Diplomacy. This was followed by the Good Neighbour Policy and now the Johnson Doctrine. Always domination and arbitrary domination.'[36] The only solution for Latin America was to achieve economic independence, without which there could be no political independence.

A few months later, Che Guevara was killed in Bolivia. The survivors of his guerrilla column desperately sought to escape. In Chile, some Socialists, including Allende's daughter Beatriz, had previously set up a support network known as the National Liberation Army (*Ejército de Liberación Nacional*, ELN). The news of Che's death was a political earthquake for the Left. Allende recalled his meetings with Guevara in a heartfelt homage in the Senate, where he showed his signed copy of Che's 'Guerrilla Warfare' where Guevara had written, 'To Salvador Allende, who seeks the same ends by different means'. Yet, even here, Allende reminded his audience inside and outside the Senate that Guevara had not blindly supported the armed struggle. Allende showed that Guevara had written that armed struggle could only take place where civic competition was no longer possible, reminding everyone that in Chile, the popular movement had, in fact, nearly reached power through these means.[37] Yet, not everyone understood or believed the message. Just over a month later, the PS held a congress in Chillán. Che's example motivated

[36] Allende speech quoted in Nolff pp. 38-46.
[37] ASD, Session 7a, 18 October 1967.

a series of resounding resolutions declaring the inevitability of the violent seizure of power. Allende was booed off the stage ('They didn't let me speak! And on top of that they whistled me off! My own comrades!' he said.), and the Congress once again refused to select him for the Central Committee.[38] Instead, the new Central Committee became even more dominated by voices that questioned the utility of the 'electoral road' and competed with each other to fetishize the role of violence in revolution. The Congress even unanimously passed resolutions that stated:

> Revolutionary violence is inevitable and legitimate. It necessarily stems from the repressive and armed nature of the class state. It is the only road that leads to the seizure of political and economic power and its subsequent defence and strengthening. Only by destroying the bureaucratic and military apparatus of the bourgeois state can a Socialist revolution be consolidated.

It continued, 'The peaceful, or legal forms of struggle do not by themselves lead to power. The PS considers them limited instruments of action incorporated into the political process, which take us to the armed struggle'.[39] It was a notable shift away from Ampuero's previously dominant position. One Socialist leader later wrote that these resolutions were really an emotional tribute to Guevara and an expression of frustration with the electoral road, which is no doubt true, but they were taken by the media and by many Chileans outside the Left to demonstrate the violent nature of the PS.

With the news that the survivors of Che's guerrilla column were heading to Chile, the Chilean ELN and the Left as a whole mobilised to receive them. At the same time, the government mobilised the security forces to find the guerrillas as soon as possible. Allende,

---

[38] Jorquera, p. 48.
[39] See Julio César Jobet, p. 130.

with his usual political nous, knew that their arrival in Chile was a hot potato for the Frei government. It could not be seen to be handing revolutionaries over to their executioners, nor could it be seen to be supporting them. As a senator, Allende was able to communicate with the government, the Cuban authorities, and with the Chilean Left. He suggested that the guerrillas be provided temporary political refuge before being flown to Easter Island and then onwards to Tahiti, where French authorities would guarantee their onward travel to Cuba. He accompanied them. The Chilean media had a field day. He was accused of being a 'guerrilla senator' and of having abused his position as President of the Senate. He was also subjected to a campaign of lies and sarcasm, which did its best to portray him as a buffoon, a man desperate for attention, and in the pay of Cuba.[40] It seemed as Miguel Labarca commented, as if his image was at the point of being destroyed.[41]

When Allende was cornered, he came out fighting. This time, he challenged the editors of Chile's main newspapers to a debate to be broadcast on TV and radio. For over four hours, Allende took apart his opponents. He reminded the listeners that the Editor of *El Mercurio* had been a member of the Chilean Nazis. The Editor of *La Segunda*, a former Leftist from Valparaíso, was left looking like an avaricious traitor who had betrayed his former comrades for money. The Editor of *La Nacion* — the government newspaper — was reminded that in the nineteenth century, his own grandfather had sought to create an army of Latin Americans to liberate Cuba from Spanish colonialism. How could such people criticise Allende's behaviour? Allende's opponents were left floundering, and his popularity rocketed.

In a second part of his defence, Allende took to the floor of the Senate. Here, he explained why his actions had been legal and

---

[40] During this period, the CIA continued to 'support' right wing media, produce radio commentary shows and funded 'CIA-inspired editorials' in *El Mercurio*. Church Committee Report, pp. 18-19.

[41] M. Labarca, p. 120.

explained, why international solidarity was vital to 'social fighters under assault across Latin America.' In this speech, Allende defended his life's work in Parliament and his reputation. Over the years, he said, 'Everything has been said of me, except that I am dishonest'. Allende continued, 'For me, politics is about principles, about convictions. I have been honourable in my public life, and my hands are free of blood and embezzlement'. As a man with an old-fashioned sense of honour, he could tolerate attacks that targeted his politics but not those against his reputation.

Allende protested that the media campaign against him had been 'planned, organised, and measured' and that having failed to undermine the popular movement in successive elections, the campaign had moved to target Allende himself, making him the victim of 'jibes, ridicule, grotesque caricature, and anonymous sneers'. He reminded the Senate of his long career that he had been the first to seriously talk about the need for agrarian reform, the first to call for the nationalisation of copper, and to call for fairer taxation — the very measures that many of them now supported. If he was ambitious, he said that it was because the Presidency was 'a means to make real what one feels, believes and desires, to put in play one's convictions and doctrines'. Finally, he reminded the Senate that he had suffered for his political opinions, having been expelled from university, imprisoned and blacklisted. He and his family had also suffered 'many very bitter hours', thanks to attacks — the kind of which 'I do not wish for any of you', he said. It was dishonourable that he be accused of being an unsubstantial man without principles when, as he reminded them, his hands had also carried out 1,500 autopsies, and he had earned his bread 'sticking them in pus, cancers, and death'.

Allende then refuted the accusation that he supported violence, repeating that guerrilla movements 'will spring up wherever implacable dictatorships impede the right of men to participate even in bourgeois democracy'. He defended the Cuban and Bolivian guerrillas as 'soldiers of Latin American independence' and underlined that since they shared a vision of a Socialist Latin America without imperialism, they were the brothers of the Chilean Left. The Chilean popular movement had a duty to support those who fought for the Latin American revolution, whether legally or with weapons. Imperialism was a key issue, and he reminded his audience that Chile could not be independent while its copper, nitrates, iron, and other fundamental riches were under foreign control and while imperialism 'strangles our destiny'.[42] With this daring defence, Allende was able to turn imminent defeat into victory.

Although he had saved his reputation and, therefore, his ability to stand as a presidential candidate in the upcoming 1970 elections, Allende clearly needed to broaden the electoral coalition that had so far failed to get him into power in 1958 and 1964. The lesson of these failures was clear to anyone willing to look back to the only time that the Left had been part of government — the Popular Front. Back then, the Radical Party had been the leading political force of the coalition, limiting the scope for change. This time, the situation was different. Firstly, the Communist and Socialist parties were both well-entrenched national forces. The union movement was strong and united. Furthermore, in the 1964 and 1965 elections, the Radical Party had been barged off the centre ground by a vigorous and foreign-supported Christian Democrat party. In power, the PDC had ruled alone and had failed to deal with Chile's structural problems. For the Radicals, the Left held out the possibility of a return to power as part of a broad coalition, albeit this time as a junior partner. Left-leaning Radicals won the argument. The problem was, would the Socialists accept them? After Chillán, the PS had seemingly rejected any possibility of an electoral alliance which included non-Marxist parties. However, this did not deter Allende from trying to build one anyway. The first signs that such an alliance was possible came in the Cautín

---

[42] ASD, session 65a, 12 March 1968.

by-election in 1968. Here, Socialists and Communists successfully voted for a Radical candidate, but the future alliance still lacked a declared leader.

By the late 1960s, there were many voices calling for a fresh face to lead the Left. Once more, Allende had to stake out his right to stand. The parliamentary elections of March 1969 would make or break his chances. Allende's choice of constituency was made as a result of events in the PS.

In July 1967, a faction of the PS under Raúl Ampuero had been expelled from the Party after a heated leadership plenum in the town of Linares. Ampuero was disillusioned with the Party's new leadership, which he said was 'two-headed', divided between the 'victims of infantilism' and 'revolutionary globetrotters' around Allende.[43] As a historic leader, Ampuero could not accept what must have felt like the takeover of *his* party, and as a theorist, Ampuero well understood the importance of unified leadership. So, Ampuero undertook to provoke a rebellion, organising his adepts around the country, highlighting that proposed rule changes intended to make the Party more 'Leninist' and shift power away from the Party base, which, for Ampuero, threatened the basis for the Party's ideological autonomy. The PS leadership found out and, after long and painful debates, expelled him. Ampuero set up his own party, bitterly contesting PS offices and decided to stand for Senate for the Magallanes Region in the far south, the region he was from. His success would lay the basis for the new party's national ambitions and would deepen the newly-developed divide in Chilean socialism. Allende decided to take advantage of this situation, and he asked to switch to the Magallanes constituency he had represented in the 1940s to directly challenge Ampuero. If Allende won these elections, he would be beating an old rival, paying back the defeat Ampuero had doled out to him in 1946, and he would be doing the new leadership of the PS a favour by

---

[43] *Ampuero Ahora: 50 Preguntas y 50 respuestas de la actualidad*, pp. 14-15.

eliminating a potentially dangerous critic and rival. Furthermore, if he won well, as he had done in Valparaíso in 1961, he would also be cementing his case as a future presidential candidate.

Allende deployed his traditional methods — speeches, meetings, dinners, and travelling — to the places where ordinary people lived and worked. Thanks to his extraordinary memory, he could recall the names of places and events from twenty years earlier, and he was able to roundly defeat Ampuero, getting ten votes to every two of Ampuero's, destroying his new party and rebuilding the PS networks in the region. The victory, as he had expected, underlined his status as the man to turn to when an important victory was required.

In retrospect, it was a turning point, one that may have helped seal the fate of the UP. For all their disagreements, Allende and Ampuero shared their views on the importance of the electoral road and were experienced politicians with a nuanced understanding of Chilean politics. Although Ampuero was viscerally opposed to any alliance with the Radical Party, he could see that the PDC was a contested space, and he was even less tolerant of 'ultra-leftism' in the PS.[44] It is tempting to wonder what might have happened had Ampuero either won back leadership of the PS or been able to build his new party into a national actor of importance. It could have provided Allende with a way out of the 'ultra-left' stalemate he found his government in later, but as one Socialist leader subsequently wrote, Allende and Ampuero 'were overcome by the rigidity of their surroundings and their incapacity to understand that they needed each other to ensure the success of the Socialist road they had forged.'[45]

The Parliamentary elections also paved the way for the nomination of a left-wing candidate for the 1970 elections. Having demonstrated the strength of his candidacy, Allende decided to

[44] *Ampuero Ahora*, p. 18.
[45] *Ampuero 1917-1996: el socialismo chileno*, (Santiago: Ed. Tierra Mia, 2002), p. 35.

leave Chile for a while in order to escape the inevitable debates and discussions. According to Miguel Labarca, he knew that events demanded the creation of a broad alliance, and he was convinced that he was the only viable candidate to lead such a coalition. This was characteristic of his political nous and his self-confidence. Allende would joke that he was — like Coca-Cola — a product well-known in the market, but it was not just that he was well-known; it was also that he truly believed he was the Left's best candidate.

By the end of the decade, Chile was once more enduring an economic crisis. Inflation had been 27.9 per cent in 1968, 29.3 per cent in 1969 and rose to 34.9 per cent in 1970. Officially, unemployment stood at almost 10 per cent. There were growing symptoms of political crisis, too. In 1969, the *Tacna* military regiment had attempted a coup in what became known as the *Tacnazo*. Allende immediately condemned the attempt and offered his support to President Frei. Notably, the PS as a whole did not. The reaction to the *Tacnazo* coup attempt also showed tantalising glimpses of the coalition that Allende thought made a future Socialist government possible. To resist the attempted coup, the PC joined a mass demonstration supporting the government, with thousands marching united arm-in-arm on the Presidential Palace.[46] The economic situation continued to deteriorate, and in 1970, Chile witnessed nearly two thousand strikes involving almost a tenth of the total population. The US-designed and sponsored 'Revolution in Liberty' of Chile had awakened popular appetites for change but had failed to produce either revolution or liberty.

Among the parties of the FRAP, two divergent responses to this social, economic, and political crisis were crystalising. The first — led by the PC and Salvador Allende — was to continue with the strategy of the popular alliance, seeking to broaden the popular coalition to include the political centre to ensure that the

---

[46] Sergio Muñoz Riveros, *A partir de la UP: el aprendizaje democratico*, (Santiago: La Copa Rota, 2013), p. 39.

changes they proposed had majority support across society and in the institutions. The second response, led by the new radicals of the PS, was to look at the crisis as evidence of Chilean capitalism's terminal condition and to seek to take the struggle to a qualitatively new level, under the general understanding that the elite and US imperialism would never allow a peaceful transition to socialism to occur. This necessitated preparing for a violent break with existing institutions and potentially for armed struggle.

The two options were incompatible, but in the atmosphere of the late 1960s, there seemed to be enough concrete evidence to sustain both approaches. Moreover, they *could* both coexist in the run-up to an election, with some convinced that they were struggling to pursue a set of democratic reforms that were revolutionary in their content, while others could equally believe that they were struggling to create the preconditions for state fracture and a subsequent seizure of power. The incompatibility began to show once the UP became the government.

In the meantime, Allende set out for a tour of North Korea, Vietnam, and Cuba. He was inspired by the dignity the people of these countries showed in the face of imperialist hostility, and he admired many of the advances they had made in education and healthcare. Allende later said his belief in socialism had been strengthened by witnessing how, in the wake of tremendous destruction, North Korea had created a universal education system. He saw factories and villages that 'have all the services that our urban population lacks: polyclinics, schools, chemists, small hospitals, nurseries, and a normal level of nutrition for children'.

In Vietnam, Allende admired the courage of a people facing massive aerial bombardment. He was taken to see a jungle university that had 35,000 students as well as hospitals, where the wards were made of bamboo, and where every bed had a bomb shelter dug out next to it. He was deeply moved by his meeting with the Vietnamese leader Ho Chi Minh. He later recalled how Ho Chi Minh addressed his visitors in the Spanish he had learnt as a kitchen hand on an Argentinean ship, thanking them for coming so far to show their solidarity with the Vietnamese people. These visits, in particular the visit to Vietnam, had a profound impact on Allende.

He imagined what Chile could achieve under socialism, if it had the chance — 'from afar, with Chilean feelings and passion, I looked on and thought of our copper, the iron, nitrates, I thought of the forests, of our sea, that emporium of the greatest riches, and I thought too of our own people, who are also heroic and selfless.'[47] Witnessing the destruction of Korea and Vietnam must have made him think of what imperialism would do to prevent Chile from achieving socialism, but it probably reinforced his conviction that the democratic road to socialism had tremendous advantages by avoiding bloodshed. The visits also reinforced his status as Chile's leading revolutionary leader by associating him with the great names of the world's anti-imperialist struggle.

Allende's travels took him away from the debates that had begun around who would lead the Left into the 1970 elections. Despite Allende's self-belief and his recent victory in Magallanes, he was by no means a certainty as a presidential candidate. For many in the political parties, it was time for a new face for the Left. They doubted that Allende could attract radicalised youth, and as they argued, he had never polled very well with women. At the same time, the Communists had made it clear that they would not back a narrow coalition as in the past. If they were going to lose, they preferred to do so with their own candidate.[48]

Each party put forward a candidate. The Communists symbolically put forward Pablo Neruda, but they were mostly concerned with achieving a consensus around the future candidate, and they seem to have favoured the Radical leader, Alberto Baltra. Within the PS leadership too, there were also many who wanted

---

[47] ASD, session 23a, 30 July 1969.

[48] Luis Corvalán, *De lo vivido y lo peleado*, 2nd ed., (Santiago: LOM Ediciones, 1999), p. 117.

a new face to lead them, as well as those who thought of the upcoming election as a symbolic gesture. These groups pushed the candidacy of Aniceto Rodríguez, the Party's General Secretary, who was planning to launch his campaign and create a *fait accompli* while Allende was away. For these 'ultra-left' Socialists, Rodriguez's failure would be a clear message of the futility of electoral politics, preparing the ground for overtly armed struggle. However, on the eve of the proclamation, Allende sent an urgent message from Cuba renouncing his candidacy and saying it was time to put the party before 'any egocentric attitude'.[49] At a stroke, Allende had prevented the imposition of a candidate by the Party leadership and the stage was set for an open discussion.

On 9 October 1969, after months of meetings and informal conversations, the UP coalition was declared. The new coalition consisted of the Radical Party, the Popular Unitary Action Movement (*Movimiento de Acción Popular Unitario,* MAPU) (which had split from the Christian Democrats in May 1969), and a small party called the Independent Progressive Alliance (*Alianza Progresista Independiente,* API), as well as the old parties of the FRAP but the UP coalition still needed to decide who would lead it into the elections.

The UP's birth was a convoluted process. Nobody in the PS had wanted to trigger the internal race to be the Party's candidate to lead the UP, so the Deputy General Secretary proposed that the Central Committee consult with the Regional Committees of the Party to see who they backed. They found that all but one supported Allende. However, he had few backers in the post-1967 Central Committee, which tended to see him as a 'social democrat', and it held back. On August 26, its members were called to vote on the matter. In the hall, as one participant later recalled, the atmosphere was 'anything but fraternal'.[50] No written record of the vote exists,

---

[49] M. Labarca, p. 162.

[50] Luis Jerez, *Ilusiones y quebrantos (desde la memoria de un militante socialista),* (Santiago: Forja, 2007), p. 214.

and testimony of the vote is contradictory. What all accounts agree on is that Allende won largely because many Central Committee members abstained.[51] As Luís Corvalán, the leader of the PC, later said that Allende's nomination as the PS candidate was a 'forceps birth.'[52] It was through the resounding backing of the grassroots that Allende went forward as a PS candidate to lead the new coalition.

In November, the PC held its XIV congress. One of the main issues debated was the danger posed by 'ultra-leftism' to the further development of the popular cause. The congress was addressed by MAPU senator Rafael Gumucio. Gumucio called ultra-leftism the worst obstacle to unity. 'Ultra-leftism could mean the failure of the UP', he warned. 'I think that the UP would gain a lot of internal consistency and homogeneity, if it could decide to do without these activists of division.'[53] While these were somewhat prophetic words, they were not new. Gumucio expressed the traditional views of the PC leadership, who had been facing the problem of Socialist cynicism about alliances and the electoral road for many years.

In the wake of the 1973 coup, some asked whether, in light of the FRAP strategy, it might not have been better to support a non-FRAP candidate as a way of building a broader coalition. In fact, the PC did initially support this option, but it was not sustainable in the face of Socialist hostility to the idea. Nor was the PDC leadership united around the issue of an alliance with the Left, even if a significant portion of its voters were open to it. In June 1969, a motion in the PDC to propose a centre-left coalition was defeated. Nevertheless, in August 1969, the party chose Radomiro Tomic — its most left-wing representative — ironically, the man who had led the campaign for the PDC not to field its own candidate but to lead them into the 1970 elections. For Allende, it

---

[51] Ibid. p.215; Eduardo Gutierrez, *Ciudades en las sombras: Una historia no oficial del Partido Socialista de Chile*, (Santiago: Editare, 2010), pp. 30-32.

[52] Corvalán, *De lo vivido y lo peleado*, p. 118.

[53] Sergio Muñoz Riveros, *A Partir de la UP: El aprendizaje democratico*, (Santiago: La Copa Rota, 2013), p. 42.

was a testament to how tantalisingly close the Left were to closing a strategic alliance with the centre. Nevertheless, Frei remained an important influence in the Party, and so the PDC remained balanced on a knife edge — depending on circumstances, it could tip to the right or to the left.

Socialist intransigence around alliances with centrist political forces meant that a non-Socialist candidate could not win the candidacy of the UP. Radomiro Tomic could have been the candidate to unite the Left with the increasingly influential left-wing of the PDC, but he was a former ambassador to the US and unacceptable to much of the UP because of it. Alberto Baltra was a Radical, but his Party was losing strength and had betrayed the Left in the late 1940s, ushering the Cold War into Chile; he was also unacceptable to the PS. Some suggested Gumucio as a candidate, but no matter who was considered, they all faced the same intractable problem — the Socialists would not accept a 'petite-bourgeois' party leading the process. And nobody in the PS could follow Gumucio's advice and act against a recently elected Socialist leadership dominated by radicals that had been strengthened by Ampuero's expulsion and subsequent electoral defeat at Allende's hands. In this situation, Allende — friend to Fidel and Guevara and also to Lafferte and Corvalán — became an increasingly likely candidate.

The coalition agreed on a political programme by December 1969 but was still unable to agree on a leader. The UP set the New Year as a deadline to decide, but the date came and went. According to Luís Corvalán, the situation was sometimes 'tense and on the verge of explosion'.[54] Although they had hoped for a negotiated consensus, the Communists finally decided to openly back Allende and the smaller parties were persuaded to withdraw their candidates.[55] Corvalán famously said there was finally 'white

---

[54] Ibid., p. 117.
[55] Some socialist testimonies assert that the Communists were pushing for their party to accept Baltra's candidacy, but this is hotly denied by the

smoke' and Allende would lead the UP into the elections.

However, as the price for his selection and to assuage all doubts, Allende was made to sign a 'Pact of the UP' which committed him to governing in accordance with the decisions of the UP leadership. This, in effect, made him a prisoner of the inter and intra-party dynamics of the UP and was a colossal infringement on his constitutional powers as president. That Allende accepted these limitations is a testament to two things — the weakness of his situation within the PS and his aversion to becoming a *caudillo*.[56] By accepting this pact, he subordinated his constitutional authority to loyalty to the party he had founded and the Left unity that he had spent his entire career building. This, together with the narrowness of his victories in the struggle to be nominated as candidate of the PS and subsequently of the UP as a whole, contributed to his relative weakness as president and was a practical reason why he could not later impose his will upon his coalition.

The creation of the UP was the culmination of a thirty-year effort by Allende and his Communist allies to create a broad alliance of all possible social sectors around a programme designed to put Chile on the road towards socialism. In many ways, it was a 1970 re-incarnation of the 1937 Popular Front, but this time, the alliance was clearly dominated by Marxist parties and had a deep structural change on the agenda. It was achieved, despite the opposition of the Chilean elite and US interventionism, and in the face of increasingly dogmatic perspectives on violence among some sectors of the Chilean Left. It was achieved in large measure, thanks to Allende's tireless campaigning over many years, which

---

PC's then-leaders. See Garcés, *Allende y la via chilena*, p. 241; Jerez p. 217; Corvalán, *El gobierno de Allende*, p. 108; Millas, *De O'Higgins a Allende*, p. 318.

[56] *Caudillo: A caudillo* is a strongman, a figure from Latin American and Spanish history, charismatic, and often with a military background. Someone who, like Juan Perón in Argentina, could subordinate a popular movement to their own will rather than reflect it.

aimed at appealing to 'a million consciences' rather than just getting votes and thanks to the efforts of those Communists and Socialists who had long backed the idea of a broader alliance of the Left and the centre.[57]

Despite his good physical condition, Allende paid a price for the intensity of his work and the pressures of campaigning. In the run-up to the election, he suffered a minor heart attack, which was kept secret. For two weeks, he was treated at home while his intimate circle staved off rumours. His closest collaborators and his daughter Beatriz, who was also a doctor, decided that the best treatment was for Allende to keep working. They did, however, prescribe a glass of whisky before bed. Allende returned to the campaign trail.

[57] Allende cited in Puccio, p. 135.

The Popular Unity Government

Those who are good at governing draw close to them
those who are far away.
— Confucius

The first duty of government is to make itself obeyed by all.
— Radomiro Tomic

On 4 September 1970, Salvador Allende won the Chilean presidential elections. As was usual in Chilean elections, nobody had won an overall majority (1964 had been an exception), and Congress was called to ratify the election result. Allende had polled 36.6 per cent, Jorge Alessandri, the right-wing candidate, 34.9 per cent, and the Christian Democrats under Radomiro Tomic, 27.8 per cent. The results hid clear support for a socialist programme, with the PDC espousing what it called 'communitarian socialism' and showed how the Left had gained from disillusion with the PDC, whose popularity had suffered after six years of government, a sorry economic record and a catalogue of massacres. The PDC had also been abandoned by its foreign backers, who had observed how the Left had come to dominate the Party. In June 1969, some in the PDC had even sought to make an alliance with the UP official policy. The debate was fierce, and the motion was narrowly lost, leading to a split in the Party.[1] The grassroots of the Christian Democrats chose to put forward Radomiro Tomic, a left-leaning

[1] Monica González, *La Conjura: Los mil y un dias del golpe,* (Santiago: Ediciones B, 2000), p. 54.

candidate who led the wing of the party opposed to Frei. The right-wing leadership of the PDC had lost control. With the failure of the CIA's programmes to develop a non-Marxist popular base and to divide the union movement, the CIA decided not to support a particular candidate and to concentrate on attacking the UP, the tactic from the 1960s that it judged to have been most successful.[2] In all, the CIA spent between USD 800,000 and 1,000,000 on the 'spoiling campaign' in 1970, with US transnational corporations also contributing funds.[3] The campaign evoked fears of a red terror with images of blindfolded prisoners before a firing squad and Soviet tanks in central Santiago, radio programmes, and other stories planted in the media. Although the campaign failed to prevent Allende's victory, it contributed to further polarisation and financial panic. Despite this, the results showed that nearly 65 per cent of the electorate had backed programmes that espoused some form of socialism.

On the day of the election, Allende went to the PS headquarters and then accompanied Tencha to vote. On arrival at the polling station, they were met with applause mixed with whistles and jeers. The couple then returned to their home on Guardia Vieja Street, where they waited with friends and comrades.[4] As usual, each party prepared its victory celebrations just in case but had to get final permission from the army, which provided security during the elections. Allende called the officer in charge to get permission for a UP celebration. The officer informed him that it had been approved. Allende put down the phone and said, 'We've won!' The people assembled in his dining room erupted into cheers and hugs of joy. At 1:00 am, Allende walked to the nearby FECH building. The people of Santiago had begun gathering on Alameda Avenue, bouncing up and down in unison, chanting 'If

---

[2] The Church Committee report states that 'labor [sic] and community development projects were deemed rather unsuccessful' and the precepts of Allende's campaign found 'almost universal support', p. 19.

[3] Equivalent to nearly USD 6 million today.

[4] Puccio, pp. 233-234.

you don't jump, you're a *momio!*[5] Throughout Chile, thousands of people celebrated victory, among them many Christian Democrat supporters. Allende thanked the people and the popular parties for a clean victory, reminding them that Chile's was a different kind of revolution, which 'does not mean destroying, but building; it doesn't involve demolishing, it involves constructing'. He finally underlined that the UP were the legitimate heirs of the founders of the nation and that together 'we will make the second independence, the economic independence of Chile'.[6] Now, although its first victory had formally been won, the real battle was just beginning.

Allende and the Chilean popular movement faced many powerful enemies both in Chile and abroad, and their influence began to be felt immediately. It was an extremely tense situation. Although Allende's victory was promptly recognised by the Christian Democrat candidate Radomiro Tomic and celebrated by many of the Party's supporters, the leader of the Party and former President of Chile, Eduardo Frei, refused to do so. The situation was further complicated because the CIA was heavily involved in trying to prevent Allende's accession, using the now notorious 'Track I and Track II' options. Track I involved trying to get Frei re-elected by having Congress choose Alessandri over Allende, with Alessandri then resigning, opening the way for a 'special election' in which Frei would be the candidate. However, it rapidly came to involve seeking Frei to instigate the military option. Track II, meanwhile, rested on identifying officers willing to lead a military coup directly.[7]

Three days after the election, on September 7, Allende went to see Frei in the Moneda palace. Allende knew that a cold distance

<hr>

[5] Momio: (lit. Egyptian mummy), what the Left called right-wing conservatives. Lisandro Otero, *Razon y fuerza de Chile: tres años de unidad popular,* (Havana: Ciencias Sociales, 1980), p. 75.

[6] *Discursos: Salvador Allende. Discurso ante el pueblo de Santiago 5 Septiembre 1970.*

[7] Peter Kornbluh, *The Pinochet File,* (London: The New Press, 2003), p. 14.

had grown between himself and his former friend, but he tried to relax the situation. After greeting each other, Allende ran to the presidential chair and sat in it. 'How do I look?' he joked. Seeing that Frei was unamused, he tried to cheer his old friend up. 'Don't worry, *flaco* (slim); I'll give it back to you in '76.'[8] Although Frei was not up to joking, he reassured Allende that he was setting up a transition team. He lied. On the day that Allende took over the Presidency, the Moneda palace was completely empty. Frei's team did not even leave the internal phone directory.[9] Despite the initial rebuff, Allende continued to try to build a relationship with Frei and asked for a mutual friend, Gabriel Valdés, Frei's former Foreign Minister, to arrange another meeting at which it became clear that Frei would not support Allende. According to Altamirano, Allende said Frei greeted him coldly, saying, 'What have you done? This entire thing of yours will fail!'[10]

Embittered by electoral defeat and jealous that Allende might succeed where he had failed, Frei warned that he could never support a government that contained Communists.[11] At the same time, Frei was now under pressure from the CIA to mount a coup against himself by appointing a military cabinet before the handover and was being informed of US intransigence and hostility if Allende were to assume power.[12] He also knew of plans afoot to mount a coup. Meanwhile, Frei remained silent in public. With the outgoing government unclear on its position with regard to Allende, attention inevitably drifted towards the armed forces. Their position would be decisive in resolving the situation.

The armed forces were commanded by General René

---

[8] Martinez, p. 318. Chilean presidential terms were limited to one 6-year term.

[9] Puccio, p. 272.

[10] Salazar, p. 263.

[11] Valdés, p. 211. A secret CIA cable dated September 5 stated that 'If Tomic finishes third, this is tantamount to a rejection of all Frei and his government had sought to accomplish'; see 'Concerns of President Frei' National Security Archive.

[12] Kornbluh, p. 14, p. 17.

Schneider, a strict constitutionalist who had been appointed by Frei to impose obedience to the law after the 1969 *Tacnazo* mutiny. Schneider's position, along with that of the parties of the UP, had remained immovable during those vital days; the army should be apolitical and subordinated to civilian authority. In 1970, thanks to this position, the onus returned to the politicians in Congress and a coup was avoided.

Within the PDC, popular pressure and fears of what the Left's supporters might do — if blocked from taking power — forced the right wing of the party to accept Allende's victory. At the same time, they predicated their approval of Allende upon the signing of a pact of constitutional guarantees that they felt would guarantee the rule of law and pluralism in Chile. Despite it being the second measure limiting his prerogatives as President, Allende enthusiastically supported the initiative and delegated a team to negotiate it immediately. 'With this, we'll begin to deliver our programme before the inauguration!', he optimistically told Orlando Millas, one of the drafters of the document. The main idea was to find all the points of agreement in the presidential manifestos of Allende and Tomic and put them together. By doing so, it 'cleared suspicions, eliminated resistance, dissipated unfounded fears, and even satisfied an understandable [Christian Democrat] desire for prominence'.[13]

Allende accepted these guarantees because they did not fundamentally contradict either his government programme or his core beliefs on pluralism and democracy. In many ways, he was simply guaranteeing to act in accordance with those beliefs. However, they clearly contained measures intended to defend the status quo, and like any defensive measure, they had the potential to be used offensively too. From a revolutionary perspective, the main problem with these guarantees was that they limited the scope of the Presidency's constitutional prerogatives and

---

[13] Orlando Millas, *Memorias 1957-1991, una disgresión*, (Santiago: CESOC, 1996), p. 68.

guaranteed freedom of action for the government's opponents under the mantle of pluralism and freedom of speech.

Their usefulness in organising subversion is clear:

The holding or diffusion of any political idea cannot be constituted as a crime or abuse', 'The expropriation [of media] can only be carried out by a law approved in both chambers [of Parliament]'; 'Written and telegraphic and telephonic communications are inviolable. They cannot be opened, intercepted or registered except in cases clearly indicated by law'; 'The liberty of staying in any part of the Republic, to move from one place to another or enter and leave its territory, as long as they preserve established legal norms and do not prejudice a third party, without it being possible to detain, imprison, exile or banish except in the ways established by law'; 'neighbourhood committees, mothers' centres, trade unions, cooperatives and other organisations that collaborate in the fulfilment of State and municipal services [...] will in no case appropriate the name or representation of the people and will not try to execute powers that belong to the State authorities.

Allende's government had no intention of violating any of these principles, but such clauses later helped protect privately-owned media as they drummed up support for violent subversion and encouraged the armed forces to 'take action' — they were just expressing political ideas. The clause on communications limited the government's ability to counter the October 1972 strike and track the activities of terrorist groups like PyL, as did the clause on freedom of movement. The final clause had implications for preventing social organisations linked to the Left from assuming activities that might help defend the process from sabotage.

When the clause on the armed forces is considered, it is obvious that one aspect of the guarantees was to ensure that no alternative military force or significant alteration to the composition of the armed forces would be possible. It stated, 'the armed forces and *Carabineros* are professional, hierarchical, disciplined, obedient, and non-deliberant', by which it meant that they were apolitical. Allende could have no problem with this because, as president, he was their commander-in-chief. The final sentence read, 'The incorporation of new members of the Armed Forces and *Carabineros* will only be done through their own specialised institutional schools' which meant that the hierarchy would have control over who to admit to the armed forces, preventing any left-wing infiltration.

In the euphoria of victory and with the political initiative behind him, Allende could emphasise the positive nature of these guarantees, particularly since they represented an agreement with the Christian Democrats, whom he would need in Congress. However, along with his commitments to the UP, they effectively curtailed his constitutional powers. The guarantees later meant that he could not create new units in the armed forces, change its doctrine, discipline the media, or effectively crack down on subversion. Admittedly, none of these were necessary in the early stages of Allende's programme of economic and constitutional reform when all was going well. Once the forces of institutional resistance and subversion began to combine to seek a non-institutional solution, it closed off options that could potentially have saved the process — such as the expropriation of *El Mercurio* or the creation of a presidential guard (the normal recourse of a governor fearing potential coups) or the mass influx of Leftists into the armed forces.

Allende signed the guarantees on 15 October. The deal allowed Allende to take power, effectively as the president of the 65 per cent of Chileans that had voted for broadly similar programmes of change.

The only option left to prevent Allende from taking office was now a military coup. The more extreme Chilean opposition found a ready ally in the US, and President Nixon ordered the CIA to begin preparations for Track II — a military coup in Chile (and possibly the assassination of Allende). Plans to destabilise the Chilean economy were drawn up as part of a project to create the psychological climate for a coup. While the CIA coordinated these plans, terrorist violence struck Chile for the first time. Bombs targeted supermarkets, the stock exchange, a TV channel, railway lines, and the main airport's fuel depot. Although the media attributed many of the attacks to mysterious and previously unknown left-wing groups, it was clear that the real instigators were right-wing groups opposed to an Allende government, which were being funded by the CIA.[14] On 22 October, things went even further; a group of assailants with whom the CIA was covertly involved, tried to kidnap General René Schneider two days before Allende was due to be confirmed. He was shot and died the next day. Schneider's killing showed the desperation of the right, and it sparked outrage and shock, ensuring that Congress voted Allende in.

Allende and his team knew that he was next on the list, although Allende was loath to adopt any extra security measures. His daughter Beatriz helped to convince him, and he approached a group of socialists known as the National Liberation Army (*Ejercito de Liberación Nacional*, ELN) who had some experience working with weapons as they had been set up to support Che Guevara's guerrilla campaign in Bolivia. They rejected this approach, wanting to focus on their main mission, so via his daughter Beatriz, Allende then talked to the MIR, who had proposed a security arrangement some weeks earlier.[15] Accordingly, after 4 September, the MIR set up Allende's first security detail, which became popularly known as the Group of Personal Friends (*Grupo de Amigos Personales*, GAP), after Allende's response to journalists asking who they were.

It was a strange partnership in many ways because the MIR

---

[14] Kornbluh, p. 20.

[15] Manuel Cortés, *Yo Patan: Memorias de un combatiente*, (Santiago: Ceibo, 2015), pp. 45-49.

leadership had no faith in the 'Chilean road'. Nevertheless, for the MIR, it was a way of gaining access to privileged information and to weapons and training. It also helped to legitimate them as part of the Left. For Allende, it was an effort to integrate the MIR into the process, preventing them from carrying out destabilising actions, while also influencing its leadership. Miguel Enríquez, the MIR's charismatic leader, jokingly told his fellows after Allende's election, they now had to turn 'this bunch of bank robbers into a political party.'[16] Allende knew this and tried to encourage it, even inviting Miguel Enríquez to become his Health Minister in early 1971. Enríquez refused. The MIR was still not a political party in the sense of the rest of the Chilean Left. It aspired to be a political-military organisation preparing for a future confrontation. The difference in the analyses and methods of the UP and the MIR eventually came to contradict each other despite Allende's efforts and led to the MIR being expelled from the protection detail in mid-1971.[17]

The MIR's presence around Allende also confused his political opponents. After all, if Allende was a democrat, why were people who called for violent revolution protecting him? During talks prior to Allende's assumption of power, Frei repeatedly asked Allende to dissolve the GAP since they were 'extremists', and it was not correct that they protect the life of the President of Chile.[18] Whether or not this was the real motive, Allende could still not rely on the police to be completely loyal, nor did they have experience in protection, since Chile had no history of assassinations. The regular contacts with the MIR led to exchanges of information between it and the UP leadership, particularly in regard to seditious activity in the military, but it was an uneasy relationship that was a testament

---

[16] Mario Amorós, *Miguel Enríquez: un nombre en las estrellas*, (Santiago: Ediciones B, 2014), p. 130.

[17] Max Marambio, *Las armas de ayer* (Santiago: Debate, 2007), p. 69; Enerico Garcia Concha, *Todos los dias de la vida: Recuerdos de un militante del MIR chileno* (Santiago: Cuarto Propio, 2010), p. 67.

[18] Valdés, p. 210.

to Allende's efforts to try to bring together the broadest possible spectrum of support for his revolutionary project.

While there were good reasons to attempt to integrate the MIR into the process in some way, it has to be asked whether the political cost was worth it. The MIR was a very young organisation. It had only been founded in the mid-1960s, the latest of a fairly regular series of radical splits from the PC-PS duopoly. Its leadership were only in their twenties or early thirties. In 1970, the MIR was a small political group, although it was influential among middle-class students, particularly those associated with the PS in Santiago and Concepción. Before the UP victory, the MIR was mainly known for a number of armed 'requisition actions' (bank robberies) that it undertook in the late 1960s. Many people, particularly among the middle and upper classes, considered them terrorists or criminals of a sort. Therefore, the extent of its positive influence outside the Left was questionable. So, why did Allende make such an effort to accommodate the MIR?

Although Allende did not share their vision of the necessity for armed struggle to achieve the revolution in Chile, he understood it. Allende's nephew, Andrés Pascal, was one of the MIR's leaders, and Allende also knew and liked the MIR's charismatic leader, Miguel Enríquez, a doctor like himself. Allende had developed a good relationship with the leaders of the Cuban revolution, and the MIR was also well favoured in Havana. Having constructive relations with the MIR was therefore important in maintaining good relations with the Cuban leadership. Allende was also aware that there were plenty of people within the PS who shared the MIR's analysis and their frustrations with the electoral road. There were groups, such as the ELN in the Party, who were engaged in paramilitary training and organisation in a similar way to the MIR, of which Allende's favoured daughter, Beatriz, was a member. Moreover, many members of the MIR were former militants of the PS or from Socialist families. Alienating the MIR could, therefore, threaten the internal stability of the PS and Allende's relationship with the Cuban leadership, which was, in turn, key to sustaining Allende's revolutionary credentials.

Allende had a soft spot for young people. Allende thought of himself as being young at heart, and he always praised young people for their revolutionary zeal and rebellious instincts. Initially, Allende had a lot of sympathy for the MIR and he, no doubt, thought that he would be able to convince or control them if he had access to them. Since similar views to those held by the MIR were well represented within the PS, perhaps Allende thought the MIR could even eventually be persuaded to join (or, in many cases, rejoin) it.[19] As his invitation to Enríquez showed, he certainly thought he could bring them into the UP. So, by engaging the MIR with the UP, in what may have seemed a relatively unimportant manner, Allende was involving them in that project in a way that echoed his method with individuals. First, they would be given small tasks that could later develop (or not) into a more stable contribution to the cause. By doing so, Allende was preventing the emergence of an autonomous Left beyond the UP. Nevertheless, in light of Allende's recognised need for PDC backing in order to govern effectively, Allende's flirtation with the MIR seems a triumph of revolutionary ego over political pragmatism, if not a crass error.

Chile's state institutions and political elite never accepted the GAP's existence since its existence challenged their monopoly of an armed organisation. Allende's security was, therefore, forced to function in a semi-clandestine way, training its members in secret, using weapons smuggled into the country, and run on a shoestring. Within a few days of the MIR running Allende's security, the ELN repented and joined the GAP. The Cubans were then approached

---

[19] With Chile having two mass Marxist parties, it was relatively common for members to switch from one to the other, or for the Socialist Party to absorb smaller non-Communist groupings. The founding of the MIR was a direct result of criticisms of the FRAP strategy inside the PS. Many MIR leaders, including Miguel Enríquez, were former members of the Socialist Party's youth section, whose parents were also Socialists.

to help train the team, but that took time, and so for the first weeks, it was a very small, very lightly armed team using three borrowed cars to ferry Allende around. Together with the Cubans, they were able to sweep the Moneda for bugs, working long into the night. They found almost every room had been bugged.[20]

During the whole period prior to his confirmation, Allende lived an itinerant life, travelling from meeting to meeting until the early hours and never sleeping at the same address twice. He usually used empty flats that were in the process of being let by an estate agent friend. His guards carried clean sheets, a pillow and a blanket in the boots of their cars, and they themselves slept on the floor covered with whatever was to hand. As Allende's collaborators had always found, it was difficult to keep up with his energy levels. However, his guards also encountered a new challenge. At every opportunity, Allende would ask them their opinion on current events, and they felt forced to read the news digests that were sent to his home at 5 am every morning so as to be able to discuss the issues with the man who insisted they call him *compañero*.[21] Despite the amateur nature of the operation at this stage, they were able to prevent at least one assassination attempt, with Allende telling one Christian Democrat friend that he had been shot at while getting out of his car some days earlier.[22]

Later on, there were several attempts on Allende's life — a truck full of ice poured onto a coastal road in Valparaíso, shots fired at his cortege on the road to the port of San Antonio, and an oil slick on the road in Santiago. Allende's detail initially drove borrowed cars, but eventually came to have their own FIAT-125s. Ever the patriot, Allende had insisted that the cars had to be made in Chile. These cars were rapidly provided with specialist rally engines and eventually armour, but they were nevertheless small cars, much

20 Espejo, p. 18.
21 Cortés, p. 84.
22 Valdés, p. 207.

smaller than the American cars that most of the Chilean upper class drove. This added to the danger posed by upper-class youths trying to block or interfere with Allende's convoy or push his little cars off the road. Unfortunately for these youths, Allende's drivers had to assume that each effort was a potential assassination attempt, and they used their skills and rally engines to destructive effect. The enraged mothers would later arrive at the Moneda carrying a torn-off bumper, a mechanic's bill, or a medical note accusing Allende of trying to murder their *hijitos* (dear little sons).[23] They were paid off. These events may seem trivial, but they demonstrate the extraordinary hostility that Allende's government was faced with and the complex security situation this created. The harassment may have initially been relatively amateurish, but it was soon to move into the institutions of the state as well. No Chilean president before or since has ever dealt with anything similar.

In parallel to the development of his security detail, Allende also promoted the development of a political analysis team, which some have compared to an 'intellectual GAP'. This team was made up of three leading social scientists, each from the Communist and Socialist parties. The team was to work for Allende and the Political Commissions of both parties. It was classic Allende, a team of young experts who could use cutting-edge techniques to analyse trends and provide accurate intelligence. One of its main jobs was to carry out opinion polls and combine this data with other sources. The team was supported by a number of leading scholars and analysts and eventually came to produce top-secret weekly analytical reports destined for Allende and a select handful of others. They also met with the other teams Allende had around him — the speechwriters and analysts such as the Spaniard Joan Garcés.[24] Finally, as President of Chile, Allende was able to begin

---

[23] See Cortés for a description of these attempts, pp. 86-89.

[24] Félix Huerta, *El trabajo es vivir: Conversaciones con Jaime Chávez*, (Santiago: Rubén Darío, 2011), pp. 121-125.

developing a more institutionalised intellectual support structure, which moreover contributed to dialogue and better understanding between the Socialist and Communist parties.

Allende took office on 4 November 1970. Eduardo Frei arrived riding a horse and carriage, surrounded by plumed cavalry. He wore the traditional top hat and tails. Allende wanted to show that he would be a different kind of president. Throughout his life, Allende had operated within the system but meticulously not of it. In 1937, when he was elected to Congress, he had asked the President of Congress to allow the Socialist deputies to take their oath the day after the others; and when Queen Elizabeth visited Chile in 1967, as President of the Senate, he had asked if he could forego the customary morning suit and wear a well-tailored dark suit instead. At his inauguration, Allende did the same. He arrived by car wearing a dark suit, and afterwards, he walked from the Congress to the cathedral through cheering crowds alongside his newly sworn-in cabinet ministers.[25]

One of the first people to come to see Allende was El Chicharra, Allende and Betancourt's old sparring partner and street-fighting comrade. Allende's aide de camp, Arturo Araya, told him that an odd-looking man was asking to see him. Allende asked for his name and was told it was Tulio Salinas. President Allende drummed his fingers for a moment before crying out, 'El Chicharra!' and running down to embrace his old friend, who was wearing tattered clothes and a different shoe on each foot. El Chicharra now lived in poverty, selling puzzles on the streets of Santiago. Allende gave him the job of looking after the fountains in the Moneda palace and arranged a salary and a new flat for El Chicharra and his mother.[26] This curious incident was testament to the ways in which Allende continued to care for the people he knew or who worked for him, even while he was president. He would arrange holidays, ensure they had jobs, send them gifts, and

[25] Puccio, p. 272.
[26] Jorquera, p. 25.

visit them if they fell ill. He did not forget his friends and found the time to look out for their wellbeing.

Allende's inauguration marked the failure of US efforts to prevent a Marxist government from coming to power in Chile. Two days later, on 6 November, President Nixon convened the National Security Council to discuss ways of bringing Allende's government down. For Nixon, Allende's effect on Latin America was dangerous. 'If we let the potential leaders in South America think they can move like Chile and have it both ways, we will be in trouble', 'Latin America is not gone', he continued, 'and we want to keep it.'[27] Following this meeting, the decision was taken to maintain an outwardly 'cool and correct' position but, at the same time, to undertake 'vigorous efforts' to ensure that the rest of Latin America understood their opposition as well as seeking their cooperation against Chile, while blocking all forms of external economic and financial cooperation with Chile.[28] On 25 November, Kissinger outlined five main points to the Covert Action Program [sic] to be undertaken against Allende's government — political action to divide and weaken the Allende coalition, extending contacts in the Chilean military, providing support to non-Marxist political groups and parties, assisting opposition media outlets and using them to 'play up Allende's subversion of the democratic process and involvement by Cuba and the Soviet Union in Chile.'[29] This programme of interference set the scene for Allende's entire time as president, providing his opposition with undreamed of resources, creating instability, undermining negotiations, exacerbating economic problems and encouraging the violent subversion of the UP process.

However, at first, the Opposition was too divided and

---

[27] See 'NSC Meeting — Chile (NSSM 97)', 6 November 1970, National Security Archive.

[28] NSC Memorandum 93, 'Policy Towards Chile', 9 November 1970, National Security Archive.

[29] See NSC, Kissinger to President Nixon 'Covert Action Program — Chile', 25 November 1970, National Security Archive.

demoralised to be able to prevent the UP from starting to implement its programme. This envisioned the expansion of democracy and the transformation of existing institutions in order to 'open the way for the most democratic government in the history of the country.'[30] It was, in essence, a summary of the measures proposed in Allende's previous campaigns. As Allende wanted and as was most practical, the coalition left the details to be worked out later during discussions between the political parties and the new mechanisms of popular power outlined in the programme.

The programme called for a new constitution and a single-chamber parliament and for simultaneous local, regional and national elections.[31] It proposed allowing the recall of public officials and politicians. Workers and social organisations would be given a role in power, helping to plan, analyse and resolve problems. The judiciary would be reformed in order to favour the poor. In defence, a new vision of sovereignty would place the Chilean people at its centre. The armed forces would be better funded and integrated into society and the economy. A series of social reforms were projected — equal pay for men and women, the provision of a living wage for all, to extend social security and a guarantee of 'preventative and curative' medical care to all. A vast new housing programme was planned and built by private and mixed firms. The programme also guaranteed equal legal status for women and 'illegitimate' children.[32] In education, a national state school system was planned, and a literacy drive would aim to end adult illiteracy. Sport would become a central part of education, and a new 'popular culture' would be promoted in society at large.

A central aspect of the programme was to be the reform of the economy into three related sectors — the social sector, the mixed sector, and the private sector — linked by a process of

---

[30] From the Programme of the Popular Unity.
[31] The existence of two chambers and staggered elections contributed to enormous delays in passing legislation, sometimes of up to twenty years.
[32] The latter was only reinstated in 1998.

democratically decided planning. The most important step would be the nationalisation of the copper, nitrates, iodine, iron and coal industries, the banking system, foreign trade (to prevent the export of vital goods for private gain), and of the country's largest monopolies. The UP also committed itself to finishing the land reforms begun under Alessandri and Frei.[33] The UP's land reform programme envisioned the creation of cooperatives and state-owned farms as well as giving land titles to individual peasants. The programme also provided for the restitution of lands and the provision of resources to Chile's indigenous communities. In foreign relations, the UP would condemn all forms of colonialism and neo-colonialism and revise or cancel all pacts and treaties that Chile had signed with the US — the programme, in effect, condensed 40 years of left-wing aspirations.

Although many of these measures may not seem particularly radical to Europeans accustomed to the existence of a welfare state, there were several important differences. In Chile, the provision of welfare was to be linked to a transformation in the way people acted and thought of themselves. They were not to be passive recipients of state largesse but active participants in a process that provided the means for a dignified life and, in return, demanded their participation in the management of the welfare system. Participation was to be demanded at every level. Workers were to participate in the management of enterprises, and trade unions and other social organisations were to be incorporated into administering enterprises and in the planning process. The government's first act in power was to sign an agreement legally recognising the Workers' United Centre of Chile (*Central Unitaria de Trabajadores de Chile*, CUT) trade union federation for the first time since its establishment nearly twenty years earlier. The deal had previously been debated in trade union assemblies and was the

---

[33] Ironically, land reform began under the auspices of the Alliance for Progress and was envisioned as a way of preventing Marxist revolution.

first step towards workers' inclusion into power under Allende.[34]

The hope was that the people could be incorporated into every aspect of decision-making in the process of democratisation that went beyond the realm of elections and made the exercise of power a daily reality. This would not only change the way Chile worked, it would change the way people behaved. It was the Chilean method of creating the revolutionary 'new man'. In practice, the government tried to channel and subordinate these organisations to the grand strategy being followed by Allende. As the situation polarised towards the end of 1972, the structures of this 'revolution from above' came into conflict with alternative ideas and structures developed autonomously outside the UP.

The UP's foreign policy was also revolutionary in that it proposed a sea change in Chile's relations with the rest of the world. Although Chile would no longer accept a subordinate place within an international system dominated by the US and would no longer accept the primacy of foreign interests, it still had to exist in an international system that was, in essence, built on foundations of military, economic and technological power. Balancing the revolutionary substance of his foreign policy with the demands of an international system that largely functioned in sharp contradiction to it was an immense challenge. Therefore, to make a strength out of Chile's weakness, the mechanisms of this sea change would be gradual and pluralistic, like its domestic programme.

The purpose of the UP's foreign policy was to strengthen Chile's autonomy and to promote anti-imperialism, Latin-Americanism, and a sense of solidarity within the Third World. It sought to strengthen Chile's relations with the socialist world, rapidly extending diplomatic recognition to Cuba, East Germany,

---

[34] Mireya Baltra, 'La participacion de los trabajadores en el gobierno popular del Presidente Salvador Allende', in *Salvador Allende: Presencia en la ausencia*, ed. Miguel Lawner, Hernan Soto, and Jacobo Schatan (Santiago LOM, 2008), p. 251.

China, and other socialist states. It emphasised sovereignty and participation in decision-making and precluded Chile's acting for the interests of any foreign power. Allende hoped that by doing so, Chile would help to 'liberate the powerful countries [currently] condemned to exercise despotism'.[35] Chile would promote self-determination and non-intervention in the affairs of states, expressing both the desire for autonomy in decision-making and respect for these decisions by other states. These principles, extended to other countries, meant that Chile had to pursue a policy of 'ideological pluralism', a readiness to deal with any state on equal terms no matter what their domestic ideology. It was an eminently practical basis for policy in the real world.

When Allende was elected, two of Chile's three neighbours, Peru and Bolivia, were ruled by left-leaning militaries, while Argentina — by far the most important due to its size, a long and in places disputed common border, and a marked cultural influence — was under the control of a nationalist and generally right-wing military regime that was beginning a crackdown on the Left. Within a year, the Leftist Bolivian government had been replaced by another right-wing military regime. Further afield but still influential across Latin America, the Brazilian dictatorship was overtly hostile. Other dictatorships dominated Paraguay, Central America, and the Caribbean. Across Latin America, there were rather authoritarian power-sharing arrangements in Venezuela and Colombia, unstable Latin American social-democracy in Ecuador, Uruguay, and Costa Rica, a Mexican government whose revolutionary credentials had been tarnished by the bloodshed of 1968 and only in Cuba, a socialist government. It was a complex environment in which there was little to be gained by ideological showboating and where the horse-trading of mutual legitimation played an important role.

Outside the region, the non-aligned movement was growing

---

[35] First Message to Congress, 21 May 1971.

and increasingly vocal as the superpowers entered a period of détente. In this context, Chile's policy of 'ideological pluralism' was part of a broader trend. Argentina followed a policy of 'heterodox occidentalism', which situated it firmly in 'the West' but sought to reach out to what it called the growing 'global middle class' of nations. In Europe, it was the period of German 'ostpolitik' and the independent Gaullist 'politics of grandeur', during which even Franco's Spain was adopting the 'Lopez Bravo Doctrine' of reaching out across the world (particularly what they called *'iberoamerica'*), based on principles of non-intervention and ideological neutrality.[36] In this context, Chile's ideological pluralism was generally met with understanding and sympathy.

The policy soon produced tangible results with governments that could have been expected to be hostile — Allende's summits with General Lanusse of Argentina reached agreements on resolving border issues and some economic cooperation. With Spain, Allende's government reached agreements on economic cooperation, including car plants, nuclear energy, and financial aid. Subsequently, both Argentina and Spain voted for Chile to be the host of UNCTAD III. Encouraged by Spain, the Paris Club provided credits to Chile (and negotiated their repayment), and Chile received loans and credits from Western Europe, Latin America, and across the socialist world. These successes indicate that Allende's approach to international relations and the way it balanced ideology and practicality was working.

This did not mean that Allende abandoned his politics in the international sphere. In August 1972, a group of Argentinean guerrillas who had escaped from the prison of Rawson landed in Chile. General Lanusse requested that Allende extradite the prisoners back to Argentina. Allende had to decide whether to privilege politics over realpolitik. According to their lawyer, Allende made his decision with the following words, 'Chile is a

---

[36] Maria José Henríquez Uzal, *Viva la verdadera amistad! Franco y Allende, 1970-1973*, (Santiago: Ed. Universitaria, 2014), p. 12.

capitalist country with a socialist government, and our situation is really difficult. The choice is to return them or leave them in prison'. Allende paused and then thumped the table with his fist, 'But this is a socialist government, dammit, tonight they go to Havana.'[37] However, while it may seem like the decision was a purely moral or ideological one, it was no doubt influenced by the news of increasing repression in Argentina, where the other escaped guerrillas had been murdered and by domestic pressure to show his socialist credentials in the wake of the unfortunate killing of a man by police during a raid.[38]

Later, in 1972, Allende also considered a visit to Franco's Spain, showing that realpolitik could trump ideology if the circumstances were right. He knew that his government carried a great deal of legitimacy and popularity abroad. He knew his visits enabled his hosts to share some of that legitimacy. He also knew that their hospitality and the ability to reach agreement with different political regimes strengthened his own claims to pluralism and legitimacy at home and abroad. At root, though, Allende's foreign policy was aimed at strengthening Chile's economy and protecting his government from external aggression, and he was willing to consider some sacrifices to achieve it. The ideological content was there as a statement of principle, a guide for practice but not as a straitjacket and fundamental to it was the emphasis on sovereignty and anti-imperialist cooperation, which precluded Chile's acting in the interests of any foreign power. Sovereignty and non-intervention are the concerns of any middling state, whether socialist or not. Therefore, this foreign policy was practical in that

---

[37] Duhalde cited in Ricardo Ragendorfer, *Masacre de Trelew la condena que falta*, Contraeditorial.
https://contraeditorial.com/masacre-de-trelew-la-condena-que-falta/

[38] The raid by the Investigations police was aimed at freeing a MIR leader who had been detained by a small ultra-left group known as the 16 July National Liberation Commando, who had seized a petrol station and detained Allende's nephew, MIR leader Andres Pascal Allende. After the coup the leader of this group, Osvaldo Romo Mena, was revealed to be a military intelligence, later DINA agent who took part in the torture of detainees.

it sought to establish common ground with other states, no matter their ideological perspective, and it was revolutionary in that it assisted Chile in its construction of socialism. All these elements of foreign and domestic policy were aimed at creating the basis for a socialist society, and by doing so, they attacked the economic, political and social sources of elite (and imperialist) power.

Allende had instructed a team of collaborators to distil the concepts expressed in the UP programme into forty specific measures to deal with Chile's 'profound crisis', echoing the forty measures of the 1930s Socialist Republic. The first seven of the government's 'forty measures' proposed limiting the pay of top public servants, ending the use of external advisers, depoliticising bureaucratic appointments, stopping the private use of government vehicles, and ending expensive jaunts abroad. The UP promised to provide pensions to anyone over sixty who hadn't been able to pay enough contributions to retire and to include small and medium businesses in the social security system. A Ministry of Family Protection would be created, and free milk and breakfast would be provided to all children. Mother and child clinics and legal advice centres would be created in every neighbourhood, and every neighbourhood would be provided with electricity and clean water. Rents would be fixed at 10 per cent of family income and no more.[39] Many of these measures would still be relevant to Chile today, where they would no doubt be labelled 'populist'.

Unfortunately, in many parts of Chile, the content of the programme was not well understood as it competed with the long-standing anti-Communist alarmism of the CIA-funded black propaganda project. One foreign resident was surprised to hear the elderly owner of a rural boarding house vehemently say, 'If any of these bastards come to take away my house and rape my wife, they will get stopped by this gun', as he took a rifle down off the wall.[40] A greater misunderstanding of Allende's democratic

---

[39] From the Programme of the Popular Unity.

[40] Kate Clark, *Chile: Reality and Prospects of Popular Unity*, (London: Lawrence

revolution is hard to imagine, but it is indicative of the gap that existed in some cases between what the UP proposed and what people thought it was proposing.

Nevertheless, for most Chileans, the UP government carried with it a tremendous weight of expectation, but its unity was fragile. While the parties of the UP had united around a path to power, the purpose of holding that power was still a divisive issue. For some, including Allende himself, holding the Presidency was a way of beginning a process of changes that would lead to the consolidation of socialism by means of gradual measures that would transform the basis of the economy, political system, and institutions of the state. 'Our country, starting from its traditions, will use and create the mechanisms that, within a pluralism based on the great majorities, will make possible the radical transformation of our political system', Allende said.[41] The country's existing institutions might serve foreign and elite interests, but Allende thought that the Chilean constitution was flexible enough to enable the UP to transform their use gradually and from within, discarding or replacing only what was necessary. The great advantage of this approach was that it built on existing foundations, saving time, resources and, most importantly — lives.

For the Communists, Allende's main allies within the UP, the UP was part of their strategy to develop a 'National Democratic Revolution' in Chile, in line with the precepts developed by the Communist movement during the 1960s. The context of these was that the creation and strengthening of the Soviet Union had put socialism firmly on the political agenda in every country across the world. As they put it:

The strength and invincibility of socialism have been demonstrated in recent decades in titanic battles between the new and old worlds. Attempts by the imperialists and their

& Wishart, 1972), p. 63.

[41] Speech in the National Stadium, 5 November 1970.

shock force — fascism — to check the course of historical development by force of arms ended in failure. Imperialism proved powerless to stop the socialist revolutions in Europe and Asia. Socialism became a world system. The imperialists tried to hamper the economic progress of the socialist countries, but their schemes were foiled. The imperialists did all in their power to preserve the system of colonial slavery, but that system is falling apart. As the world socialist system grows stronger, the international situation changes more and more in favour of the peoples fighting for independence, democracy and social progress.'[42]

So, for the Communists, the principal feature of the times was that socialism was becoming stronger and imperialism weaker. This defined the possibilities for change within countries across the world.

The strategy they pursued was the product of a long debate within the Communist movement. Back in the 1920s, the international Communist movement had argued over the forms of revolution and the political alliances necessary in the 'colonial and semi-colonial' world. This discussion eventually settled on the possibility of revolution in stages through worker-peasant alliances. The first revolutionary stage was the struggle for 'bourgeois democracy' in alliance with the local petite-bourgeoisie and even those wealthy sectors with contradictions with imperialism. This broad alliance was built on the material interest that all these sectors had in land reform (anti-feudalism), economic development (anti-imperialism), and democracy. Together, these interests enabled these groups to end the domination of the landed elite and what would be called today 'transnational corporations'. This 'bourgeoise-democratic revolution' would, at a later stage,

---

[42] Statement of 81 Communist and Workers' Parties Meeting in Moscow, 1960. https://www.marxists.org/history/international/comintern/sino-soviet-split/other/1960statement.htm

develop into an outright socialist revolution led by the worker-peasant bloc.

After the Second World War, as the decolonisation movement gathered steam, this 'stageist' approach to revolution became more sophisticated. It was recognised that even where the material conditions for socialism were absent, a 'national democratic state' could pursue measures under the umbrella of a 'national democratic revolution' that would create a 'non-capitalist' or socialist 'orientation', which could then develop into socialism. While these concepts were outlined in the International Meetings of the Communist and Workers' Parties after 1960, Chilean Communists argued that they had de facto followed this policy since the 1930s. Chile's Communists could, therefore, not only claim to have been early initiators of this approach but also that it was an approach deeply rooted in Chilean reality, a perspective that Allende fully agreed with.

This may seem a somewhat esoteric discussion, but such definitions were important because, as Corvalán wrote, 'From them depended both the programme and the policy of alliances that we [Communists] ought to formulate and apply'. In Chile, the Communists defined their alliance policy as the creation of a national liberation front, a front of anti-colonial and anti-feudal struggle.[43] In practice, this meant 'agreements and collaboration' with 'various parties and organisations' and, by doing so, grouping together the 'majority of the people'.[44] This definition meant that all political forces outside the oligarchy could become part of the alliance. Accordingly, Chile's Communists did not think it was necessary to over-emphasise the socialist nature of the revolution. Since 'a revolution cannot be defined wilfully or on a whim', then revolutions — even ones that hoped to build socialism — first needed to develop the right conditions for socialism. For

---

[43] Corvalán, *De lo vivido y lo peleado*, pp. 99-100, 115.

[44] Luis Corvalán, 'Nuestra via revolucionaria', in *Camino de victoria*, (Santiago: PCCh, 1971), p. 24.

the Communists, revolutions were determined by reality, by the 'social and political evolution of the country and the international situation'.[45] Therefore, it made little sense to alienate potential allies over labels and superficial issues. Communists also believed that where the National Democratic Revolution was led by revolutionary forces and the proletariat (especially where Communists played a leading role), these processes could lead directly into a socialist revolution; in other words, the stages, rather than being totally distinct, could flow into one another.

This then was the intellectual framework used by both Chilean Communists and the Soviet Union in analysing Chilean reality, while acknowledging that the revolution would be different in every country. It was also the framework that the US and the Chilean opposition were familiar with. Although, in their understanding, this theory was merely window-dressing for the inevitable violent revolution. The Communists' perspective was very close to Allende's own views on revolution and helped explain the irreconcilable differences Allende and the Communists had with other Left groups and sectors within the PS. It is also why the PC demonstrated such loyalty to the 'Allendista' programme over time.

For others within the UP, particularly in the PS and the MAPU, the purpose of taking the Presidency was to open the way to smashing the old institutions in order to replace them with new ones. They thought that since the old institutions served the bourgeoisie and the interests of US imperialism, they could not be transformed. This meant creating parallel institutions that would then overcome existing ones after a victorious confrontation. This focus made the role of the military and the existence of a popular alternative 'own force' an important aspect of policy.

This did not mean that Allende had ignored or forgotten the importance of the military. Allende and his closest collaborators

---

[45] Corvalán, *De lo vivido y lo peleado*, p. 99.

had, in fact, developed a 'military policy' of their own. Allende's strategy was 'to act upon the social, economic, political, and ideological factors that regulated society', in order to avoid losing the initiative to those who wanted to shift the conflict into the arena of physical violence.[46]

In other words, the UP government had to maintain legitimacy, social approval, institutional cohesion, and foster economic development in order to ensure the military deploy its arms to defend the government. It assumed that the military factor was best neutralised by going with the force of Chilean military tradition, not against it. One of its originators, Joan Garcés, has called it the 'indirect' approach to revolution. It was certainly an approach intended to avoid the introduction of violence to the process. It initially worked well, and it enabled the UP to assume the Presidency, despite Schneider's assassination, and to defeat the efforts (to overthrow Allende) of late 1971, March 1972, October 1972, and April and July 1973. Though it eventually failed, it is not evidential of that it was wrong-headed.

Unfortunately, this strategy was not well understood within the Left. For many in the Left, the 'military policy' was not about a strategy to politically neutralise the Chilean military but instead to develop the means to defeat it in open conflict. This more 'traditional', confrontational vision of the revolution increasingly entered into conflict with Allende's. This problem was exacerbated by the fact that both Allende and the PC still justified their vision using the traditional framework of revolution.[47]

The Left was blinkered by this traditional framework, by this 'revolutionary formula' that began with the bourgeois revolutions of the eighteenth century and ran on through the Paris Commune of 1871, the Russian Revolution of 1917, and which was then turbocharged by the combined impact of the Cuban revolution

---

[46] Joan Garcés, *Allende y la experiencia chilena: las armas de la política*, 3 ed. (Santiago: Ediciones BAT, 1991), p. 148.

[47] See the work of Tomás Moulian for more on this.

and the dogged heroism of the Algerian and Vietnamese struggles against imperialism. Each success had culminated in a violent struggle, and the result was a fetishization of armed struggle. Allende was forced to pay lip service to this fetish, but the price he paid was that he was then unable to properly articulate or defend his own unique military policy.

The UP was put forward as a new way of achieving the goal of traditional revolution, but this hampered Allende's ability to develop and disseminate a distinct theoretical approach to the issue of the state's apparatus. This ensured that Allende's military policy, which was at the heart of the policy towards the state as a whole, was poorly understood, even by those in the leadership of the UP. Some of those who understood it thought it was simply wrong. After all, history showed that to build socialism, the old institutions and classes had to be violently smashed.

Still, there was a further problem. Everyone in the UP agreed that they wanted to build socialism eventually, but how this socialism was defined depended on who was talking. For Allende, pluralism, anti-imperialism, a mixed economy, free speech, and individual liberty were key parts of socialism, but many others within the UP had not given much thought to whether the UP would be a stage on the road to Soviet-style socialism or whether it would be the beginning of a new version. Many, no doubt, thought that such issues could be worked out along the way, in the interplay of discussions within the Left. Regardless, the influence of existing models of socialism was difficult to resist. Only the Communists had a clear and coherent vision, at least at the level of their party leadership. Although the Communists were important and arguably the most effective of the parties in the UP, in terms of size and discipline, they could not impose their views on the rest. Nor could Allende. Decision-making in the UP was democratic, but nobody had the role of ultimate arbiter and executive. As President, Allende could have been given this role, or he could have taken it, but amid the traditional rivalry between Socialists and Communists, each party carefully protected its prerogatives. This meant that each party confused its own position with both the ideologically correct position and the popular interest, in a combination that was toxic to the compromise that was to prove essential.

Allende could have insisted that he be the arbiter — his status as president would have made it quite a natural move — but he did not. It is likely there were two reasons — firstly, Allende saw each of the parties in the UP as the representative of a legitimate set of currents that were all part of the popular movement in Chile — Radicals, Socialists, Communists, and Social-Christians. Without ignoring their shortcomings, he accepted their view that they were the embodiment of the people. Therefore, he could not impose his will on them without imposing it on the masses in some way.

Secondly, Allende was an anti-*caudillo*. These charismatic leaders had been characteristic of Latin America since independence. In the twentieth century, men like Perón in Argentina came to define the *caudillo* as a national leader, but there were many political leaders who developed mass appeal and the ability to enforce their views, men such as Ibañez in Chile or perhaps Gaitán in Colombia. These men defined and gave life to the movements they led. It was their overshadowing of and autonomy from the popular movement that created the danger of authoritarianism that was anathema to Allende. Allende felt that the political leader was subordinate to the movement. It was a profoundly democratic perspective and also a legacy of the Marxist idea that the masses threw up the leaders they needed at a particular time. However, there were practical reasons for Allende to subordinate himself to the UP leadership — Allende was a president without a political apparatus of his own. Without the two main parties of the UP, Allende had no way to turn rhetoric into action and without the smaller parties, he had no hope of winning a majority in Congress. So, the uncomfortable truth was that he needed them, and he risked losing their support if he ignored their views.

The two perspectives on the nature of the revolution demanded different approaches to the issue of power. For those wanting to smash the 'ancient regime', the development of class-based unity and of alternative 'popular' institutions that could challenge those of the state were essential. They believed that violent conflict was inevitable, and they, therefore, focused on mobilising the people for violence and on developing some form of a popular army or militia. They never got very far in this.

For those who sincerely believed in the Chilean Road, either as a method on the way to conventional Soviet-style socialism or as a means to a pluralistic and libertarian form of socialism, this was a mistaken approach. They needed to build a broad coalition for change in order to strengthen popular control over existing institutions and make them function in new ways. In the military sphere, instead of building an alternative armed force, what the Left needed to do was strengthen the position of the constitutionalists and Leftists within the armed forces while giving it a new constructive mission in society. The two visions within the Left were always in competition and, in many ways, directly contradicted each other.

The lack of clarity on the definition of socialism and whether the UP was a stage on the way towards it or simply the beginning of its development was practical in that it minimised the scope for disagreement within the UP. However, it made it difficult for the UP to make allies beyond the Left, among sectors whose understanding of socialism was limited and heavily distorted by decades of anti-socialist and, more specifically, anti-Communist propaganda. If traditional socialism was the goal, what would happen to the Chilean bourgeoisie or middle class? The non-Marxist parties were presumed to pass into opposition at some point further down the road, and the Communist leader, Luís Corvalán, invented a metaphor for this, stating that the UP was like a train travelling from Santiago to Puerto Montt — passengers would get off at stops before the final destination. The problem was, what would happen to them once they did?

For those Chileans outside the Left, many of them members of the middle class, the 'traditional' framework of revolution was frightening. This fear of class violence was ably intensified by the right-wing media using propaganda designed in the USA, and which played on decades of negative reporting of the USSR, Cuba, and socialism in general. The fear was that at any moment, the 'cloak' of democratic and pluralist socialism would be discarded for the 'reality' of a repressive authoritarian regime. Allende, it was feared, was a Chilean Kerensky; because of this, the Left's language became increasingly important. So, when the PS leadership declared in 1971 that 'Revolutionary violence is inevitable and legitimate [...] and is the only road that leads to the seizure of political and economic power' and that 'the PS considers the peaceful or legal forms of struggle limited instruments of a political process that leads us to the armed struggle', it struck icy fear into the hearts of many.[48]

Gabriel Valdés, a leading Christian Democrat and Frei's former Foreign Minister, recalled the outgoing President Eduardo Frei telling Allende that he had become alienated from Chilean socialism since it was 'even more revolutionary and frenetic' than the Communists and that together, they would end up 'exercising dictatorship'.[49] He led the party that the UP needed to bring on side, if they were to succeed. Within the Left, the apocalyptic language of the extremists may have been confined to a minority, but it was a vocal minority. Moreover, it was a minority that controlled much of the leadership of the main party of the UP government. While

[48] Resolutions of the XXII PS Congress, La Serena, February 1971.
[49] Valdés, p. 211.

much of this violent language was for internal consumption, the effect on UP's potential allies was an understandable alarm. While they may not have feared Allende, they feared those who stood beside him. With both left and right-aligned with regard to a traditional vision of revolution, this vision became the framework within which the UP government developed.

Politically, this issue was important because it formed the biggest barrier to cooperation with the PDC but also because, alongside social unrest, it opened questions around the legitimacy of the UP government. This latter issue was crucial to the attitude of the armed forces because it was difficult to justify seditious action against a government that was both legally elected, legitimate in its use of power and providing social stability. Still, if it could be argued that the government was using power illegitimately and contributing to civil unrest, then its overthrow could be seen as legitimate, even if illegal. This was increasingly the angle that the opposition took as the relationship with the Christian Democrats deteriorated.

While the UP programme was unique in its goals, the Christian Democrat programme had also promised many similar measures. It also envisioned the nationalisation of copper, the continuation of agrarian reform, and even mentioned the creation of 'Communitarian Socialism' with an enlarged state role in the economy. Meanwhile, the Christian Democrats were torn on how to respond to Allende's victory. The Party had not shown great skill in building alliances prior to winning the government, and nor after 1964 did it feel that it needed them. In the words of one of their then leaders, 'Our words and our conduct were marked with arrogance'. Despite this, and as the Party's support fell, the Christian Democrat youth section argued for the need for a future electoral alliance of all Chile's progressive parties. In 1969, this wing of the Party even managed to force a vote within the Party leadership on whether to go into the 1970 elections with their own candidate or to join a broader coalition. The decision to field their own candidate won narrowly by 233 votes to 215.[50] There were, therefore, good reasons to expect the PDC to support Allende's government.

Much of the PDC grassroots supported the UP process, while the leadership was consumed by arguments over the approach to take towards the government. Although Tomic and many others wanted to cooperate with the UP, Frei was still convinced that it was best that Allende's government fall as soon as possible. In the shadow of his public silence and assisted by American dollars, the right wing of the PDC regrouped.[51] The Left of the PDC, led by the party's candidate for the 1970 elections, Radomiro Tomic, Allende's old friend from the Senate, were convinced that Allende's proposed revolutionary path could not succeed without unity between left-wing Marxists and Christians. For both Tomic and Allende, Chile's problems could not be solved within capitalism.

Frei, Tomic, and Allende knew that unless the UP could make some form of alliance with the PDC, the Chilean political system would stall. In this system, the president had broad powers, but Congress could act as an effective block. There was no institution that could act as a referee if the two were at loggerheads. Furthermore, Chile was traditionally politically divided into 'three-thirds'. This meant that no political force tended to absolutely dominate Congress and required either a UP alliance with the PDC or a plan that would enable the PDC to support those UP policies that were held broadly in common. Therefore, Allende knew that he had to nullify the threat of confrontation with Congress and avoid conflict with the PDC if his programme was to succeed. The PDC's support for Allende's confirmation as president and their reaction to the assassination of General Schneider showed that with some

---

[50] Ricardo Hormazabal, *La Democracia Cristiana y el gobierno de Allende*, (Santiago: Copygraph, 2014), pp. 74-78.

[51] The CIA provided significant funds to the PDC and the PN throughout Allende's government. See Kornbluh, p. 89. According to Garcés the money was actually given to the Frei faction of the PDC, strengthening its right wing.

compromise, the UP could reasonably hope for such an alliance to succeed. As Tomic said to Allende in late 1970, the PDC just needed a 'gesture' from the UP. This could have taken the form of an agreement not to stand a UP candidate in the election to replace Allende's senate seat, another that the UP invite the PDC to join the government. Allende thought that this was the way forward, but he knew that his Party and the UP, more broadly, would never accept it. As Corvalán, leader of the least sectarian of the UP's parties later ruefully recalled, ' … the intoxication of victory and the sectarianism that shortens foresight impeded us from seeing […] the need to seek a great accord with the DC'.[52]

Therefore, Allende asked his personal advisers to come up with an alternative plan in mid-October 1970. They presented it to him on 25 October. The plan consisted of a referendum that would link the nationalisations of a list of large companies and of copper and other natural resources, with the participation of workers in decision-making in housing and planning, and allow the president to dissolve parliament and call elections once during his term. The plan was intended to resolve the potential impasse between the president and Congress, and it was hoped that by giving way to the ability to dissolve parliament, the idea would get broad support since there was great enthusiasm for the nationalisation of copper.[53] This referendum would link the economic to the political and capitalise on Allende's victory, forcing the PDC to support the government or be exposed as a de-facto opponent of change. It would also provide Allende with the tools necessary to push through the reforms promised in the UP manifesto.

Allende then took the two ideas to the UP leadership. Either an alliance needed to be made with the PDC while it was still led by its left-wing, or the UP needed to try the referendum. Allende preferred the latter option, but his problem was in the nature of

---

[52] Luis Corvalán, *El gobierno de Salvador Allende* (Santiago: LOM, 2003), p. 10.
[53] Joan Garcés, *Allende y la experiencia chilena: las armas de la politica*, 3 ed. (Santiago: Ediciones BAT, 1991), pp. 220-221.

the UP leadership. Although they were ostensibly united, Allende characterised the UP leadership as lacking 'homogeneous central thinking' and 'tactical ideas'.[54]

The inter-party divisions were, on occasion, severe. Luís Corvalán, the Communist leader, recalled that his Party had the 'greatest affinities and the greatest differences' with the Socialists. This meant that each party used the UP meetings to defend its positions rather than articulate or develop a common strategy. So much so that Allende preferred to meet with the party leaderships individually.[55] This can be exemplified by an anecdote recalled by Corvalán: Shortly after Allende's election, the PC leadership, including Pablo Neruda, visited Allende at home to discuss their role in the upcoming government. As they were leaving, Neruda managed to accidentally gather up some of Allende's papers from the table they had been sitting around. Among them, they later found a letter to Allende from the PS leadership demanding that he ensure that several ministries not be given to the Communists under any circumstances.[56]

This was the leadership that Allende had agreed to subordinate himself to, so when he approached the UP, he had to contend with a divided group that could not agree on the issue of compromise with the Christian Democrats. For the more dogmatic Left, it seemed the PDC simply had to choose which side it was on or split but that the UP should make no deals with them.

The referendum proposal also ran into stiff opposition, particularly from the PC, with many worrying that the new rules around holding referendums would allow the centre-right dominated Congress to shape the questions, and others were concerned that the UP would not get over 50 per cent in a referendum. They preferred a gradualist approach, hoping that the

---

54 Interview in 'La Gran Encuesta', 10 September 1972, in *Discursos: Salvador Allende* (La Habana: Ciencias Políticas, 1975), p. 428.

55 Espejo, p. 11.

56 Luis Corvalán, *De lo vivido y lo peleado*, (Santiago: LOM, 1999), pp. 115, 125.

UP's economic reforms would develop further electoral support. Allende felt that this was a mistake, but as Garcés later noted, 'Allende was alone'.[57] Even though he was president, Allende thought he could not impose the referendum against the will of the UP parties or that of the Minister of the Economy, whose plan had already been approved.

By the third week of November, the idea had been abandoned, although Allende tried to get versions of it approved several times in 1971 and early 1972. Allende's failure to push through this proposal against the wishes of the UP leadership risked making the government hostage to the PDC. A few months later, Allende asked the Christian Democrats to share the UP's 'historic responsibility', showing their 'accordance with the principles and manifestos they offered the country so many times'.[58] Towards the end of 1971, Allende tried to consolidate an alliance with the PDC, given the repeated rejection of a plebiscite by the UP leadership. He offered Tomic a ministerial role, but Tomic rejected it, feeling that he and the left-wing of his party had been hung out to dry by the UP leadership. Soon afterwards, Tomic lost control of the PDC, no doubt aided by the funds the CIA was disbursing to Frei and his supporters.[59]

Despite this, one of the UP's most important victories was achieved with unanimous support in Congress, showing how far Allende and the Left had managed to make their proposals a centrepiece of popular common sense. Demand for nationalisation had become so widespread that the bill passed unanimously. After more than 30 years since it was first proposed, Allende's dream had been realised. The decree nationalising the copper industry was signed on 22 November 1970. It was, in effect, the foundation of modern Chile and perhaps the UP's most lasting legacy since

---

[57] Garcés, p. 228. See Garcés for a description of how the UP leadership misfunctioned.

[58] First Message to Congress, 21 May 1971.

[59] Garcés, pp. 211-212.

copper has been the largest contributor to state coffers ever since.

Allende called the day the decree came into effect — 11 July 1971 — 'the day of national dignity' and said that it marked the moment that Chile started out on its road to its second, definitive independence. Allende always had an eye for historical symbolism, and he spoke his words in the city of Rancagua, the site of a famous 1814 battle in Chile's Wars of Independence and a few miles from the famous El Teniente copper mine. In his speech, Allende explained to the people the problems that the nationalisation process had encountered and would yet have to confront, thanks to the foreign copper companies. These copper companies had begun a race to get as much copper ore out before the nationalisation took place. They stopped investing in machinery and left rubble in the mines. Furthermore, the US mining experts who had managed much of the industry began to leave Chile, leaving unqualified Chileans to deal with the mess.[60] Two teams of mining specialists from France and the USSR confirmed that the mines were in a sorry state and that it would take heavy investment just to get them up and running at capacity.

Lacking an industrial elite in Chile, the state played a key role in the development of the economy. The Popular Front had set up the CORFO, and by 1970, the Chilean state-owned many enterprises. Allende's plans for nationalisation simply sought to expand this area of the economy in order to allow the redistribution of surplus in a way decided by the government and other social forces. The UP programme envisioned nationalising ninety-one mostly industrial companies that held monopoly positions in the market. By the end of 1971, 70 per cent of these had either been nationalised or taken under state control.[61] Then, in May 1971, after months of work, the government signed an agreement with the CUT, which

[60] Speech on the Day of the Nationalisation of Copper, 11 July 1971.
[61] Andres Valera, 'Gestion de los trabajadores en las empresas del Area de Propiedad Social: un análisis testimonial', in *Salvador Allende: Presencia en la Ausencia*, p. 232.

fixed the rules for worker participation in decision-making in the nationalised Area of Social Property (*Area de Propiedad Social*, APS).

The structure of this participation was as follows: the top instance was the Workers' Assembly, followed by Productive Unit Assemblies of the departments of an enterprise, Production Committees within the sections of these, a Workers' Coordinating Committee chaired by the leader of the trade union and finally the Administrative Council (like an Executive Board). The Administrative Council was made up of five workers' representatives, five state representatives and a representative of the Presidency.[62] In modern terminology, it was a tripartite structure with the main distinction being the workers' active role in decision-making around production.

Giving workers a role in decision-making was an essential socialist measure since Marx had argued that relations of production and workplace relations, were important factors that underlay and influenced other relations in society. In other words, they were crucial to the continuance of capitalism or the construction of socialism. Every other socialist revolution had also attempted to change workplace relations to benefit workers. The purpose was to change the way surplus value was produced and give workers a collective voice in how it was distributed. That, at least, was the theory. Nevertheless, it was not an easy process to begin.

Miguel Labarca, one of Allende's oldest friends and collaborators, was appointed to run the nationalised nitrate company, Chemical and Mining Society of Chile (*Sociedad Química y Minera de Chile*, SOQUIMICH), and he has left a rather negative testimony of his experience. At first, production increased to unprecedented levels. The workers were motivated by the UP victory but also by actions like the reduction of managers'

---

[62] Ibid., p. 241.

salaries, Labarca's included, and the shift from paying managers in inflation-resistant dollars to Chilean Escudos. However, the elections also brought party politics into the workplace. The bulk of the workers in the nitrate fields were affiliated with PC unions, and a small minority to Christian Democrat and socialist organisations. As the national situation deteriorated, the committees fell to defending party positions that reflected the sectarianism developing in national politics. The debates began to affect production. As the material impact of the economic blockade began to be felt both by the workers and the company, morale fell. It was the economic reflection of the problems caused by division. As Labarca observed, 'the struggle among the parties along with the materialist demands that a handful promoted among the workers created an unsustainable situation.' Efforts to keep the company functioning and profitable were 'sterilised by a maddening and senseless agitation.'[63] In despair, Labarca resigned from his post at the end of 1972.

Yet, other participants had a somewhat different view of the experience. Andrés Varela ran several APS enterprises under Allende. Years later, after meeting with former workers in these enterprises, he recalled:

> On balance, we can come to a positive evaluation. Without doubt, there were many difficulties, but I am convinced that the chance to participate, dignified the workers, made them feel like direct actors in the process, and they gave a lot to overcome the difficulties. [...] The working environment changed, there was a relaxation of discipline, an increase in meetings and lost production time, yes, in addition to a lot of sectarianism and appointment by political quotas ... but at the same time, there were many shop floor initiatives in production, there was voluntary labour on weekends and in

---

[63] M. Labarca, pp. 204-207.

general, a better atmosphere that translated into improved productivity.[64]

In fact, Varela recalls that the APS followed the general tendency of the Chilean economy under Allende — rapid growth until mid-1972, followed by a 'negative tendency' caused by external problems.

Furthermore, in the nationalised industries, the government felt an acute shortage of cadres of people with both professional skills and political commitment. This also exacerbated problems in the nationalised enterprises, with workers without enough relevant experience often being left to run things.

The way worker participation was organised demanded that their trade unions change their methods and their structures too. Allende was calling on workers to 'win the battle of production', but how could unions shift from attitudes and structures designed to defend pay and improve working conditions towards structures and attitudes that sought to improve productivity? In other words, if under a capitalist government, unions fought for redistribution of wealth with no consideration for the impact on the economy as a whole, for a bigger slice of the cake as it were, under a socialist government, unions had to fight to work harder, to increase the size of the economic cake for all. That way, there would be more to be distributed over time. It required a political understanding that to defend these workplace demands; workers needed to defend the overall process. It required workers to consider the interests of the working class as a whole against their own immediate interests.

Unfortunately, as with individuals, social and institutional habits die hard. This problematic process can be clearly seen in relation to wage demands. In the first year of the UP, wages rose rapidly (wages by 55 per cent, salaries by 48.5 per cent),

---

[64] Varela, 'Gestion de los trabajadores', in *Salvador Allende: Presencia en la Ausencia*, pp. 241-242.

and unemployment also dropped to record lows. The result was a shortage of goods that increased prices, which led to rising inflation. Inflation then devalued the wage increases. The situation required that wage demands be held back. Allende referred to this in his 1 May Speech in 1971, where he spoke of the 'battle of production':

> Before, when the state was at the service of the capitalists, the workers in both the public and private sectors had to adopt an attitude of demands — proposing wage increases to compensate for the rising cost of living. They fought to defend their claim. But today, you have to understand; the workers *are* the government, the people *are* the government. The public sector is not financing a minority. It is putting the economic surplus at your service, at the service of the people of Chile.'[65]

The issue was one of the distribution of the costs and benefits of the revolution, of the relative weight of its material gains and those which might be called 'non-material' or 'moral' (such as the change in the social status of workers, and their increased political voice). After months of debate in many enterprises, the solution arrived at was to split an individual's wage into a static amount, while linking any earnings over this level to the productivity results of that worker's immediate team. This way, individual material improvements were linked to increased production, which benefitted society. As in other revolutionary processes, the egalitarian demand for redistribution gave way to a form of collective performance-related pay as society fought to build more wealth for collective allocation. In the process, trade unions 'increasingly adopted the role of auditors, of defending individuals, of ensuring good working conditions, and of creating opportunities for collective recreation', and they gradually left

---

[65] Speech on International Workers' Day, 1 May 1971.

the tasks of production, including wage demands, to the work collectives themselves.[66]

Allende's economic programme and the nationalisations were intended to give workers a strong role in the economy to create the engine of Chile's further development. The CUT-UP agreement demanded new trade unions and a new generation of trade unionists who could both manage and balance shop floor demands and their relation to national issues and who were both workplace leaders and communicators of national priorities to the workers. Quite simply, the UP process did not last long enough to allow this new generation to fully develop, but this vignette provides a flavour of the way that Allende envisioned the democratisation of the economy would impact workers as well as the complexities involved in the process of transformation.

Another key point in the UP programme was that the completion of the land reform began in the 1960s. At the same time, the nationalisation of copper would allow the government to plan future economic growth based on the production of copper and other minerals. The agrarian reform would enable small and medium-scale farmers, alongside state-run and collective farms, to produce enough food for domestic needs and for export. It would also go some way to providing redress for Chile's indigenous peoples. Together, they would create an internal market for the Chilean industry. The nationalisation of copper would be combined with the creation of an international copper organisation aimed at regulating prices to the advantage of copper producers. Copper, the wage of Chile, together with Chile's other minerals, would

---

[66] Varela, 'Gestion de los trabajadores', pp. 244-245. The issue underlines the distinction between the functions of trade unions in countries building socialism and the functions of those in capitalist societies. Why would unions in socialist countries seek to confront management or government, if they themselves were a part of that management, if the government acts in the general interest of society as a whole? In fact, unions in many social-democratic countries also avoid zero-sum confrontation through works councils and other trilateral bodies.

fund the vast transformation of society that Allende and the UP planned.

The economic aspects of the programme were highly optimistic and made several assumptions that underestimated the potential effect of political events. This was largely due to the technocratic bias of the experts convened to develop this programme. While there were young experts from within the various UP parties, there were also a large proportion of independent economists and social scientists whose previous experience had been in international organisations such as the CEPAL and Chile's universities.

Although their technical qualifications were excellent, these people were not accustomed to thinking about the political ramifications of their proposals, and therefore, there was a tendency to 'not take responsibility for the content of the policies they were proposing', which helped create problems later.[67] For example, it was assumed that nationalisation and a progressive wage policy would soon create bulging state coffers and an enlarged internal market. However, the nationalised mines needed massive investment. Wage increases allowed people to spend on food, but agricultural production was disrupted by the agrarian reform, and the combination created shortages and inflation. It was also assumed that the Chilean elite would take advantage of an enlarged market to invest in business. Instead, many began moving money abroad, fearing further nationalisations. In combination with the problems created in the economy, the imposition of price controls also helped enlarge the black market. The government could have dealt with these problems, but in combination with growing political polarisation, foreign interference and an economic blockade, the situation began to spin out of control.

Despite this, with the opposition in disarray, during its first year, Allende's government made many advances in its legislative programme and its economic strategy showed promising signs of

---

[67] Clodomiro Almeyda, *Reencuentro con mi vida*, (Santiago: Las Ediciones del Ornitorrinco, 1987), pp. 172-179.

success. As one foreigner living in Chile noted, after a year, 'US imperialism has lost its copper, the Chilean oligarchy has lost its biggest industries and banks, the land-owning class has all but lost its *latifundios*'.[68] Inflation was brought under control, from over 30 per cent to under 15 per cent, and GDP grew by nearly 8 per cent (in comparison to less than 3 per cent under the previous government). Industrial production, mining and agriculture all showed increases. Importantly, this all had immediate impacts on ordinary people. 'The revolution', one Minister recalled, 'was translated above all into calories, proteins, healthy diets, clothing, housing, urbanisation, school-building, better education, the extension of medical attention ... '[69] Some problems were beginning to show such as the increasing shortages of food products — thanks to increased consumption — but the government was still optimistic. Chile was living through an unprecedented boom, with masses of people having access to more and better food and consumer goods.

This optimism was bolstered by the results of the April 1971 municipal elections, when the UP increased its support to over 50 per cent; it was an unprecedented success achieved, despite US financial support for opposition media and candidates. An improvement in the share of the vote was unheard of in Chilean politics, and it moved Allende to push the UP to call a plebiscite on designing a new constitution for Chile. However, most within both the Socialist and PC leaderships opposed it, fearing that despite the municipal results, the UP would lose a plebiscite that went beyond economic measures and proposed a massive restructuring of the political system.[70] Allende felt that he could not push it without their support. The idea was shelved.

This period was the zenith of the UP government. It appeared

[68]   Clark, *Chile: Reality and Prospects*, p. 98.
[69]   Orlando Millas, *Memorias*, p. 79.
[70]   Eduardo Gutierrez, *Ciudades en las sombras: Una historia no oficial del Partido Socialista de Chile*, (Santiago: Editare, 2010), p. 38.

to be in control. It was also the high point of Allende's life, the culmination of his life's work. The economy was booming, society was enjoying a revolutionary 'fiesta' of participation and a cultural carnival, and US intelligence noted that Allende's policies 'enjoy wide popular support'.[71] However, the honeymoon could not last forever. As the same US intelligence report noted, 'Now inflationary pressures are rising, as accumulated stocks are exhausted, and production has not kept pace with demand', indicating that the contradictions of the economic and political programme would soon bite. Furthermore, US intelligence noted Allende ' ... has still not gained sufficient political strength to carry him surely through the difficult times ahead.' Indeed, the UP still had no majority in Congress, and this gave the PDC the key to the situation. Unfortunately, while Allende, the Communists, Radicals and the smaller parties of the UP wanted to reach an agreement with the PDC. The official Socialist position, expressed in their January 1971 Congress, was that, 'the bourgeoisie is gathering around Christian Democracy' and that 'the so-called Left of the Christian Democrats, by staying in that party and being indecisive, is serving as a screen for the right and reactionary sectors'. They demanded a 'growing acceleration of the revolutionary process' to force the PDC-left to choose sides.[72]

For their part, for much of 1971, the Christian Democrats wavered on the position they ought to take with regard to the UP. Some supported the UP and largely agreed with the construction of an alternative social system. Some saw that the vast popularity of the UP's programme meant that, for the time being, outright opposition was politically impossible. Others wanted to bring the PDC into a total opposition, allying it with the right. In December 1970, the former position won out temporarily and therefore,

---

[71] Special National Intelligence Estimate 94-71, Washington, 4 August 1971, Foreign Relations of the United States, 1969-1976, Volume E-16, Documents on Chile, 1969-1973.

[72] Partido Socialista, *Resolución Política del Congreso de La Serena*, Enero 1971.

until mid-way through 1971, the PDC de-facto cooperated with the UP in Congress. This position was even made official in a PDC national congress in May 1971, in which they expressed their support for the UP's objectives and called for 'all Chileans to redouble their efforts to make real the achievement of the objectives put forward'.[73] Allende knew that the UP needed to build on this and proposed that the UP not present a candidate for the July 1971 Valparaíso senate by-election.[74] If the UP promised to vote for a PDC candidate, it would provide tangible proof to Christian Democrat waverers that allying with the government could bring them benefits, helping to prevent them from being led into the arms of the right by Frei's supporters within the party. Instead, the PS leadership insisted on putting forward a Socialist candidate. The opportunity and the election were lost. The PDC candidate won, supported by the right.

The Christian Democrats' rightward turn had already begun. On 8 June, Frei's friend and former Interior Minister, Edmundo Pérez Zujovic, was gunned down by members of an obscure extremist group called the Popular Organised Vanguard (*Vanguardia Organizada del Pueblo*, VOP). It claimed to have killed Zujovic in revenge for a 1969 massacre of unarmed shanty town dwellers in Puerto Montt, but Zujovic had also been a leading proponent of a PDC alliance with the UP. The killing had a massive effect on the PDC. Rushing to express his solidarity, Allende, who had known Pérez Zujovic for many years, called it a 'crime against Chile', declaring three days of national mourning. He said that the killing had been intended to 'create a climate of confusion, of mistrust and of political vengeance against the Popular Government', but Frei accused the UP and Allende of 'bringing violence to Chile' and the opposition media took advantage of the murder to excoriate the Left in general, blaming Allende for his

---

[73] Corvalán, *De lo vivido*, p. 169.

[74] Carlos Prats González, *Memorias: Testimonio de un soldado* (Santiago: Pehuén, 1985), p. 209.

amnesty of political prisoners, including some members of the VOP earlier in the year.[75] Despite this, several leading Christian Democrats believed the killing to have been motivated from abroad, given its suspicious timing just after the PDC had agreed to cooperate with the UP and just before the by-election.[76] The assassination also came at a time when the CIA was spending large amounts of money on the Freista sectors of the PDC in an effort to turn it into an outright opposition party.[77]

Whatever the truth, the killing of Zujovic and the failure to support the PDC in Valparaíso were major factors in turning the Christian Democrats against the government. The right of the Party was also helped when a group of left-wing PDC congressmen, against Allende's advice, split from the PDC, creating a new party called the Christian Left (*Izquierda Cristiana*, IC). They were accepted into the UP, where they soon took up radical positions. This wing of the UP, together with the MIR, were active opponents of reaching an agreement with the PDC, and they repeatedly blocked Allende's efforts. In July 1971, the PDC voted to replace the UP President of Congress with one of their own. The phase of cooperation was over.

The failing relationship with the PDC was not completely the fault of the extreme Leftists within the UP, but they undoubtedly hampered Allende's ability to lead the process forward and contributed to the deteriorating situation by attacking the

---

[75] Carlos Toro, *Memorias de Carlos Toro: La Guardia muere pero no se rinda ... mierda, La Vida es Hoy*, (Santiago: Partido Comunista de Chile, 2007), p. 352.

[76] Luis Corvalán, *El Gobierno de Salvador Allende*, (Santiago: LOM, 2003), p. 191. According to Carlos Toro, the detective in charge of the investigation, a witness claimed that the Panamanian doctor exiled from Panama for organising an anti-Torrijos guerrilla group was the intellectual author of the killing. Since Panama was the home of Southcom and several US military bases, suspicion remains that the CIA was somehow involved. It is also known that the CIA deployed 'false-flaggers' to Chile (see Kornbluh). However, the case was never solved. Toro, p. 353.

[77] Garcés, p. 212.

government strategy from the Left, while it was increasingly under siege from abroad and from the right. Already by the end of 1971, these attacks were beginning to spin the UP process out of control.

Thus, although Allende thought the balance of the first year of his government was positive, his anniversary speech noted some major issues, several of which had to do with the effect that the extreme Left was having on the process. 'We need public order [in order] to change the structures [...] we are against the indiscriminate seizures of farms that create anarchy in production and end up pitching peasant against peasant'. Knowing the respect that many in the extreme Left had for the revolutionary classics — a leaning Allende himself did not share ('We set a lot more store by actions than by words here', he said to Debray in an interview) — he quoted Lenin to the 'minority groups', who pushed for ever more radical action. 'By revolutionary phrase-making, we mean the repetition of revolutionary slogans irrespective of objective circumstances at a given turn of events. The slogans are superb, alluring, intoxicating, but there are no grounds for them.'[78]

Unfortunately, for Allende, the MIR did not always limit itself to 'phrase-making'. Throughout the UP period, Allende struggled to prevent and reverse the MIR's practice of encouraging the popular seizure of small-scale private farms and businesses. The UP's nationalisation programme had been limited to the largest monopolies in each sector, and the seizure of these properties by the MIR was a major headache when Allende was trying to build bridges with the Christian Democrats. Allende tried to negotiate with the MIR over this, and in one example following the seizure of a farm in the south of Chile, he called the MIR to a meeting with himself and the Interior Minister, José Tohá, who had been discussing the nationalisation of the farm with the owner. Miguel Enríquez was accompanied by comrades from the MIR's central committee, all with tousled hair and wearing rather scruffy jeans.

---

[78] Speech in the National Stadium on the First Anniversary of the Popular Government, 4 November 1971.

Tohá complained that the MIR had not only occupied a farm but had encouraged the destruction of property, including the killing of a valuable prize bull. Allende and Tohá eventually convinced the MIR to return the property, but as he left, Allende paused and asked the Miristas, 'So which of you ate the bull's testicles?' (a Chilean delicacy) and before they could answer, he said, 'Next time, come dressed properly — you're meeting with the President of Chile'.[79, 80]

Another major problem was that similar views to those of the 'minority groups' that Allende mentioned were present within Allende's own PS and within some of the smaller parties of the UP coalition. In early 1971, the PS had elected a leadership that was committed to making real the resolutions of the 1968 Congress, electing Carlos Altamirano — a tall, bespectacled firebrand — to put them into effect. That Congress had passed resolutions that directly contradicted Allende's Chilean road to socialism, stating, for example, that 'revolutionary violence is inevitable and legitimate', that 'we consider the national bourgeoisie as an ally of imperialism and is in fact its tool' and that the 'so-called left-wing of the PDC is serving as a screen for the right'. This leadership clearly had little faith in the Chilean road to socialism. It did not want an alliance with the Christian Democrats and instead leaned towards like-minded revolutionaries outside the UP coalition, pushing for confrontation. These positions were so influential within the PS at the time that even within Allende's family, there was much sympathy for them. Beatriz, Allende's daughter, had been trained in Cuba and had a close relationship with the MIR leadership. Although Beatriz remained in the PS, she shared the MIR's apocalyptic vision of the future, and like many of her generation, she was highly critical of her father's 'reformist' politics.

Despite their political differences and the difference in age,

[79] In Spanish the ending '- ista' denotes belonging. Examples include *Mirista* (belonging to the MIR), *Frapista* (belonging to the FRAP), and so on.

[80] Espejo, p. 68.

Allende had developed a close friendship with Altamirano. Allende liked debate, and Altamirano provided it, and they also shared a similar social background. The two men were both former athletes, and it is likely that Allende saw something of his own impatient youth in Altamirano.[81] Allende probably thought the experience might mellow Altamirano and that he would be able to control him if not.[82] In the La Serena congress, Allende threw his weight behind preventing Altamirano's rival, Aniceto Rodríguez, from retaining his position as general secretary. Although they shared a faith in the potential of the electoral road, Allende probably suspected Rodríguez's political judgement since he had supported Ibañez's second government. In 1970, Rodríguez had exacerbated these concerns by heavily pressuring Allende to give him the Ministry of Interior. Allende refused, fearing it would concentrate too much power in his hands.[83] Allende probably feared that supporting Rodríguez would strengthen the right wing of the PS. Since, in the 1940s, the Popular Front had been brought down by a rightward shift in the leadership of the PS, it is likely Allende sought to avoid a similar mistake. Yet, Allende's decision to block Rodríguez opened the road for Altamirano, who later seriously damaged possibilities of an alliance with the PDC when, throughout 1972 and 1973, he pushed for the creation of alternative mechanisms of power, striving to push the Chilean road to socialism into the channel of a 'traditional' revolution.

In this, Altamirano and the people he represented in the PS were following a similar path to that offered by the MIR outside the UP. Here, too, the MIR was arguing for the radicalisation of

---

[81] It did but not until after the coup. In 1979, Altamirano split the PS, calling for its renovation which eventually led the PS to abandon Marxism and become a centre-Left party that shared government with the PDC after the fall of Pinochet.

[82] There are testimonies that provide evidence that the two had a somewhat competitive relationship. See Salazar p. 234 and Felix Huerta, *El trabajo es vivir* (Santiago: Ediciones Rubén Dario, 2011), p. 118.

[83] M. Labarca, p. 163.

the process, carrying out the seizure of small farms and small businesses by landless labourers and workers and, trying to develop a military force and mobilising the people around confrontation. For the Communists, the frustration with this position was intense. One Communist trade unionist expressed it succinctly: 'The youngsters of the MIR want confrontation now. I can't accept that they attack us Communists as bourgeois and unrevolutionary. We have fought for years. We have suffered repression. The working class has been dying for a hundred years to reach a situation like this, and the MIR wants to throw it all out of the window in three days of fighting.'[84] However, the idea that 'the revolution' could be made quickly was attractive to many, especially the young. Ironically, after Allende's election, the MIR had begun to abandon its original political-military structures and started working more like a political party, organising shantytowns and some rural areas. Yet, this mobilisation took place outside the state and often in opposition to it, seeing Allende and the UP as 'reformist'.

At the end of 1971, Fidel Castro, one of the icons of the extreme-left in Chile, arrived for a visit scheduled to last ten days but which extended to over three weeks. It was Castro's first visit to mainland Latin America, since the revolution, and he revelled in the chance to get to know Chile and its revolutionary process. His enthusiasm was paralleled by that of the Chilean people, who turned out in hundreds of thousands to hear him speak. Castro's visit provoked an outraged response from the Chilean right, for whom he was a terrifying figure. 'Never has a more open and barefaced intervention in the internal affairs of a country been seen as in Chile by that "Caribbean adventurer",' said one military officer later linked to the coup.[85] The close relations between Allende and Castro seemed to them to confirm that no matter what Allende said, his goal was to turn Chile into another Cuba. Castro tried to support Allende and the 'Chilean road'. In public,

---

[84] Óscar Ibañez cited in Arrate and Rojas v2, p. 45.
[85] Colonel Arellano Stark quoted in González , p. 121.

he exhorted the masses to unite behind Allende's government and in private meetings with the MIR leadership, Castro also warned them that in Chile, the revolution would be 'made by Allende or by no-one'. Castro's very presence increased the polarisation, and he was able to see with his own eyes how it developed, and it worried him.

Two days before he left, a semi-clandestine opposition organisation known as 'Feminine Power' had led a 'March of the Empty Pots', where women from the wealthy neighbourhoods, accompanied by their maids, marched, led and flanked by masked detachments of baton and chain-wielding young men from the fascist (and US-funded) paramilitary group Fatherland and Liberty Nationalist Front (*Frente Nacionalista Patria y Libertad* or simply *Patria y Libertad*, PyL).[86] It was the first anti-government march the opposition had felt able to stage, the first that had Christian Democrat support and the first concrete evidence that the US strategy to prevent a UP-PDC alliance was succeeding. The march ended in violence, as organised gangs of demonstrators split from the main route, attempted to burn down the building being built to host the UNCTAD that coming April, and attacked offices belonging to the Radical Party and the Communist Youth. The result was another first — the first time in Chilean history that the state's coercive institutions had acted against the elite. Police fired tear gas and batons and charged the PyL gangs. That night, Central Santiago was the scene of bonfires and barricades. A student leader from the right-wing Catholic University told the press that the government had transformed the *Carabineros* into 'a shameless ally of Marxism' demanding that the Minister of Interior, José Tohá, be impeached.[87]

Fidel Castro closed his visit the day after the march with an unprecedented speech at a packed National Stadium. As the host, Allende introduced him with a speech of his own. He

<hr>

[86] Garcés, p. 168.
[87] Garcés, p. 170.

drew out the similarities and differences between the Cuban and Chilean revolutions, underlining, in a way that contradicted the general tone of his message, that the Chilean people did not want violence but would 'respond to counter-revolutionary violence with revolutionary violence'. Allende then highlighted that the successes of the Chilean Revolution had affected vested interests and provoked hostility and even 'seditious attitudes'. Allende admitted that a 'fascist seed' was germinating among some sectors of the elite youth, but he underlined that, 'the people should not forget some things — that when the people is in Government, public order favours the revolution'; therefore, they shouldn't let themselves be provoked. 'I have used, and will use, the measures that our government constitutionally enjoys, which is why I have declared Santiago an Emergency Zone, to clearly show our resolution and by acting within the law to seek sanction'. This then is what Allende really meant by revolutionary violence — the use of the state to defend law and order, not the creation of a revolutionary alternative. Allende ended by introducing Fidel Castro, saying, 'I know that you will receive him with the warmth, the respect and affection with which we greet a brother'.[88]

Castro then gave a speech that was an extraordinary discussion of the Chilean situation, part theoretical musing, part analysis, and part revolutionary motivational. As such, it is worth quoting from at length. He reminded the massed audience that no social system and set of institutions was eternal, 'each form of society was succeeded by another', but each had defended itself with 'tremendous violence throughout history'. He continued, asking a question that revolutionaries around the world were asking, 'Whether the historical law of the resistance and violence of the exploiters will play out here'.

Castro questioned the elite's commitment to Chile's democratic institutions, reminding the crowd that, in general,

---

[88] Farewell speech for Fidel Castro, National Stadium, 2 December 1971.

when institutions no longer serve an elite, 'they simply destroy them.' 'There is nothing as anti-constitutional, as anti-legal, as anti-parliament, as repressive and violent and criminal as fascism', he continued. 'Fascism in its violence liquidates everything — it assaults the universities, it closes and crushes them, it assaults the intellectuals, it represses and persecutes them, it assaults the political parties, it assaults the trade unions, it assaults all the mass and cultural organisations. There is nothing as violent or as retrograde as fascism!'

Then Castro answered his earlier question, 'We have seen in this unprecedented and unique process how this law of history is manifesting: that the reactionaries and the exploiters in their desperation, supported mainly from abroad, generate and develop this political phenomenon, this reactionary current called fascism'. He reminded his audience that in Chile, as compared to Cuba, the opposition was much better prepared, organised and equipped to resist the UP's process of changes. 'They have created all the instruments to fight on every terrain against the process. A battle in ideology, a battle in politics, a battle for the masses — note it well — a struggle among the masses against the process!' Castro outlined how the opposition was using lies and slander, particularly around his visit, spreading fear and awakening chauvinism so as to win over the middle classes in order to divide the people.

Castro also discussed the issue of violence at length, and here, we can more clearly discern shades of difference with Allende. 'Once a revolutionary regime is installed, violence does not depend on the revolutionaries. It would be absurd, incomprehensible, and illogical for revolutionaries who have the possibility of advancing, of creating, to promote violence. However, it isn't the revolutionaries who, in these circumstances, create violence.' 'You are living a process that is very special, but it isn't new in relation to the class struggle. History has uncounted examples. You are living a moment when the fascists, to call them what they are, are trying to win the streets, trying to win over the middle strata of the population.'[89] Castro's unspoken question was, 'what do peaceful revolutionaries do when their opponents react with violence?'

Castro then listed examples of successful resistance to fascism — in Cuba and the Soviet Union in the Second World War. Even the French Revolution had been forced to fight off foreign invasion. Example after example of resolution, unity, and heroic resistance. It was a speech dizzying in its breadth but one that did little to resolve the stalemate within the UP because while it was superficially supportive of Allende, its subtext raised questions about the viability of the Chilean road. Allende argued that with a revolutionary government, 'public order' favoured the process, but Castro argued that once institutions no longer served an elite, they simply destroyed them. So, whom did Chile's institutions really serve? Allende spoke of a 'fascist seed' among some *hijitos de papa* (posh kids), and Castro spoke of a battle of ideology and politics 'among the masses'. Allende highlighted peaceful struggle; Castro highlighted that revolutionary success was correlated with violent resistance by peoples with their 'motivation developed to the maximum' by the revolution.

Yet, really, those who supported Allende's institutional road heard that revolutionary violence was illogical. Those who wanted a confrontational transition heard that it was the only way to defeat fascism. Perhaps the contradictions arose from the tension between Castro's respect for Allende and his fears that the Chilean process would succumb. The two leaders continued their discussions later in the presence of General Mendoza of the *Carabineros* police and General Pinochet, who had been detailed to accompany Castro throughout his visit. These public and private discussions indicate the level of confusion that Allende's 'road' was provoking among both friends and opponents. This confusion gradually got worse, and from this point on, the opposition grew more united and more aggressive, and the government's supporters more divided.

---

[89] Fidel Castro farewell speech to Chile, National Stadium, 2 December 1971.

In February 1972, the UP leaders met in the Santiago suburb of El Arrayán to discuss solutions to the internal and external problems that the government fuent now clearly faced. Following the impeachment of Tohá, all the members of the UP were clear that the opposition was intent on overthrowing Allende, whether politically or by force. Although the discussion was intended to deal with this fundamental issue and the meeting's report focused on this, there was no decision on what to do. One participant from the IC recalled that he felt 'like a deaf lion among mute lions' because there was never an answer to this question.[90] The report expressed the need to deal with three big problems: sectarianism (both within the UP and between it and other parties), bureaucratism, and 'dishonesty'; but it did not answer the fundamental political question of what to do to prevent a coup. Allende's proposal on putting constitutional reform to a referendum was discussed, but the UP took no decision.[91] As a solution to the internal sectarianism identified at El Arrayán, he also pushed for the creation of a United Party of the Socialist Revolution (*Partido Único de la Revolución Socialista*), but this was met with caution by Altamirano and other Socialists, who claimed that the time was not yet right. No doubt, they understood that the new party would be led by Allende and, therefore, undermine their positions.

Allende knew that the lack of understanding of the 'Chilean road' of his revolutionary democracy was a serious problem. He tried hard, through his daily practice, to educate people about the measures the government was taking and why. 'Unfortunately,' he said, 'people live the Chilean process a little superficially with less than 5 per cent of those who act and take part in the political process, having read, for example, the "Messages" sent to Congress.' 'The political parties', he complained, 'did not carry out this work

[90]	Bosco Parra in Pedro Milos, *Chile 1972: Desde El Arrayán hasta el paro de Octubre*, e-book (Santiago: Universidad Alberto Hurtado, 2013).

[91]	Lisandro Otero, *Razon y fuerza de Chile: tres años de unidad popular*, (Havana: Ciencias Sociales, 1980), p. 252.

of explaining the government's actions with the depth that they ought to.'[92] These efforts show that Allende and others in the UP leadership were aware of the problems they faced, but they were unable to find a decision-making formula that would resolve the impasse created by debate.

In March 1972, documents were released showing US transnational ITT's efforts to undermine the government, along with lists of civilians and military personnel linked to the plotting. The same month, the leaders of the civilian opposition, the heads of the employers' associations, along with retired military officers met near the town of Melipilla to plot Allende's downfall. The right-wing media, now largely funded by the United States, began to openly call for a coup in violation of Chilean law and yet Allende did not move against them. 'This', wrote Corvalán many years later, 'was the product of idealist concepts' and showed that Allende 'did not understand that the revolution that gives liberty to the people, must not allow the counter-revolution to prosper, specifically in order to defend that liberty.'[93] The Party wrote to Allende, in August 1972, to say that 'Our first and principal duty to the people and the country is to put a straitjacket on those who want to drag Chile into a bloodbath' arguing that he should make use of his prerogatives to apply the law to those 'spreading lies, insults and slander'.[94] As President, Allende prioritised the use of the judiciary to disincentivise sedition, but this institution used its margin of autonomy to avoid action that would have a dissuasive effect. Allende complained of this when he told journalists that 'when there were incidents on the streets of Santiago, 600 or so people were detained in one week. Not one of them was imprisoned'.[95]

---

[92] Allende interviewed on 21 October 1972, *Octubre 72: Pensamiento politico de Allende*, Presidential Publication, no date, p. 185.

[93] Corvalán, *De lo vivido*, p. 166.

[94] Communist Party of Chile Report, *Pleno de agosto de 1977 del Comité Central del Partido Comunista de Chile*, (Colo-Colo, 1978), p. 24.

[95] Allende speech, '*Este pais le pertenece a los trabajadores*', 24 October 1972, in *Octubre 72: Pensamiento político de Allende*, Presidential Publication,

In fact, it was difficult for Allende to repress seditious activity without undermining his government's democratic credentials, which were vital if he hoped to create an alliance with the PDC. As the experience with the judiciary showed, Allende could not rely on it to appropriately punish those who were brought before the law. Nor could he promote the organisation of a popular response to right-wing violence without destroying the already difficult path being followed by the 'Chilean road' because it would play into fears that the government was a sheepskin slung over a wolf's back. It would undermine the state's monopoly on coercion, and it would allow opponents to question the government's democratic legitimacy, facilitating the task of those seeking to turn the military against the UP.

Allende had to rely, therefore, on the institutions of the state, and he did institute a state of emergency in Santiago after the 'March of the Empty Pots', which the armed forces and police enforced. In his farewell speech, Castro had noted that revolutions needed 'audacity, audacity, and audacity' in order to succeed. For him and many others, the UP's (and Allende's) commitment to pluralism and free speech was translating into giving the opposition a free hand to do what it liked. They thought that Allende needed to be more decisive in dealing with his opponents, and for this reason, Castro privately encouraged the UP to take steps to prepare for the violence that the reactionary elite and its allies in the US were clearly preparing.[96]

The right was definitely on the move. Two days after the 'March of the Empty Pots', the Christian Democrats in Congress voted with the PN to impeach Allende's Minister of Interior, José

no date.

[96] According to East German reports, cited by Harmer, the Cubans had 'reservations and doubts' about the extent to which the UP's strategic goals could be achieved by democratic means alone, about Allende's tactics against the right and they voiced concerns that the armed forces might become the referees of the situation. Tanya Harmer, *Allende's Chile and the Inter-American Cold War*, (University of North Carolina, 2011), p. 152.

Tohá, on the false grounds that he was supporting paramilitary groups. In January 1972, the right-wing PN called for a united front of all non-Marxist parties. In February 1972, the PN and the PDC allied during by-elections in two provinces, forming the basis of a political alliance that would last until the coup. In March, leading figures from across the opposition — the PDC, PN, Church leaders, business leaders and members of the judiciary met to plan coordinated actions for the future. In April, a 'March for Democracy' united the PDC, the PN and other opposition forces to protest what Patricio Aylwin, the PDC President of the Senate, called 'the threats and violations that [our] democratic rights are being subjected to increasingly and more openly every day'. In answer to Allende's calls for moderation, he warned, 'We will be inflexible in exercising our rights'. The UP responded with an even larger mobilisation, where Allende underlined that those gathered had come to defend 'authentic democracy and authentic liberty'.

Yet, the possibility of a political agreement still existed. Key to this was the discussion around a constitutional reform put forward by the Christian Democrats, the Hamilton-Fuentealba proposal, which sought to define the three areas of the economy — the social area, private area, and mixed area; as well as which companies would fall under each area. The proposal was approved by the opposition-dominated Congress in February 1972, but in April, Allende vetoed those parts of it that were not in line with UP policy. Part of the problem for Allende was that the projected reform shifted the centre of political power to Congress, which obviously limited his capacity to lead the country. Furthermore, it could be used by the opposition to block further socio-economic reforms. Then, in June, Congress passed the reform, but Allende argued that it did not have the required majority to do so. It was a struggle of legal and constitutional interpretation. The opposition argued that Allende ought to put the proposal to a referendum, but Allende stated that 'we aren't going to do it as they'd like' because the way the proposed reform had been passed was unconstitutional.[97]

Nevertheless, Allende sought to reach an agreement on those areas that were not controversial for either side. Initially, the PS opposed it, but it eventually relented. The sides finally agreed that a reduced number of companies would be nationalised (eighty out of ninety-one proposed by the UP) and that 150 companies that had already been nationalised would be returned, among other measures. In future, rather than Allende using presidential decrees to nationalise companies, a new law would regulate this, with the government and PDC agreeing to postpone a vote on the constitutional reform to allow bills to be submitted on this. The Executive Council of the PDC agreed, and the signing was arranged, but from a meeting with the Christian Democrat International in Europe, Eduardo Frei phoned several senators to tell them not to make any agreement. On the day of the signing, two PDC senators left the chamber, meaning that the Senate did not reach quorum, and the agreement sank.[98]

These negotiations help explain why Allende did not feel the need to push a constitutional reform during the first half of 1972, despite the fact that he was not blind to the danger of institutional stalemate. At the meeting of the UP in El Arrayán in early 1972, Allende had raised the need for constitutional reform, but the response was lukewarm. The Left as a whole saw the Chilean constitution with its strong presidential powers as an ally to their process, not an obstacle, and the possibility of an agreement with the PDC seemed so close as to make a broader reform unnecessary.

However, with the failure of the negotiation with the PDC, Allende began to publicly discuss the need to reform the state, as envisioned in the UP programme, saying that 'we should mobilise the Chilean popular masses around the project for a

---

[97] Allende speech '*Aqui reside la fuerza de Chile*', speech to the Popular Unity, 5 September 1972, in *Octubre 72*, p. 233.

[98] Joan Garcés, Allende's former political adviser, recalled this incident at an event called '25 years after the military coup', held in Santiago in September 1998.

new constitution; a constitution that won't be that of a socialist country because Chile at this stage is not a socialist country, but which also cannot be that of a capitalist country'.[99] In the middle of 1972, he nominated a Commission to develop a blueprint for a new constitution. On 5 September, at a UP plenary meeting, he officially presented the UP with the Commission's proposal, intended to become the basis of a nationwide debate and to act as a rallying call for the upcoming elections in March 1973:

> We need to proclaim a great platform that signals to the people the task that it must fulfil. We need to say that we need new reforms, an educational reform, a new tax code, a new labour code, and new social security. We need to make possible the rights and duties of the workers. […] Chile cannot function indefinitely with a systematic and irreconcilable obstruction against the government. This afternoon I want to give the people of Chile this task, the study, discussion and analysis of these fundamental bases of a new constitution which with effort, tenacity and drive we will put into movement […]

Allende then outlined the basis of the new constitution. 'It must give more freedoms', allow indigenous peoples the right to their 'cultural personality', while also establishing the basis for overcoming the differences between manual and intellectual labour and between the city and the countryside — which was and remains a key objective of Marxist practice. Allende wanted constitutional recognition of the unions and the workers' role in running enterprises. He wanted education as a right from the cradle to the grave and to 'especially protect the single mother'. 'It must establish the principle that the country's economy is at the service of the people; it must clearly define our concept of the necessary coexistence between the economy, industry, mining,

---

[99] Allende in *Octubre 72: Pensamiento político de Allende*, Presidential Publication, no date, p. 179.

agriculture and services'. The new constitution would also enshrine the right and duty to work and reserve the natural wealth of the country for the state. The police and armed forces should have a 'broad social labour' in addition to their existing purpose. The judiciary needed to be democratised, and the legislative system needed to be simplified. Allende also proposed administrative reforms that helped decentralise and democratise planning. At the local level, 'the people should undertake directly the responsibility for central control through community organisations'. Overall, the new constitution had to 'recognise the power of the workers at the local level, in the workplace and in the state institutions'. 'The main question', Allende said, was 'how to ensure that the workers can come to control the economy of the country, control political power'. 'This', he said, 'is indispensable for Chile to resolutely progress down the revolutionary road that history has traced for us'.[100]

An incomplete draft of this constitutional project survives, outlining this deep re-imagining of Chilean society, economy and politics. For the first time, the constitution would recognise Mapuche and other indigenous groups and enshrine their linguistic and cultural rights. It also enshrined equal pay for women and young people and, befitting Allende's long-standing concern with healthcare, made social security a public service and 'the exclusive and primary function of the state', which ought to be particularly aimed at protecting women and children. The project gave women, particularly in their role as mothers, specific rights and established a Family Code and family courts.

The blueprint also outlined a new structure for the state's political institutions. Allende favoured a single-chamber congress. However, the constitutional blueprint provided another option, which was to have a second 'Chamber of Workers' to replace the Senate. Along with the president and direct popular petition,

---

[100] Allende speech '*Aqui reside la fuerza de Chile*', speech to the Popular Unity, 5 September 1972, in *Octubre 72*.

this elected Chamber would have powers to initiate legislation that would then be debated by Congress. The idea was to give workers a preponderant level of control in politics, echoing the way the Senate had favoured the elite during the early years after Chile's independence from Spain. The state was reenvisioned as a decentralised structure where, at every level, democratic assemblies cooperated with state and social bodies to approve, develop and apply plans and exercise oversight.

For example, at the lowest level, trade unions and social organisations would be represented in a Neighbourhood Council. Another council, known as the 'Corporation', would be directly elected, and together, they would compose a municipality. The Corporation would be responsible for the development, administration, and execution of a local plan. Meanwhile, the trade unions and social organisations in the Neighbourhood Council would feed information on local problems to the Corporation, as well as propose solutions.

The Neighbourhood Council would also approve the local development plan and have oversight of it. In this way, directly elected bodies interacted with local civil society to identify problems, plan solutions, and ensure their effective execution. A similar structure of overlapping councils and state bodies would exist at other levels.

The planning system was at the heart of the new institutionality and one of the main responsibilities of the state. The planning system was topped by the president and a Council of Socio-Economic Development, made up of national representatives of trade unions and of small and medium businesses. At each level, state and elected representatives were responsible for the delivery of the plan so as to ensure that it was 'democratic in gestation, central in formulation, and decentralised in execution'. The proposed document also defined taxation as progressive or proportional taxation, called for the protection of the 'ecological system', nationalised all riches of the 'soil, subsoil, and the bottom of the sea within 200 miles' and made it effectively illegal to nationalise small or medium-sized 'rural or industrial, fishing, mining or service enterprises' or land areas under 40 hectares.[101] These latter proposals clearly aimed at reassuring the middle class and offering an olive branch to the Christian Democrats.

The document could have formed the basis for a broad discussion of the problems afflicting Chile. It could have provided the detail needed to overcome the party-political debates. If linked to a referendum, it would have given Allende a mandate for the needed reforms. It was probably the last true opportunity to seize the political initiative and force the opposition to fight on Allende's territory. However, only the CUT and two of the smaller parties officially approved it. The Socialists and the Communists simply did not respond, and the initiative died.[102] In retrospect, it was a real lost opportunity.

In the meantime, the government also faced the problem that the increased opposition in Congress and in the media also acted as a catalyst for the activism of the 'ultra-left', who saw it as evidence that the process had run out of steam and considered that the government's role should now be to stimulate the creation of alternative institutions that could push the process forward. Miguel Enríquez, the MIR's leader, spoke of a government that had carried out some positive economic measures but which had failed to 'mobilise the people, to push the combative energy of the masses [...] against its enemies, who were the entire dominant class, and not just a part of it.' As an alternative to what they considered a failed strategy, the MIR fought hard to create a 'revolutionary pole' in Chilean politics. Faced with what it called 'the evident exhaustion' of the government's policy, the MIR identified two currents in the Left — one 'reformist and timid' and the other

---

[101] See the available text at the website of the CUT:
        https://cut.cl/cutchile/2020/09/08/las-bases-de-la-reforma-constitucional-
        de-allende-a-50-anos-del-triunfo-de-la-unidad-popular/
[102] Garcés, pp. 248-250.

'revolutionary'.[103] What they sought was, in its substance, the latest iteration of the PS's 'Workers' Front' — a class bloc that could force through the revolution with mass support but without the need for compromise with the middle class.

During the early part of 1972, in the wake of the UP meeting in El Arrayán, which had identified sectarianism as a problem, the government and the PC, in particular, sought to reach a deal with the MIR, but the MIR insisted that the government make a 'qualitative turn'. They argued this was necessary because 'the revolutionary nature of a period is not just in the quantity of sources of wealth that are nationalised'; it was in the 'problem of power'.[104] The mobilisation led to fighting in the streets and also forced the governor to call on the police to break up the demonstrations, leading to the death of a youth. The national UP parties disavowed the action of their local branches, but the MIR emphasised the unitary nature of the decision, stating that the local CUT, peasants, and students had all supported the mobilisation. The MIR accused the Communist governor of repression, called for his resignation and framed the issue as one of a reformist government that was retreating under opposition pressure and which was 'not capable of controlling the repressive apparatus'.

Instead, the MIR proposed a revolutionary alternative, which would channel and push popular mass mobilisations against the enemies of the process and the elite in particular, as well as developing mechanisms of 'popular power' — an Assembly of the People, Communal Councils of workers and peasants and finally, create 'a revolutionary alliance within the forces of the Left'. In late July, the MIR, working with the local Socialist and Radical parties, duly created an Assembly of the People in Concepción.

Allende was livid, in a letter to the UP leadership. In July, he wrote, 'I don't hesitate to qualify this as a deformed process that

---

[103] Mario Amoros, *Miguel Enríquez: Un nombre en las estrellas*, (Santiago: Ediciones B, 2014), p. 179.

[104] Amoros, *Miguel Enríquez*, p. 180.

serves the enemy of the popular cause'. 'Popular power', he wrote, 'will not arise from the divisionary manoeuvres of those who want to create a lyrical mirage derived from political romanticism'. For Allende, the idea that Chile needed a 'Popular Assembly' when he legitimately governed the country was 'absurd', 'crass ignorance', and 'irresponsibility'. He wrote that 'dual power' had come about in other revolutions when faced with a reactionary government lacking in popular support 'and plunged into impotence'. How could that be relevant in Chile, where there was a legitimate socialist government with mass support and which 'in its composition and class content is a government at the service of the general interest of the workers'?

Furthermore, the institutions have resisted elite and imperialist aggression so far. 'Therefore', he wrote, 'it is my duty to tirelessly defend the institutions of the democratic regime'. Allende admitted that these institutions needed reforming, but he wrote that this must happen in line with the will of the majority of the people, 'through the pertinent mechanisms of democracy'. The Assembly in Concepción, if it had any real revolutionary content, would have been targeted by the opposition. Instead, the opposition media had done all they could to promote it, 'because they know', Allende wrote, 'that it is useful to promote any process that distracts the people from its real tasks' in the government's political programme. Instead of playing about with irrelevant and dangerous 'Popular Assemblies', the UP needed to focus on winning the March 1973 elections in order to push through the much-needed constitutional, economic, and social reforms.[105]

The MIR leadership later argued that the UP had misrepresented the Assembly, that it was not an attempt at 'dual power', but instead was aimed at creating 'an agitational and propagandistic assembly, to create political conditions that would later extend into

---

[105] Letter to the heads of the Popular Unity, July 1972, *Discursos: Salvador Allende* (La Habana: Ciencias Políticas, 1975), pp. 409-413.

Communal Councils.[106] In retrospect, this seems rather convenient. How could an Assembly outside the state institutions and outside the control of the governing coalition not become a challenge to it? The opposition joyfully used the Assembly's proclamations to attack the government. As two Chilean scholars of the event have argued, the Assembly 'clearly disputed the UP government's leadership of the Chilean political process.'[107] Nor did the people involved in the Assembly see it as merely propagandistic, with one Socialist councillor stating that the tasks of the Assembly were to 'reject the representativity claimed by Parliament in respect of the workers' and act as 'a democratic instance of revolution'. What was this, if not an effort to create 'dual power', a Chilean 'soviet' of workers, peasants, and students?

Although ultra-left critics might categorise the UP as a 'reformist' process if it achieved the hegemony of the working class in the economy, society, and the political system and, broke that of the Chilean oligarchy and prevented foreign interference, was this not revolutionary? If it created a new morality, a new political culture, if it transformed the way the *pueblo*, the ordinary people saw themselves, was this not revolutionary? Did the Chilean oligarchy need to be physically eliminated or forced into exile to make a revolution? Marx and Engels, in their discussions of class, drew the distinction between a class 'for itself' and a class 'in itself': Classes and competing groups exist in any society, but not all are conscious of themselves as a class. Those that are, acquire a sense of class mission and develop the tools with which they attempt to mould and control society beyond themselves.[108] The UP's political programme and its forms of activism threatened to eliminate not the elite or private property per se but the ability of the elite and their foreign networks to mould and lead society. What made the

---

[106] Amoros, *Miguel Enríquez*, p. 194.

[107] José Diaz Nieva and Mario Valdés Urrutia, 'Desencuentros en las izquierdas y reacciones contrarias a la Asamblea del Pueblo en Concepción (Chile, 1972)', *Revista Austral de Ciencias Sociales*, No. 36 (2019), p. 283.

[108] See Marx, *The Poverty of Philosophy* or Bukharin, *Historical Materialism*.

UP a revolutionary project was that it was not limiting itself to claiming a larger share of an economic or social pie controlled by the upper class, as occurred with Western European social democracy — the UP wanted to control all the economic, political, and social levers of society, in order to build a fairer and more developed country for the people of Chile. Allende, in effect, proposed allowing the elite to continue to exist as 'a class in itself, but shorn of the power and mechanisms needed to act "for itself"'. While it is true that Allende and the UP sought to carry out this process gradually, in a reformist manner, their ultimate objective was not to reform capitalism, but to overcome it.

The events in Concepción were evidence of a growing polarisation across Chile. During 1972, university campuses and the streets bore witness to growing violence between youths affiliated to political groups. Sometimes, the fighting was between left and right, at other times, even between Leftist groups. People argued and fought in the queues for the everyday goods that were becoming scarce.

Behind the façade of violence and political obstructionism in Congress, the right made more use of its wealth and its extensive social networks to develop plans to overthrow Allende. At the same time, the CIA, US transnationals, and even European money contributed to the opposition's development. This opposition was multifaceted and in practice, consisted of a political wing (the PDC-PN alliance in Congress and in elections), a social wing (demonstrations by organisations such as 'Feminine Power'), a propaganda wing (the right-wing media and radio stations setting a hostile news agenda), an economic wing (the actions of transnationals, the leading Chilean landowners and capitalists and their various economic associations), and a coercive wing (groups such as PyL that carried out terrorist attacks and street violence that intimidated UP supporters). These inter-related wings interpenetrated the institutions, contributing to challenging the balance of what Allende called the 'social forces' within and around them. These wings needed coordinating so that their actions would support each other and produce the maximum effect. This coordination occurred at secret meetings and dinners, in social engagements and in meetings with US intelligence and embassy operatives. It was here that the threads of conspiracy were gradually woven ever tighter together around Allende's government.

In August 1972, the parliamentary opposition united in a 'Democratic Confederation' and in October, the Congress they dominated passed a vote declaring the government to be 'outside the law'. The National Confederation of Transport began a national strike that they had begun planning in March, using the pretext of opposition to the government's proposal to create a state-owned transport company for the far south. The strike was organised and supported by business leaders, the PN and the Christian Democrats, and was primarily funded by CIA monies.[109] Hundreds of lorries were stopped and disabled in strategic locations, blocking transport hubs and causing shortages and chaos. The truck owners attacked strike-breakers, and PyL carried out other violent attacks. Outside the trucking sector, the strike failed to mobilise many workers, and despite the participation of the Medical Association, even the hospitals stayed open. Allende's response to the opposition mobilisation was to declare a state of emergency in several provinces and to rally popular support. Despite the difficulties, the government's support held up, with workers at one pro-government demonstration holding a sign reading, 'We prefer to eat bread standing on our feet than chicken on our knees'. Hundreds of thousands of people mobilised voluntarily in supply depots and at railway stations to allow the flow of food and other products to continue. The government also made use of a network of computers akin to an early internet that had been installed by British scientist, Stafford Beer. The system

---

[109] See Kornbluh, p. 90.

provided a rudimentary method of linking together factories and ministries in order to provide an accurate picture of the state of the economy. Cybersyn, as the system was known, helped the government to allocate resources effectively in the face of the blockade.[110] The Government tried to negotiate with the strikers, but the strikers' demands were basically political, not economic. Allende persisted. On 1 November, the government brought the top ranks of the armed forces in to manage the Ministry of Interior, the Ministry of Public Works, and the Ministry of Mining. The negotiations continued, and after an agreement not to prosecute those involved, the strikers brought their actions to an end.

Enormous damage had been done to the economy. Furthermore, the inclusion of the military in government was highly controversial, and for some, it marked the end of the socialist stage of Allende's government. Allende's sister Laura, a Socialist deputy, stormed into his office afterwards, crying out that, 'The government is over! Salvador, this is the limit! You've betrayed us, the revolutionary movement is over!'[111] The inclusion of the military into the government did nothing to resolve the debate over whether to supersede the institutions of the state, or rely on them. However, it is often forgotten that at the same time as he brought the military into the government, Allende also made CUT president Luís Figueroa the Minister of Labour, and CUT general secretary, Rolando Calderón the Minister of Agriculture, bringing organised labour directly into government for the first time in Chilean history. Within the unions, this provoked unease in some quarters with a concern that the unions were trading in their autonomy and potentially stimulating division among the workers, not all of whom were organised in Socialist or Communist-led unions.[112]

---

[110] Eden Medina, 'Designing Freedom, Regulating a Nation: Socialist Cybernetics in Allende's Chile', *Journal of Latin American Studies*, No. 38 (2006).

[111] Espejo, p. 81.

[112] Jorge Arrate and Eduardo Rojas, *Memoria de la Izquierda Chilena, Vol. II*

The issue also exacerbated tensions between the historic organisations of the working class and the new organisations that had also played a key role in overcoming the challenge of the 'bosses' strike'. These included the Councils of Supply and Prices (*Juntas de Abastecimientos y Precios*, JAP), which had been set up in 1971 to link shops and communities in neighbourhoods in order to ensure fair distribution of basic necessities. By the end of 1972, there were over 600 in Santiago alone. Women played a key role in these organisations and in the social base of the UP government. According to Michèle Mattelart, 'Working class women participated with ardour and combativeness in the demonstrations of the Left'. This was partly due to the way in which the government's support for the JAP and Mothers' Centres created spaces for women to actively participate in practical political life for the first time.[113] It is also indicative of the ways in which Allende's government helped stimulate the activism of new social groups whose organisations had to be integrated into the process in a somewhat ad hoc manner. Among these were the organisations of the *pobladores*, the inhabitants of the shanty towns that circled Chile's cities, and those of landless itinerant peasants, women, and indigenous peoples.[114] Other organisations included the 'Vigilance Committees' set up by workers to prevent acts of sabotage and eventually also the 'industrial belts' which were made up of the trade unionists active in particular localities, which organised demands and oversaw production and developed as well as grew spontaneously during the October strike. Yet, while these organisations represented a broadening of the UP's social base, their autonomy threatened the grand strategy being followed by Allende. As one CUT leader later wrote, ' … most of the industrial belts in practice transgress those ends [of maintaining production

---

(1970-2000), (Santiago: Zeta, 2003), p. 96.

[113] Arrate and Rojas, *Memoria de la Izquierda Chilena, vol. II*, pp. 94-95.

[114] *Pobladores*: They are shanty town dwellers who have migrated from the rural areas to the big cities.

and bringing new social groups into revolutionary activism], becoming an alternative, parallel and opposed source of power to that of the CUT and the government.'[115]

The new organisations were another aspect of the debate around the relationship that ought to exist between the old and the new. In the state, it was the question of whether to rely on the institutions of the state or supersede them; in society, the question was whether to subordinate to the 'traditional' organisations of the Left or supersede them — a question that became increasingly divisive. Allende was not hostile to these new groups. He saw their growth and development as natural, stemming from 'a deep social concern' that doubted 'the speed and depth of the process, of the revolution'. To bring these groups onside, Allende argued that the political parties of the UP needed to be more disciplined in their effort to reach out to them so as to 'channel and reinforce them so that they become a factor of support to the revolutionary process'.[116] With the industrial belts, the government rapidly switched from suspicion to trying to subordinate them to the CUT and the UP programme.[117] Unfortunately for Allende, the demands of the new organisations were not always coherent with the government's priorities. The UP created the environment for the growth of new movements and organisations, but there was no effective mechanism for integrating them into the project that did not mean their subordination to trade unions or political parties, a subordination that they often resisted. The situation was further complicated by the influence of the MIR among many of these new organisations, which encouraged the MIR to increase its activity in promoting 'popular power'.

---

[115] Arrate and Rojas, *Memoria de la Izquierda*, p. 98.

[116] Allende in *Octubre 72: Pensamiento político de Allende*, Presidential Publication, no date, p. 179.

[117] Franck Gaudichaud, 'Construyendo "Poder Popular": El movimiento sindical, la CUT y las luchas obreras en el periodo de la Unidad Popular', in Julio Pinto Vallejos, *Cuando hicimos historia: La experiencia de la Unidad Popular* (Santiago: LOM, 2005), p. 99.

Meanwhile, the UP was paralysed by the debate over how to deal with these multiple challenges. It was a terrible weakness. The UP project and Allende's government, was at root based on the possibility of some sort of agreement with the Christian Democrats to pursue the institutional and economic changes the Left thought was necessary. This agreement could be made either from a position of strength, after some kind of clear expression of public support for the UP's agenda or from a position of weakness without it. Once the possibility of an alliance became a marginal prospect after October 1972, it required a re-assessment of the political context. Allende clearly sensed this, but he was unable to take the action required because he had subordinated himself to a UP leadership that was divided over the best course of action to follow.

In lieu of an agreement with the PDC, after October 1972, the UP, as a whole and Allende as its leader, faced a narrow set of options.

Allende and the UP could have made an agreement with the PDC, their primary objective, recognising the obstacle formed by the ultra-left. This would have meant taking action against the ultra-left outside the coalition and strictly redefining the extent of the Left coalition, in essence, declaring the 'ultras' to be outsiders.[118] This was a variant of the unenviable choice faced by revolutionaries many times before. Such a move, by putting clear water between the UP and the 'ultras' would have enabled Allende to show the PDC that he meant business that his 'revolution of red wine and empanadas' was different. Unfortunately, there were no clear dividing lines between the ultra-left and the UP, with many within the UP using similar language to the MIR, participating in its efforts at 'popular power' and criticising the government and Allende from a Left perspective with Socialist leader Carlos Altamirano a notable example. The blurred lines were not just

---

[118] This is referred to in Politzer's 1990 interview with Altamirano.

political, they were personal. Allende's own sister was a Socialist deputy with political views not far removed from the ultra-left; his daughter, Beatriz, worked for the government but also shared the MIR's analysis, and Allende's nephew Andrés Pascal was a MIR leader. Taking action against the 'ultra-left' outside the UP would not have been possible without action against the ultra-left within it, and this would have meant the expulsion from the UP of many leading members of the PS, alongside those groups that had split from the Radical party and the PDC — like the MAPU and the Christian Left — which had rapidly adopted the language and some of the political positions of the MIR.

The presence of so many 'ultras' within the UP made this redefinition immensely difficult to achieve in practice, and it would not have resolved the problem of the MIR's land and property seizures. Here, Allende would have needed to order the use of repression to block or reverse them, to find and arrest leading members of the group, including his own nephew. The political consequences would have been severe. The very idea ran against the grain of Allende's most profound beliefs. Moreover, the UP would have been numerically reduced and engaged in the internal witch-hunts and recriminations that have destroyed more than one political movement. Outside the UP, the 'revolutionary pole' would have been strengthened and substance provided to their accusations of Allende's 'reformism'.

Nevertheless, if a deal with the PDC was the only way to save the process, this price ought to have been considered. The difficulties posed by this action against the ultra-left would have been immense, but they could have been overcome, although probably not by a politician such as Allende, who had made a life of building alliances and who refused to see enemies among Socialists. Olive branches and sacrifices must be offered at the right time and for this option to have succeeded in guaranteeing an improved relationship with the PDC, it needed to have been carried out before 1970, when Frei was in government or when the UP was at its zenith before and shortly after the April 1971 municipal elections in which the UP won over 50 per cent of the vote. Allende could have publicly explained why the alliance with the PDC was necessary and demanded that all the political forces backing his government sign up to this. It would have forced every member of the UP to decide whether they really wanted an insurrectionist revolution and been a clear indication of the sacrifices Allende was willing to make in order to guarantee the Chilean road to socialism. Instead, Allende's first address to Congress in May that year focused on a theoretical explanation of the Chilean road to socialism, appealing to the common sense of the ultra-left and the right-wing opposition but saying nothing to the PDC.

Another option open to Allende was to make a turn against the existing institutions and effectively adopt the ultra-left's armed strategy as his own. However, this would have meant he abandoned any pretence of constitutional legitimacy, provoked an immediate military reaction, and gone against Allende's entire political philosophy. Allende could possibly have secretly encouraged the gathering of arms by left-wing forces prior to a violent clash, but the likelihood of this remaining secret was very low. Furthermore, if a unified command is important in politics in war, it is essential. Would all the parties of the UP get weapons? What about the MIR? Would each party have its own structures, or would they pool their resources? Who would be in charge? Where would the weapons and ammunition come from? Where would they be stored? The issues in this area were intractable. Any hint of a secret strategy to hoard weaponry would have severely affected perceptions of Allende's legitimacy among members of the military, as they, in fact, did during 1973. Allende also knew that the Left had no meaningful military force of its own, and therefore, even this option required the support of some part of the military if it was to succeed.[119] So, this was also unrealistic. Perhaps Allende

---

[119] Shortly before the election, Allende had called together representatives of the Socialist 'military apparatus' and the MIR and asked them about their

could have sought to create a Presidential Guard, a loyal military unit under his direct command, but this would have violated the Constitutional Guarantees he had provided in 1970. Taking all these factors into account, we can see that the option of 'arming the people' was not realistic.

Another option was to encourage the opposition to return to institutional, legal opposition through social coercion, without armed or 'acute' violence. Of course, some level of this took place spontaneously in fighting between youths from different sides, but it was not organised from above. It would have meant making active use of the government's popular support to intimidate the upper-class opposition at those points when it sought to come together. This could have taken the form of mass mobilisations such as that suggested by the Women's Committee of the UP during Fidel Castro's visit.

Mireya Baltra, one of Allende's ministers and a leading member of the UP's Women's Committee, described their idea. Prior to the opposition's 'March of the Empty Pots', members of the Committee had gone around the boroughs of Santiago to alert women of the dangers this march posed and assess how they wanted to react. Their argument, as one of them recalled, was simple, 'They [the opposition] had started the terror campaign, and now it was up to us to make them feel the same fear.' With the cooperation of the construction workers' union, workers on the UNCTAD site collected the details of 38,000 women willing to counter the opposition march. Among the ideas proposed by the women consulted was the capture and simultaneous release of thousands of rats during the demonstration. Others suggested that the rich women would be really scared, if people tore off their pearl necklaces and watches.

strength (See Huerta, *El trabajo es vivir*, p. 116). The MIR exaggerated somewhat, but the PS told him, 'We had very little'. After his election, Allende would have known of any support provided to either organisation by Cuba or any other state.

The purpose of this intimidation was to deny the opposition the time and space within which to come together, express themselves and develop a group identity. By coming together to express their opposition and by coordinating their actions, the opposition was beginning to force choices on the UP government, to seize the initiative from it. The UP women were, in effect, discussing how they could take it back, because individuals in a social group facing intimidation have to choose between flight, being cowed and fighting back between retreat and radicalisation. The discussion that follows within the group prevents effective action for a while, time that can be used well by their opponents. It almost happened.

The plans for a counter-march were first proposed to and approved by the PC leadership, then by the UP leadership. However, the UP told the women that they would also need Allende's approval. Allende heard them out, but his response was negative. 'Have you thought that PyL could create a provocation of such a scale that some of these upper-class women might be killed? This is serious. You can't forget that this is a democratic government, and we can't deny them the right to demonstrate.'[120] Allende had earlier expressed his fears of a violent provocation if the government called people to counter-demonstrate against opposition marches, 'not necessarily [violent provocations] from the right but from provocateurs, mercenaries, at the service of small fascist groups, who are at the service of foreign interests.'[121] This, Allende feared, would create worse problems for the government.

The UP women were downcast by Allende's refusal, asking themselves how emboldened the opposition might be by the march and how far the government could maintain democracy when facing a violent counter-revolution. When did liberty become licence? Similar challenges during the later truck-owners' strike

---

[120] Mireya Baltra, *Del quiosco al Ministerio del Trabajo*, (Santiago: LOM, 2014), pp. 93-94.

[121] Interview in 'La Gran Encuesta', 10 September 1972, in *Discursos: Salvador Allende* (La Habana: Ciencias Políticas, 1975), p. 458.

met with the same response. The *Carabineros* would deal with the unrest, but the people were to stay out of it. Although the MIR and PS armed structures did take some actions to clear roads blocked with trucks and, later in the process, other groups also attacked far-right groups. In general, the UP's supporters largely defended the government through voluntary work and social organisation, leaving the active defence of the government to the police.

In a variation on the theme of forcing the opposition to back down, Allende's former adviser, Joan Garcés, has argued that the solution was to ensure that the popular movement was more directly connected to the military. Allende asked him to prepare plans for this, creating mechanisms by which military actions would be coordinated with unions and other organisations, reducing the military's capacity for autonomous action by embedding it further into society. There was civil defence legislation from the mid-1940s that provided the legal basis for this kind of measure. However, despite the plans, no action in this area was never taken seriously by either the military or the UP. Nor did Allende look to build and support a network of constitutionalist officers within the military, which could, if necessary, have been reached outside the framework of their institutions and which could have formed the basis for a loyal military response to the coup.

While the insistence on an institutional solution to the problem of opposition violence was coherent with Allende's strategy and worked temporarily, its passivity and predictability gradually emboldened and strengthened the opposition while demobilising government supporters. This, in turn, reduced the incentive for accommodation in Congress and exacerbated infighting among the parties of the UP. Although it is obvious that allowing an active, coercive defence of the UP carried serious political risks, it is surprising that a man who had fought far-right thugs in defence of democracy in the Valparaíso of the 1930s was unwilling to allow a new generation of Leftists to do the same in defence of a revolutionary government striving to start the construction of socialism.

In these stalemated circumstances, Allende needed to do something drastic. In retrospect, it seems that the most promising option was one that Allende considered throughout but only decided upon when it was too late. Allende could have called a referendum over the heads of the UP leadership in a direct appeal to the masses, creating a political fact that would have forced the entire Left to define its position. It would have divided the opposition while creating immensely strong incentives for left-wing unity over a practical issue. It would have pitted Allende, the consummate electoral campaigner and champion of the people, against a declining PN, the elite media, and a divided PDC led from the shadows by an ex-president with blood on his hands. With the opposition increasingly organised around a supposed 'defence of democracy', it would have put them in an unfavourable position to reject the referendum and wrongfooted the United States as well. Unfortunately, Allende would not take a decision that would have, in effect, made him the *caudillo* of the Chilean process. He needed the backing of the UP leadership to avoid this, but he could not get it.

Therefore, instead of taking any of the options outlined above, Allende continued his dogged pursuit of the now routine strategy of trying to convince the UP leadership to agree to a referendum, at the same time as trying to build the basis for an understanding with the PDC.

Faced with such a complicated and intractable domestic situation, Allende set out to hit back at the opposition's foreign backers while also seeking renewed overseas support for his government. Perhaps here, he could gain some breathing space for his embattled government, reinforce his domestic legitimacy through diplomacy, and find some respite from the relentless pressure at home. Allende headed out on a short tour of Latin

America, also visiting the USSR before returning via New York, where he addressed the General Assembly of the UN.

In the USSR, Allende was looking for ways of shoring up Chile's economy. Allende was to be disappointed. It was not that the Soviets were unwilling, despite a complex international situation of competing interests in which détente with the US was a strategic priority. For example, the Soviets and various East European countries had already provided over 200 million Roubles in credits and assistance, although Chile had only used 2 million of this.[122] However, the Soviet leadership did have well-founded concerns about the Chilean process. In 1972, they sent a delegation of experts to Chile who produced a report which was quite realistic about the situation. While it predicted Allende's government would survive to 1976, it highlighted the problems the UP was encountering. The report noted the way in which the statute of constitutional guarantees prevented a more active defence of the revolutionary process. The report also noted the lack of ideological unity within the UP, stating that 'between the Communists and Socialists, there exist important discrepancies and contradictions over problems as important as agriculture, the attitude towards extreme-left groups, relations with the right-wing opposition, among others'. The report contrasted this with the unity of the opposition and the government's tendency towards moderation.[123]

The report highlighted that despite a 'qualitative change' in the relations between Chile and the USSR, the Chilean government was 'characterised by a tendency to focus on this primarily from the point of view of achieving economic, technical, and financial assistance from the Soviet Union and other Socialist countries'.[124] The report summarised Soviet-Chilean commercial relations and

<hr>

[122] Corvalán, *De lo vivido*, p. 146.

[123] Olga Ulianova, 'La Unidad Popular y el golpe militar en Chile: percepciones y análisis soviéticos', *Estudios Públicos* No.79, (2000), pp. 97-99.

[124] Ulianova, p. 100.

analysed Chilean proposals for future cooperation. 'These', it stated, 'imply that the Soviet Union would have to accept conditions that have never been contemplated in the relations of the USSR with developing countries. The Chileans expected the USSR to annually supply them with great quantities of essential products that were scarce in the USSR, such as wheat, meat, butter, cotton, etc., on the basis of long-term credit. At the same time, it supposes that the Soviet Union will import products of which it has little need and pay for them in hard currency [...]'. Furthermore, the Chileans did not expect to pay until after 1976. This report was followed by others from the Soviet Embassy in Chile, which began mentioning the potential for a military coup against Allende.[125] Brezhnev and other Soviet leaders were also receiving KGB reports sceptical of the UP government's apparent confidence in the neutrality of Chile's armed forces.[126] Furthermore, the Soviets must have also been put off by the sometimes-overt anti-Sovietism of some of the Chilean Socialists.[127]

The overall result was that, unsurprisingly, Allende failed to receive the economic support he had been seeking. In his disappointment, Allende accused the Soviets of not understanding him, but it seems obvious that they understood the situation only too well. Chile's internal problems were weakening its international position. The Chileans overestimated Soviet economic power as well as their own bargaining position. They also underestimated or did not understand the complex parameters of decision-making for the weaker of two superpowers. Why would a country engaged in a global life-or-death struggle sink resources into a country

---

[125] Ulianova, p. 101.

[126] Ulianova, p. 103.

[127] In an earlier visit to the USSR by socialist deputies and youth leaders, some had referred to Soviet 'red fascism', see Juan Azocar Valdés, *Lorca: vida de un socialista ejemplar*, (Santiago: Radio Universidad de Chile, 2015), p. 80. Corvalán cites Gonzalo Martner writing that among the socialist negotiators 'an anti-soviet sentiment predominated', which was sometimes not disguised. See Corvalán, *De lo vivido*, p. 146.

that it could not defend, that did nothing to improve its military-strategic balance of power, that offered minimal future economic opportunities, whose government seemed on the back foot and potentially vulnerable, whose coalition included hostile elements and whose political benefits had already been harvested? Would these same resources not be better invested in more stable socialist governments or key Cold War battlefields such as Vietnam, Syria, Egypt, or Yemen? From the Soviet point of view, the answer was clear and unequivocal.

In Latin America, Allende's reception was better, but the economic possibilities were virtually nil. The region's economies were not integrated, with the vast majority of their trade aimed at and controlled by the US. This left Allende denouncing the intervention against his country in the UN, 'We find ourselves facing forces that operate in the shadows, without a flag, with powerful weapons, and posted in the most varied places of influence', 'we are victims of almost imperceptible actions, generally disguised with phrases and declarations that express respect for the sovereignty and dignity of our country'. Unfortunately for Allende, the international community that gave his speech a standing ovation was not in a position to help. The Chilean popular movement with Allende at its head had to face its enemies alone.

Outside a national referendum, Allende's only realistic hope for success lay in reaching an understanding with the Christian Democrats, and Allende fought tooth and nail to achieve it. In March 1972, Allende asked his Justice Minister to open channels with the PDC, but the talks foundered. From mid-1972 onwards, his government was increasingly on the defensive. The possibility of an agreement with the PDC remained, but like a will o' the wisp, every time it seemed on the verge of being signed, it receded into the distance. Was it a game being orchestrated by Frei, or was it a genuine reflection of the dilemmas facing the Christian Democrats? Given the power balance within the PDC, it increasingly resembled a game, particularly once Patricio Aylwin became president of the PDC in May 1973. Aylwin was a hard-line opponent of the UP, a protégé of Frei's, and he increasingly side-lined the progressive majority within the PDC. Unfortunately for Allende, the possibility of a deal was so attractive that it reduced the incentive to look at other options. It also contributed to concealing the urgency of the situation.

In March 1973, despite the political crisis the country was enduring, the UP was still able to increase its showing in Parliamentary elections. The opposition had expected that they would win a majority, big enough to impeach Allende, so the result was an immense shock for them. With the next electoral opportunity, not until the presidential elections of 1976, this defeat cemented the view within the opposition that their political strategy would not work. Only by breaking the political system could UP now be stopped. It did not take long for them to take action. PyL stepped up the training of militants and then increased the number of terrorist actions. At the end of June 1973, Allende had to face a serious coup attempt, the 'Tancazo', in which twenty-two people were killed and others wounded.

The uprising was triggered by the discovery of the coup plot by the Military Intelligence Service on the night of 26 June, which led General Sepúlveda, the loyal Commander of the Santiago garrison, to order the arrest of several military officers in the capital's Second Armoured regiment. The Army High Command met the following day to discuss the issue, but the enemy was already on the move. The ground for the uprising had been carefully prepared. Retired officers had recently written to Allende to protest that the situation in the country was a national security risk. The Army conspirators knew of like-minded groups in the Airforce and the Navy; PyL had also promised support. The political situation was also conducive — Christian Democrat workers in the El Teniente copper mine were on strike demanding a massive pay rise, and Congress had approved the impeachment of another two of Allende's ministers. On 20 June, *El Mercurio* had published a statement from the

PN which claimed that 'Nobody was obliged to respect or obey a government that was no longer legitimate'.[128] That same night, there were nine terrorist attacks on targets connected to the government, the PS, Cuban and Soviet offices. The conspirators expected several army units to join their uprising, so they acted.

The first action was to attempt to force General Prats to resign and, if not, then, to damage his reputation as far as possible. After the meeting with the Army High Command, General Prats' car was forced to a stop by several vehicles. Two people in one car insulted him and made obscene gestures. Prats, with Schneider's assassination in mind, got out of his car and fired a shot in the air. He was rapidly surrounded by an angry crowd, shouting insults. His car was vandalised, and the tyres were slashed to prevent escape. Upper-class women waved white feathers in the General's face. Reporters were on hand to record the public humiliation of the Commander of the Chilean armed forces. Prats was inches from being beaten when a taxi driver recognised him, dragged him away, and drove him to the nearest police station. Prats was very shaken by the carefully planned and executed attack.[129]

The next stage was the uprising by the 2nd Armoured Regiment, whose commander drove his tanks to surround the city centre. On hearing that troops were moving on the Moneda, Allende ordered the GAP to accompany him there from his residence on Tomás Moro. General Prats took immediate action, also heading to the city centre. Prats, accompanied by General Pinochet in full combat uniform, approached the troops in their tanks and, at pistol point, convinced the officers to surrender. General Sepúlveda and General Pickering, the commanders of the city garrison and the military schools, also acted to prevent other units from joining

---

[128] See Luiz Alberto Moniz Bandeira, *Formula para el caos*, (Santiago: Debate, 2008), p. 441.

[129] The attack was organised by Patria y Libertad, with the codename 'Charly', assisted by Keith Wheelock of the US Embassy, who carried out a psychological assessment of General Prats. See Moniz Bandeira, pp. 431-432.

the rebellion. At the same time, the PS paramilitary structures mobilised and took strategic points in the city. Allende called for workers to gather at the Moneda. Meanwhile, the Moneda was secured by the GAP along with *Carabineros* and members of the Investigations police.

The government survived. The defeat of the military uprising was an example of the institutional-revolutionary alliance that Garcés and Allende saw as the most effective military policy. In the Moneda, after the rebellion had been put down, Allende spoke to his National Security Council. He stated that the people would meet violence with violence and that he would not resign. At the end of the meeting, he told Orlando Millas, one of his Ministers:

> I threatened them with popular violence because I couldn't not do it. But this has no chance of success and would end in a bloodbath. I think the stronger threat is that they'll have to kill me to get me out of here.[130]

Despite the defeat of the uprising, it was notable that in contrast to Allende's behaviour in 1969, the Christian Democrats did not express any support for either democracy or Allende's government during the fighting. It was also notable that the crowd that gathered at the Moneda that evening chanted for Allende to close Congress. Allende refused.

The reactions of the different groups to the failed coup attempt illustrate the divisions across the Left. The Communists expressed their support for Allende and welcomed the success of the combined efforts of the masses and the institutions of the state. Meanwhile, the Socialist leader Carlos Altamirano gave an interview in which he called for Allende to use an iron hand — 'An iron hand against the fascists, create and strengthen popular organisations, equal rationing for all, the social area [of the economy] to be dominant

---

[130] Jorge Arrate and Eduardo Rojas, '*Memoria de la izquierda chilena*' volume II, (Santiago: Grupo Zeta, 2003), p. 125.

and hegemonic, more effective participation for workers and peasants, the firing squad for the black marketeers, the denunciation and rejection of all bureaucratism, and exemplary punishments for dishonest functionaries.' It was as far from 'wine and empanadas' as could be imagined. Outside the UP, the MIR warned that the uprising was being used by 'the hesitators and the recalcitrant reformists [to] attempt class conciliation once again'.[131]

Meanwhile, the government's opponents in the military had seen the way their efforts had been stymied by effective communication between the government and the masses and between state institutions and civil society. They also took note of the RPGs and AKMs that had been displayed for the first time by Allende's guards. For some, it was evidence that the Left was preparing for mass defence, which in their understanding, was a prelude to civil war. Their exaggerated analysis was that within six months, the Left would be capable of mounting a serious challenge. A month later, Pinochet received a national security memo stating that 'respect for human life has been lost, people are killed without fear or scruple. Nor is private property respected. The government shows no sign of wanting to put a drastic end to the extremism of all its organisations. The desired and hoped for peace will not come from the government or its followers'. The time had come, it stated, for decisions of 'transcendental importance'.[132]

After the Tancazo, it was clear to everyone that the situation was reaching breaking point. On 26 August, Allende called a meeting of all his bodyguards at the country house of El Cañaveral, where he spent much of his time towards the end of his government. The guards thought it was a political-educational meeting but soon realised it was something different. Three members of the PS leadership were in attendance, including the heads of the Party's military and intelligence apparatuses. The commander of the

---

[131] Altamirano cited in Muñoz, *A Partir de la UP*, p. 86, on the MIR, p. 90.

[132] Patricio Quiroga, *Compañeros: El GAP: la escolta de Allende*, (Santiago: Aguilar, 2001), p. 125

security detail gave a report on the national situation, criticising Allende's inability to impose discipline on the UP and the failure to capitalise on Chile's popular mobilisation or to advance with a military plan to counter a coup. Allende listened in silence, and then he spoke, saying that a military coup was coming and that he no longer had complete faith in an agreement with the PDC. Allende spoke of his government being 'orphaned' by the bickering of the parties of the UP, which could not even agree on a plebiscite. He told them what he was planning — a huge popular demonstration to celebrate the third anniversary of his election, the appointment of a new cabinet, redoubled efforts to get an agreement with the Christian Democrats and agreement on a plebiscite to resolve the impasse between the president and Congress. Afterwards, Allende shook hands with them individually, thanking them for their dedication. He also thanked them as representatives of the peasantry, the youth and the impoverished *pobladores* of the cities. He then offered them a way out. If any of the guards wanted to leave, they should do so, and he would understand it not as cowardice but as an expression of disagreement with his political project. To reinforce his point, Allende ordered their commander to give an assault rifle and a pistol to every man who left. Knots in their throats, not a single man moved. Several of them spoke, reiterating their loyalty.[133] Allende's fate would be theirs.

So, despite the increased tension and the growth in violence, Allende continued to try to reach an agreement with the Christian Democrats. Allende refused to let the right wing of the PDC win. In talks with the PDC, he expressed confidence that he would be able to find a way out by doing so.[134] An agreement with Aylwin could bring the entire PDC on board, so Allende went over Aylwin's head and convinced Cardinal Raúl Silva Henríquez to talk to Aylwin about reaching a deal. The Cardinal pushed hard for

---

[133] Patricio Quiroga, *Compañeros: El GAP: la escolta de Allende,* (Santiago: Aguilar, 2001), pp. 129-131.

[134] Valdés, p. 239.

Aylwin to come to an agreement with Allende. In July and August 1973, talks between the two took place, but the PDC continued to block the government in Congress, and a sector of the PS rejected any retreat on the government's programme.

Allende knew it was time for desperate measures. 'I am in your hands', he told Gabriel Valdés, in words he could easily have addressed to Carlos Altamirano. 'One hundred years of workers' struggle and social progress depend on you'. On September 10, the day before the coup, Allende received a final 'no' from the PDC and a 'yes' from the UP, finally enabling him to play his last remaining card — that of a plebiscite on the constitutional reforms proposed by the UP and in effect, a plebiscite on his government. It was too late.

The Army and the Coup

To kill the man of peace
To strike his nightmare-free forehead
They had to become a nightmare
— Mario Benedetti

The inability to resolve the crisis in the political arena made the military's position increasingly important. The Chilean armed forces were proud of their professionalism and their subordination to constitutional power. Still, in reality, throughout their history, they had played an important role in shaping the Chilean state and, on occasion, in defining political outcomes — as in the 1920s and 1930s — but had then acquiesced to a much-reduced role.[1] In the 1960s, the military command underwent a generational change, in which the influence of General Ibañez faded, replaced by US training programmes that introduced a concept of national security that identified communism as a key threat. In an environment of cuts and low social esteem, the national security role provided an attractive raison d'etre for some within the armed forces.[2] On the other hand, Chile's chronic socio-economic underdevelopment and the nation's subsequent military weakness influenced a strong 'developmentalist' strain of thought too. The top brass was also affected by military involvement in politics

---

[1] Alain Joxe, *Las fuerzas armadas en el sistema politico de chile*, (Santiago: Editorial Universitaria, 1970), pp. 42-43.

[2] Veronica Ortiz de Zarate Valdivia, *El golpe despues del golpe: Leigh vs Pinochet Chile 1960-1980*, (Santiago: LOM, 2003), pp. 35

elsewhere, from Nasser's Egypt to the Latin American coups. Such examples contrasted with the neglect that the Chilean military were subjected to by the political elite, leading to increasing resentment.[3] Therefore, by the time Allende came to power, competing ideas regarding the legitimacy of military intervention and the solutions to national problems existed within the armed forces.

A 1969 'Synthesis of the National Situation', written by the General Staff, noted that 80 per cent of armed forces' personnel were of 'non-Marxist centre-left political tendencies' while the remaining 20 per cent were a 'small sector of the top and high-ranking officer corps of rightist inclinations and another, also small sector within the medium and lower ranks of the officer corps, that is infiltrated by Marxist propaganda'. While the numbers seemed stacked in favour of the Left, in reality, the concentration of right-wingers at the top of the hierarchy made all the difference. A constitutionalist officer, Colonel Pickering, recalled officer reactions to Allende's election as 'indifference among a few; surprise, disappointment, irritation — and even fear among the rest.'[4]

Seditious groups and the CIA began making contact with the military to provoke them into action against the UP as soon as it was elected. One opposition group linked to the navy formed a sailing club, where retired and off-duty officers could innocently mix with the civilian groups, plotting against the UP. Other officers shared friendships and family connections with people determined to bring Allende down. These spaces provided the arena for the discussions of what needed to be done to help unseat Allende's government. Initial contacts showed that naval officers in Valparaíso were motivated for a coup, but the reverse was true of

---

[3] Felipe Aguero, 'A Political Army in Chile: Historical Assessment and Prospects for the New Democracy', in *Political Armies*, ed. Kees Koonings and Dirk Kruijt, (London: Zed, 2002), p. 117

[4] Pickering quoted in González, p. 32.

the army. Even Pinochet, who later led the coup, was not involved in the plotting at this stage. In these early days, the anti-Allende forces in the military were on the back foot. Some were fearful of civil war — one high-ranking naval officer recalled a secret intelligence report that said that the 1970 election results had provoked shouts of 'Viva Comrade Allende!' in the majority of the barracks in the country.[5] Others were forced to wait for a better opportunity after the assassination of General René Schneider on 22 October 1970. In the investigation that followed, it was clear that several senior officers were involved in the plot, among them two generals and a former commander of the navy, all with links to the civilian elite and to the CIA. Schneider's killing and its fallout prevented any further action by the military opposition for a while.

In their 1969 Synthesis, the General Staff had noted that whatever government took over in 1970, it had to ensure new political, economic, and social transformations but 'without allowing the penetration of Marxism to the sources of power'. Yet, this was exactly what the UP aimed to do. In 1970, the Operations and Intelligence Secretariat of the Army produced a report on the upcoming elections. In this report, the military predicted the political tensions that would be produced, and each outcome would result in military intervention. If the right won, the Left would turn to subversion, and to contain it, the armed forces would be used.

Meanwhile, if Allende won, the report predicted an initial period of calm since 'the public forces antagonistic to him [Allende] have not yet showed any pronounced tendency to provoke public disorder'. However, this period would not last long and would depend on the government's capacity to control 'extremist elements' outside and inside the government. If these extremists began to act, the government would have two options — to seek an alliance with other political forces and use repression, or it would

---

[5] Admiral Merino quoted in González pp. 38-39. Merino was one of the coup plotters.

react 'timidly without trying to control popular excesses'. In either case, the armed forces would need to prepare 'a long and costly deployment' to enforce internal order.[6]

The army report was right. With the constellation of forces conspiring to destabilise the new government, it would not be long before social unrest became a regular occurrence. As politics became stalemated in Congress, it spilled out onto the streets and the countryside. It seeped into the lives of every Chilean — in the queues for food, in disturbances at university, in people's voluntary labour, in the fields and the factories. It was scrawled on the walls of the cities and on the rocks of Chile's mountain roads. Politics was optimistically and colourfully painted on the river embankments and city walls and angrily blaring from the TV and the radio with the opposition calling for Chileans to 'gather their rage'. As Allende said, 'Every day, in every minute, two worlds are in confrontation, two concepts of social order and human coexistence'. One was the world that 'has existed'. The other world was the new revolutionary process that Chileans had to build together in the face of the desperate resistance of the 'structures, institutions, classes and men that have the continuity of their privileges threatened'.[7] In these circumstances, it was inevitable that the armed forces became a political factor.

The problem for Allende was that his programme of transformations had no active policy for how to accommodate military politicisation. The assumption was that if the UP provided economic growth and social development, this would translate into greater national 'power' and, therefore, please the military. As he expressed to the High Command in 1972, 'there are no powerful armed forces, if there are peoples decimated by illness or punished by ignorance. There are no powerful armed forces in countries that are economically, culturally and sometimes, all too often, politically

6   Report quoted in González , pp. 26-27.
7   Second Message to Congress, 21 May 1972.

dependent'.[8] Greater control over the nation's resources would allow the government to improve pay and conditions, modernise military infrastructure and provide more modern equipment. Its incorporation into the process of development would also resolve the military's political frustrations and gradually make it identify with the problems of the people. Allende's project envisioned a medium to long-term transformation of the armed forces alongside the transformation of society and the state.

For this strategy to succeed, the government needed to emphasise the positive traditions of the armed forces, the government's historical continuity with the fight for independence, and, crucially, prevent the development of an alternative military force by the Left. The military's tradition of constitutionalism thus became a keystone of the process, which Allende tried to encourage by not to interfering in military appointments or promotions. Unfortunately, these efforts were undermined by a section of his own party, which was bent on creating its 'own military force', and the MIR also claimed the right to build a 'popular army'. Whilst in reality, these efforts were minuscule and largely symbolic, they were magnified out of all proportion by the opposition-controlled and CIA-funded media and by the militants themselves.[9] Many officers believed the hype, fearing the development of 'popular militias' and a potential civil war. This was but not the only problem. For any military, the question of 'order' is crucial. For many officers, as the 1970 intelligence report predicted, the government was being

---

[8] Allende quoted in Veronica Ortiz de Zarate Valdivia, 'Salvador Allende y las fuerzas armadas en la transicion al socialismo', in *Salvador Allende: Fragmentos para una historia*, ed. Fundacion Salvador Allende, (Santiago: Fundacion Salvador Allende, 2008), p. 115.

[9] On the day of the coup the MIR had 50 armed and trained men ready for action, with another 400 trained but unarmed, and the PS 100, with a few more in Allende's security team, Patricio Z. Quiroga, *El GAP: La escolta de Allende*, (Santiago: Aguilar, 2001), pp. 150-152. The Communists later admitted to 1,000 members trained in the use of automatic weapons, but these were unarmed and dispersed across the country. The Chilean armed forces in 1973 consisted of over 60,000 men.

lenient on 'extremist elements' and was, in their view, promoting social unrest, which in turn weakened the nation in the face of potential threats from abroad. Furthermore, the government's foreign policy, in particular, its relations with socialist countries, further increased the potential threat to the country from its neighbours and the United States.[10] To make things worse, the increasing economic disorder was also weakening the country's ability to go to war. For practical and ideological reasons, the military opposition could justify its position. The overthrow of Allende was a matter of national salvation for the survival of the *patria*.

However, the military opposition was not able to act, while the army High Command remained loyal to the constitution. The position of the army was crucial to the success of any coup, and within the army, the attitude of the commander-in-chief, the commander of the Santiago garrison and the commander of the military schools were critical. The coup plotters controlled none of these posts until days before the coup. For two years, the coup plotters had been unable to gain a strong foothold within the army, but from early 1973 onwards, their position grew in strength in parallel with the growth of the rest of the opposition. In October 1972, the armed forces helped the government weather the transport owners' strike and the following month, Allende incorporated the top brass into his government, giving General Carlos Prats, the Commander of the Army, the Ministry of Interior. While this temporarily quieted the opposition, it also overtly politicised the military. Then, on 29 July 1973, the army's second Armoured Regiment staged an abortive coup attempt. After some fighting, the rebellious troops were brought under control by loyal forces. Carlos Prats and other constitutional officers played a notable role and were lauded by Allende. However, the 'Tanquetazo' showed that the opposition within the armed forces had re-emerged from

---

[10] Valdivia, *El golpe despues del golpe*, p. 79.

the shadows. Days later, on 9 August, the top brass was reluctantly brought into the government again.

The pressures on the military were immense, and they gradually bore fruit. General Sepúlveda later recalled that 'for weeks, every day, the men received this pressure [from the opposition], through their wife, their children, their relatives and friends, with regard to the situation they were living and how long were we going to tolerate it'.[11] Those in important commands were particularly targeted. The constitutionalist officers were forced out of their positions at the top of the hierarchy by a virtual rebellion of lower-ranking officers committed to the coup. On August 17, General Ruiz, the commander of the air force and Minister of Transport, resigned from his ministerial post. At dinner that night, Allende desperately tried to convince him to stay, but Ruiz was adamant. 'You are no longer a friend and have lost my trust', Allende told him, rising from the table.[12] He replaced Ruiz with his second-in-command, General Leigh. Ruiz was not the only one considering resignation. Carlos Prats was also torn. If he resigned, then he 'had the contemptuous role of rats when they flee a sinking ship', but if he remained, the attacks against him would increase.[13]

The situation required decisive action to be taken against the coup plotters within and outside the armed forces, but this was not forthcoming because it was feared that it would provoke a coup. Prats told Allende that he would need to fire '12-15 Generals, and this would provoke civil war'.[14] Allende's hopes hinged on a deal with the Christian Democrats since, if this could be achieved, it would pull the rug from under the military plotters. He was not prepared to consider illegal action. 'We cannot break legality because we are the government. We have always fought for the law to be respected because, in a democratic state, it prevents

---

[11] General Mario Sepúlveda quoted in González, p. 246.
[12] Prats, p. 471.
[13] Prats, p. 452.
[14] Prats, p. 485.

despotism and arbitrariness, avoiding Chileans killing each other and guaranteeing the conquests made by the workers', he said.[15] Unfortunately, the opposition preferred breaking the system to preserve their power, and they did not mind killing Chileans to do it.

On 26 July 1973, after returning home from a reception at the Cuban embassy, Allende's naval aide, Commander Arturo Araya, was shot and killed. Allende was distraught. Over the past two years, they had developed a close friendship. Allende rushed to the hospital, donned a white surgeon's overall and desperately massaged Araya's heart. When Araya failed to revive, Allende looked up and, with tears in his eyes, said, 'Gentlemen, Commander Araya has died. This is fascism!'[16] Allende appointed a team of investigators from each branch of the armed forces and the police to find the perpetrators. The next day, the *Carabineros* reported having arrested a member of the PS, who confessed that he had been involved. The suspect alleged a group of Cubans and the leader of Allende's GAP security team had been involved. The media created a scandal by picking up the accusation. The *Carabineros* then denied that an arrest had been made. Then, the investigations police interviewed the witness and found that he had been severely tortured into giving a false confession. The investigation showed the involvement of PyL, although the murderers have never been found.[17] Then, in August 1973, sailors from Valparaíso requested a secret meeting with Altamirano and Oscar Garreton, the leader of the MAPU, where they denounced coup preparations in the navy. The sailors involved were then arrested by their superiors and brutally tortured for alleged links to 'extremist organisations'. Reports of their treatment reached the government, but sticking to

---

[15] Quoted in González, p. 326.

[16] Alfredo Joignant, the Director of the civilian investigations police, quoted in González, p. 210.

[17] *La Nacion*, 20 April 2008, 'Guillermo Claverie — yo no mate al comandante Araya'. Suspicions remain that members of Naval Intelligence took part in the killing, since they had been cooperating with PyL for some time.

the law, Allende called for an official investigation without acting to punish the coup plotters, saying to Carlos Altamirano, 'We can't base an accusation against the High Command on the testimony of some sailors'.[18] The pressures on the government grew by the day, and in mid-August, Allende began to keep a small bottle of Valium by his bed.[19] In a July speech to the workers of the CUT, he admitted that often 'doubt and bitterness tighten my throat', but he steeled himself by remembering 'the ordinary woman who believed in me' and 'the children of my country', no doubt recalling the injustice, poverty, and desperation he had witnessed so often during his life.[20]

Meanwhile, the pressure and the media attacks on the constitutionalist officers continued. Prats was a particular target of these. On 20 August, military wives demonstrated outside the Ministry of Defence. On the 21 August, they did so outside his house, where he was ill with flu. Over a thousand irate women screamed abuse, hurling stones at his home. Prats ordered the police not to clear the road, fearing that they might injure some of the demonstrators. The following day, Prats asked his fellow officers to express their solidarity with him, but Pinochet returned with the news that many of his comrades had refused to do so.[21] On August 24, the isolated Prats resigned from the army — it was not, after all, 'his revolution'.[22] He hoped this would give Allende time to reach an agreement with the PDC and, at the same time, avoid staining his hands with blood. Unfortunately, Prats' resignation removed 'the main factor mitigating against a coup'.[23] It was now a matter of time.

Prats was replaced by his trusted second-in-command,

[18] Salazar, p. 290.
[19] Gaitán, p. 118.
[20] Speech to the CUT, 25 July 1973.
[21] Prats, pp. 478-480.
[22] Altamirano recalls Prats telling him, 'I have an enormous appreciation for the president, but this is not my revolution', in Salazar, p. 242.
[23] Kornbluh, p. 111.

Augusto Pinochet. Even on 9 September, his position remained unclear to the other plotters. Without his inclusion, the likelihood of a civil war increased since it might split the army. Yet, on 10 September, Pinochet officially joined the coup and took it over. Pinochet first appeared on the CIA radar in August 1971, when a report stated that both his wife and son were 'turning against the Allende government' and hoped to influence Pinochet. In March 1972, another CIA source stated that Pinochet was involved with coup plotters linked to General Canales; in September 1972, Pinochet was reported to be 'harbouring second thoughts' about Allende, but there is no evidence of his coordinating with other officers.[24] We may never know if Pinochet was merely playing it safe, giving the appearance of loyalty to both sides before making a final decision. He may have seen the government in disarray over how to confront a coup, its inability to agree on a plebiscite and calculated that it could never win a confrontation.[25] He had no reason to stay loyal to Allende, for as he said to Arellano on 8 September, 'I'm no Marxist, dammit!' However, once Pinochet came down on the side of the coup, its victory was almost assured.

Admiral Montero, the head of the navy, remained, but he was isolated and due to be replaced on 12 September by Admiral Merino, a committed coup plotter. On the night before the coup, a team of sailors cut Montero's phone lines and disabled his car. By one means or another, in early September, the top constitutionalists in the army had been isolated or removed.

The coup plotters had set a date — 11 September 1973. Starting at 6 am, naval forces would take the city of Valparaíso and cut communications there and in Santiago. At 8 am, the army would move to Santiago. An inner circle of troops from the Santiago garrison would overthrow the government and take over energy,

[24] Kornbluh, p. 95.
[25] According to Jaime Gazmuri, then president of the MAPU, at a meeting with the CUT, Allende and Prats, Pinochet proposed to develop a defence plan based on combining military units with workers. Interview in *El Mercurio*, 12 October 2003.

water and telecommunications installations to prevent workers from disabling them. Columns from outside the city would then eliminate any resistance in the outskirts. The air force was on hand to destroy government radio stations and, if necessary, the Moneda palace and any points of resistance. Pinochet based himself in an army communications centre in the foothills of the Andes on the outskirts of the city. Others took up positions just opposite the Moneda palace in the Ministry of Defence — three floors of which were dominated by the US Military Advisory Group. Reports of strange troop movements in Valparaíso and towns near Santiago began coming into the UP party leadership and to the government. The Defence Minister, Orlando Letelier, later killed in Washington by Pinochet's secret service, was the first government figure to be detained when he arrived to clarify the situation in his Ministry.

Reports of suspicious troop movements began to arrive at midnight. Allende was woken at about 4 am. He began trying to find out what was happening. Eventually, he decided to go to the Moneda, where he arrived at about 7:20 am, wearing charcoal grey trousers and a turtleneck jumper covered by a tweed jacket, accompanied by a group of his bodyguards and some *Carabineros*. He carried an AKM rifle given to him by Fidel Castro during his 1971 visit and headed straight for his office, relieved that the long wait was over. He called Tencha, his wife of 34 years, 'Tencha, the navy has rebelled … I don't know if we'll be able to withstand it'. They bid each other farewell, not knowing it would be for the last time. At 7:55 am, Allende addressed a nation uncertain of what was happening. Many felt relief that the army had acted at last. Many more felt dread and trepidation. In a calm voice, Allende informed the people that part of the navy had mutinied and that the city of Valparaíso had been taken, but he expressed his hope, his certainty that the 'soldiers of the fatherland' would know their duty. 'I am here, and I will stay here defending the government I represent by the will of the people.' In the meantime, the people, the workers, had to mobilise themselves to their workplaces in order to defend their government. Beatriz, his daughter, arrived — six months pregnant and insisted on helping to defend the Moneda. She had military training, after all. She called Miguel Enríquez, the leader of the MIR, to whom Allende sent a message — 'Miguel, it's your turn now'. Throughout the early morning, friends, comrades, and colleagues arrived at the Moneda.

Allende called the various branches of the armed forces, and at 8:15 am, he again addressed the nation. He confirmed the rebellion in Valparaíso but said that he had ordered loyal troops to the city and he expected that 'the loyal forces [...] alongside the organised workers will crush the fascist coup threatening the fatherland'. As the military edicts began to come over the air, he and his followers in the Moneda soon realised that not a single unit was staying loyal. He again addressed the country. 'In this edict, they demand the president resign. I will not do it. I notify the country of the incredible attitude of soldiers that are breaking their word and their commitments'. He reminded the country that General José Maria Sepúlveda, the official commander of the *Carabineros*, was by his side. A jet passed overhead. Allende continued, 'In this instant, planes are passing over the Moneda. They will probably machine gun it. We are serene and calm. Our holocaust will mark the infamy of those who betray the fatherland and the people'.

At 8:30 am, the first military pronouncement made clear that Pinochet was part of the sedition. At 8:45 am, Allende picked up the phone and made another address to the nation. 'The situation is critical', he said, 'We are facing a coup in which the majority of the armed forces are participating. In this dark hour, I want to remind you of the words I said in 1971; I say them calmly, with total tranquillity — I do not have the makings of an apostle or a messiah. I don't have the makings of a martyr; I am a social fighter fulfilling a task given to me by the people. But let those who want to rewind history and ignore the will of the majority of Chile know without being a martyr; I will not take a single step backwards. Let them know it, let them hear it, let it be deeply engraved in them — I will leave the Moneda when I have fulfilled the mandate that the Chilean people gave me'. He continued, 'I will defend this government, and I will defend this revolution because it is the mandate given to me by the people. I have no alternative. Only by riddling me with bullets will they be able to impede the will to complete the programme of the people. If they kill me, the people will continue its route; it will follow its road with the difference may be that things will be much, much harder, much more violent because it will be a clear, objective lesson to the masses that these people stop at nothing. I had that possibility accounted for. I do not offer it or facilitate it. The social process will not disappear because a leader disappears. It may be delayed, it may be prolonged, but at the end, it cannot be halted.' Allende finished and drummed his fingers on his desk, muttering, 'three traitors, three traitors ... '[26]

One of Allende's comrades asked if they should try to contact Prats. Allende made a disappointed gesture and said, 'Let's not talk about him'. In any case, Prats preferred to lie low rather than risk a civil war. At the end of 1972, he had told a meeting of generals that a civil war would mean at least 100,000 and possibly up to a million dead. On 7 July, Allende had invited Prats for dinner, where he asked him whether he thought part of the army would remain loyal. Prats avoided the question, reminding Allende that in 1891, when the army had stayed loyal, it had caused civil war and much bloodshed. Prats did not want any blood on his conscience, and he refused to take sides.[27] Pinochet had no such qualms. Just over a year later, Prats was killed in Buenos Aires by a bomb planted on his car.

Just before 9:00 am, Isabel, Allende's youngest daughter, arrived at La Moneda. Allende begged both his daughters to leave. The junta demanded immediate surrender. Allende refused. At 9:03 am, he again addressed the nation; this time via Magallanes Radio, a PC station, and the last remaining on air. 'The planes

<hr>

[26] Garcés, p. 385.
[27] Prats, p. 485.

are passing overhead. It is possible they will gun us down. But let them know that we are here, at least with our example; they will see that in this country, there are men that know how to fulfil their obligations'. He repeated his condemnation of the Generals and expressed an unshakeable optimism for the future, 'In the name of the most sacred interest of the people and in the name of the fatherland, I call on you to say, have faith. History cannot be stopped by either repression or crime. This is a stage that will be overcome. This is a hard and difficult moment; it is possible that we will be crushed, but tomorrow belongs to the people, belongs to the workers'. Conscious of the imminence of defeat, he urged the people 'to be alert and vigilant'. It should not allow itself to be provoked nor massacred, but it should also defend its conquests. It should defend the right to build a better and more dignified life by its own efforts'.

He then organised the defence of the building, posting defenders at the windows of the upper floor. Six regiments with tanks surrounded the Moneda. Allende's final battle would take place here, sandwiched between the US Embassy on Constitution Square and the US military group stationed in the Ministry of Defence. The Moneda's defenders fired from the windows and from some of the surrounding buildings. There were less than sixty of them. Another message was received from the generals — immediate surrender and Allende to go over to the Ministry of Defence. Allende responded, 'A President of Chile does not surrender, and he receives people in the Moneda. If Pinochet wants me to go to the ministry, tell him not to be such a coward and that he should come and get me personally!' Allende then told the palace police guard that they could leave. An emissary from the PS leadership, which had so often proclaimed the inevitability of violence, arrived wanting to find out what the situation was and asking Allende to move to a defensible position. Allende bitterly replied, 'I'll fulfil my duty here; let the Party fulfil its own'.[28]

At 9:15 am, Allende gave his last speech to the people of Chile. Most of the defenders gathered to hear it. Allende held the phone, communicating him to Radio Magallanes in one hand and his AKM in the other. A military helmet sat atop his head and contrasted with his tweed jacket and turtleneck jumper. This last speech was an emotive farewell. He called Radio Magallanes; the phone was lifted up at the other end. 'Who's speaking?' 'Ravest, comrade'. 'Comrade, I need you to get me on air immediately'. For days, he had known that his time was coming. In his speeches, he had repeatedly made it clear that 'only by riddling me with bullets will they get me to leave the Moneda'. Nine days before, he had told his Colombian lover, Gloria Gaitán, 'I am a man who has but two hours of life left, a week, or maybe a month … ' On 11 September, Allende was a man who knew he was living his last hours. The radio crew barely had time to play a few bars of the national anthem before putting him on air while they scrambled to record what Allende would say, forgetting to switch off their own microphones: 'This is probably the last opportunity for me to speak to you'. Allende began.

> The air force has bombed the towers of Radio Portales and Radio Corporación. My words contain no bitterness, just disappointment. May they be a moral punishment for those who have betrayed the oaths they took: the soldiers of Chile, the titular commanders-in-chief, Admiral Merino, who has designated himself the commander of the Navy, and Mr Mendoza, that despicable General who only yesterday was declaring his fidelity and loyalty to the Government and who has also designated himself Director-General of *Carabineros*. Faced with these actions, the only thing I can say to the traitors is, 'I will not resign!'

[28] Gutierrez, p. 20.

Placed in a historic moment, I will repay the loyalty of the people with my life. And I say to you that I have the certainty that the seed we have sown in the dignified conscience of thousands and thousands of Chileans cannot be destroyed definitively. They have the force; they may overcome us, but social processes cannot be stopped, neither by crimes nor by force. History is ours, and peoples make it.'

Workers of my fatherland, I want to thank you for the loyalty that you have always shown, the trust that you deposited in a man who was just an interpreter of your great desires for justice, who gave his word that the Constitution and the Law would be respected, and who did so. In this defining moment, the last in which I can address you, I want you to learn the lesson: foreign capital and imperialism united with the reaction, created the climate for the armed forces to break the tradition that was taught to them by General Schneider and reaffirmed by Commander Araya, victims of the same social sector that today is in its houses, waiting for power to be reconquered by the hands of others, in order to continue defending their profits and their privileges.

I address myself above all to the modest woman of our land, the peasant who believed in us, the worker who worked harder, the mother who understood our concern for the children. I address the professionals of the fatherland, the patriotic professionals who continued to work against the sedition supported by the professional organisations, those class organisations that defended the advantages given to them by a capitalist society.

I address the youth, those who sang and gave your joy and your spirit of struggle. I address the man of Chile, the worker, the peasant, the intellectual, those who will be persecuted because fascism has been present in our country for many hours now — in the terrorist attacks, blowing up bridges, cutting railway lines, destroying oil and gas pipelines right before the eyes of those who had the duty to act. They, too, were committed. History will judge them.

Radio Magallanes will surely be silenced, and the calm tones of my voice will no longer reach you. It doesn't matter. You will continue to hear me. I will always be with you. At least the memory of me will be of a dignified man who was loyal to the fatherland.

The people should defend themselves without sacrificing themselves. The people should not allow themselves to be devastated nor gunned down. Nor can they allow themselves to be humiliated.

Workers of my fatherland, I have faith in Chile and in its destiny. Other men will overcome this grey and bitter moment when treachery tries to impose itself. Go on knowing that much sooner than later, you will again open up the great avenues upon which the free man walks in order to build a better society.

Viva Chile! Viva the People! Long live the workers!

These are my last words, and I am certain that my sacrifice will not be in vain; I am certain that, at least, it will be a moral lesson that will punish felony, cowardice, and treachery.

His remaining followers, about forty people, including his daughters and his lover and secretary, Mireya 'Payita' Contreras, stood in choked silence as he finished. He replaced the telephone receiver. Tears were flowing down many cheeks. Some of his closest collaborators, his daughters and his friends embraced him.

Allende released anyone in state service. He gathered his three military aides and told them, 'Tell your commanders that I'm not leaving here, and I will not surrender. That if they want me to resign, they come and ask me to do it themselves. They should have the courage to do it personally. They won't get me out of here even if they do bomb us'. Allende told them that his last bullet would be saved for himself 'like this', and he gestured, jabbing his fingers upwards under his chin.[29] The aides left, taking the military cooks and the *Carabineros* palace guard with them. The civilian detectives stayed. Next, Allende tried to convince the women to leave, and he finally managed to get his daughters to go, inventing a message for Fidel Castro. Once outside, Beatriz repented and frantically knocked on the door to be allowed back in. Nobody opened, and Isabel dragged her away to the shelter. Payita had hidden from Allende and remained in the palace until the end. Then Allende sent away all those who did not know how to shoot. Joan Garcés, the Spanish social scientist who had tried to theorise Allendismo, was sent away along with ministers and other collaborators. 'You must tell the world about our government and what has happened here today', Allende insisted. The Air Force Hawker Hunter jets arrived in the skies above the city.

The wife of the US ambassador, Nathaniel Davis, described their flight as they fired their missiles at the Presidential Palace — 'It was an eerily beautiful sight as they came in from nowhere. The sun glinted on their wings'. The first rockets hit the front of the palace, blasting through the thick walls. The explosions were deafening, and the defenders sheltered from the blasts and the fire. Allende covered Payita's body with his own. He had told her that the military would not dare bombard the Moneda. 'Looks like they did dare after all', he joked to her as they lay amid the dust and smoke. The next aircraft fired its rockets down through the roof, setting the building ablaze. The fires began to spread. Some reports state that the police fired tear gas into the inferno from circling helicopters. The defenders choked on the fumes. The shooting was incessant. Allende fired from the windows of his offices over Constitution Square, almost diagonally opposite the US Embassy.

---

[29] This is the testimony of his air force aide, Commander Roberto Sánchez, who after the coup was in a particularly vulnerable position with regard to the junta.

Smoke billowed from the windows, and the national flag burned on its pole above the main entrance.

At the Moneda, the attack continued. Tanks tried to force the main doors. Allende and a GAP bodyguard fired RPGs at them, forcing them back. GAP members posted in nearby buildings covered the approaches to the palace. Allende ordered someone to call the Tomás Moro residence. A bodyguard answered and informed them that the house had also been rocketed by aircraft, destroying much of it. One aircraft missed its target, hitting the Air Force hospital next door. Tencha hid under a desk while the house disintegrated around her. Allende's face creased in pain. He headed upstairs, where he fired at the attackers from the balcony of this private secretary's office.[30] Escorted by members of the GAP, Tencha escaped to a friend's house. The bodyguards then tried to reach the Moneda. The house was later ransacked by the army and by neighbours, and paintings and the library were stolen or destroyed. As with so much else looted from UP supporters after the coup, most items have never been returned or found.

In the centre, ministry functionaries cowered in basements or in the inner rooms of the solid buildings. Gloria Gaitán was in one when the planes attacked the Moneda. 'Finally, they've killed that son of a whore!' shouted one woman. Gaitán dashed over and shook her by the throat before being dragged away in tears by her friends. In the wealthy neighbourhoods, some people began hanging out Chilean flags in celebration. In the Moneda, Allende still fired from his exposed position on the balcony. One of the doctors in the building grabbed him by the feet and dragged him back inside. 'Let me go, *huevon*!' shouted Allende, before turning and saying, 'Oh, it's you Jironcito.'[31]

Soon afterwards, one of the defenders, Augusto '*Perro*' Olivares, Allende's close friend and the head of National Television, committed suicide. It was a harsh blow to morale. Allende asked

[30] Payita quoted in E. Labarca, p. 352.
[31] Jorquera, p. 88.

the defenders for a minute's silence in his honour and then ordered four of the defenders out to negotiate a truce with the attackers, probably in the hope of saving their lives. At one point, he ordered the GAP to 'knock down all those shitty old men', referring to the plaster busts of Chile's past presidents, 'except for Balmaceda and Pedro Aguirre Cerda'. The busts were smashed, and the floor of the halls was littered with broken plaster. The attack began again, the air thick with bullets, explosions, smoke, dust, and tear gas.

With ammunition running low and the defenders exhausted, alone, isolated and without hope of relief, Allende called them together and ordered them to surrender. The GAP in the buildings covering the Moneda had also run out of ammunition and began their escape from the centre. As the defenders discussed surrender, troops smashed their way in through the Moneda's side door, known as Morandé 80. Shots rang out, and boots could be heard crunching on the debris downstairs. One of the several doctors in the Moneda, Oscar Soto, bumped into the advancing troops on the stairs. An officer saved him from being shot and sent him upstairs to negotiate the surrender. Allende ordered all the defenders out, 'All of you, go downstairs, leave your weapons, don't leave anything in your pockets. Leave with dignity; surrender because this is a massacre.'[32] Allende said that he would be the last to leave. The defenders organised themselves in a line. Payita was put first, wearing Augusto Olivares' jacket, with Chile's Declaration of Independence hidden in one sleeve.

It is at this point that what happened next becomes unclear. The current official version of events has several inconsistencies. It is based upon the testimony of Doctor Patricio Guijón. Guijón's story goes as follows:

As the defenders began to descend, Allende suddenly stepped from towards the back of the line, opened the door of the Independence Salon and closed it behind him. Two men heard

---

[32] Patricio Guijón quoted in E. Labarca, p. 354.

him shout, 'Allende doesn't surrender, dammit!' The men in the line were confused. 'Where's he going?' asked Dr Arturo Jiron. 'To commit suicide,' answered Dr Ruiz. Downstairs, boots and rifle butts were used to hurry the defenders outside, where they were forced down onto the ground, hands on their heads. Payita had Olivares' jacket torn off her shoulders; a soldier ripped up the Declaration of Independence that fell out.

Upstairs, 'Jano', one of the GAP defenders, opened the door Allende had closed behind himself. The others crowded around him. Through the smoke and dust, they saw Allende sitting facing them on a red sofa, wreathed in smoke, diffuse light pouring in from two large windows on either side of him. Behind him, a large painting of the Proclamation of Independence hung on the wall. Allende saw their faces and shouted, 'Shut the door!' Before anyone could react, President Allende seemed to rise off the sofa, his face becoming smudged, as if dissolving in the smoke. The men heard a shot. Dr 'Pachi' Guijón rushed in and took Allende's pulse. He was dead. 'What do I do now?' he thought to himself. Allende's wristwatch continued to tick. Others stood by the door observing the scene. One of them burst into tears; they turned and began to descend the staircase leading out of the burning palace. Dr Guijón remained by Allende's side. On the staircase, Enrique Huerta, one of the defenders, shouted out, 'The President has died! Viva Allende! Don't surrender, comrades!' but others grabbed his gun.[33]

Dr Guijón states that he remained by Allende's side for 10 minutes or so, sitting on a small stool. Realising that he was too near Allende's AKM, he moved it a little further away, across the President's body. Two soldiers entered; Dr Guijón raised his hands. Firemen followed the soldiers, and behind them came General Palacios — the man in charge of the operation — to take the palace. He observed the scene. Allende lay back over the red sofa, his assault rifle across his lap. His hands were blackened

[33] Testimony of these final moments is confused. This account is based on the various testimonies collected by E. Labarca, pp. 409-412.

with gunpowder. His face was hardly recognisable; the top of his head was missing. Palacios then radioed out to Admiral Carvajal. 'Mission accomplished. The Moneda is taken. The President is dead'. A few minutes later. Carvajal, in turn, informed the junta, in English — 'They say that Allende committed suicide and is dead now'. Then in Spanish, 'Tell me if you understood'.

Unfortunately, there are no surviving witnesses to attest to the veracity of Dr Guijón's account. We, therefore, only have his word for what happened. Guijón's testimony has contradicted itself on occasion; for example, in one interview, he stated that Allende fired two shots into his head, and in another that he only fired one. In one version, he said that he had witnessed the moment of Allende's death; in others, he had not. Some of those who later shared their incarceration with Dr Guijón on Dawson Island have stated that they did not believe his version because of these inconsistencies.

In fact, for many years, the dominant version among the Left was that Allende had fought, been fatally wounded and then died from his wounds surrounded by a handful of GAP, who were later killed. Again, this version has no surviving witnesses of Allende's death. Variations of this version were written by Gabriel García Márquez, Jorge Timossi (the head of Cuba's Prensa Latina in Chile), Eugene Propper, and others. They were largely based on the testimony of 'Eladio' (Renato González), the sole member of the GAP to survive the battle inside the Moneda and upon the statements made by military officers in the moments after the coup, which were recorded in the extraordinary East German documentary, *Mas Fuerte que el Fuego* (*Stronger Than Fire*).[34]

Given the uncertainties, it is only fair to give the other version of events based on testimonies provided by soldiers and military officers, and Eladio. That version goes like this :

As the doctors and other civilians headed down the stairs

---

[34] The film can be watched on Vimeo here:
       www.vimeo.com/459008807
       (1978).

on Allende's instructions, the attacking soldiers led by General Palacios filed upwards. As they reached the landing, they came under fire from Allende and the remaining GAP defenders. The soldiers recall that the defenders were defiantly yelling, 'The people do not surrender, dammit!', and 'Come and get it, you sons of whores!' One officer was hit twice in the helmet, and General Palacios was wounded in the hand by shrapnel or a ricocheting bullet.[35] The Moneda was full of smoke from the burning fires; attackers and defenders were crawling about in semi-darkness, choking on smoke and soot. Visibility was poor. Testifying the intensity of the fighting, after the battle, General Palacios told the German documentarists that 'the most difficult part for us was inside the Moneda'.[36]

It is possible that Allende was wounded in this first engagement at the top of the stairs. Certainly, one soldier states that a civilian wearing a gas mask was hit by a burst of fire from the groin upwards to the chest.

Years later, Palacios also told an old friend in confidence that once the defenders had been beaten back, he had checked the bodies and had noticed an expensive watch on one of them. He said that he had pulled off the gas mask covering the face and realised it was President Allende. Palacios then pulled out his service pistol and shot Allende through the head. The week after the coup, Palacios was in Colombia, where he told journalists that 'Allende had been firing the whole time because his hands were covered in powder. The magazine of his machine gun was empty. There were many casings in the window. He had a pistol by his side, and when I identified him, he also had on a helmet and a gas mask'.[37]

In Timossi's version, based on Eladio's testimony, it also states that Allende was heavily wounded as the soldiers reached the first

---

[35] Ravanal and Marin, p. 99.
[36] Ravanal and Marin, p. 93.
[37] Ravanal and Marin, p. 141.

floor, but it continues stating that Allende's guards grabbed him and, under covering fire from their comrades, dragged him from where he lay to a sofa in a nearby room, leaving a blood trail that firefighters witnessed later. They took a Chilean flag from beside a desk and covered his body in it. As they were doing this, soldiers burst in, and in the firefight, Allende's guards were either wounded or killed. Perhaps, this is where Palacios found Allende wearing the gas mask. We will likely never know. In Propper's version, which is based on interviews with US intelligence agents, a wounded Allende was finished off by another Chilean soldier called René Riveros.[38]

What is certain is that at 2.35 pm, Palacios radioed General Sergio Nuno saying, 'Mission accomplished. Moneda taken. President dead.' Ten minutes later, General Carvajal communicated with the Army High Command stating in English that Allende had killed himself.

If it is true that Allende's suicide had to be set up, then General Palacios' Military Intelligence men now moved to do so. Fresh clothes were found in Allende's wardrobe in the small anteroom by his office, where he took his 20-minutes after lunch siestas. Allende's shirt and trousers were removed (one of the inconsistencies of the battle is that surviving witnesses say that Allende took his jacket off since the temperature inside became unbearable once the fire took hold, and yet the photograph of his body shows him wearing one) and fresh ones put on. His body was placed on a colourful woven blanket before being dragged and lifted onto the sofa. His AKMS was placed between his legs, and somebody fired at least one shot up through his chin, blasting remains over the tapestry behind the sofa. Then, the detectives were brought in to witness the scene. The survivors of the battle were taken outside the Moneda, where they were lined up on the floor in front of a tank whose

---

[38] Eugene M. Propper and Taylor Branch, 'Labyrinth' (New York: Viking, 1982).

commander threatened to run them over. Afterwards, they were taken to a military base, where all but two of them were tortured and disappeared.

Whichever version is closer to the truth, Allende was now dead, and the UP was over.

The Contested
Versions of
Allende's Death

I have always maintained that how Allende died matters less than how he lived. Whatever the truth may be, his was a heroic death full of dignity. By refusing to surrender, he made it a death of his own choosing. Nevertheless, it has to be acknowledged that in a largely Catholic society such as Chile's, a widespread belief in Allende's suicide could be useful to those who overthrew him. Firstly, because it reduced emphasis on the actions of the military and doing so helped indicate the fatal nature of the UP's own internal contradictions. It made the coup seem less like a murder and more like a spontaneous abortion. This also had the benefit of reducing any potential legal recriminations against the officers concerned. Secondly, it could be seen to weaken the symbolism of Allende's last stand and, therefore, reduce the likelihood of some kind of popular revolt. For the opposite reasons, the Left always tended to believe that Allende had died in combat. As mentioned, this was actually the version that dominated until the 1990 exhumation and autopsy of Allende's remains, which concluded that he had shot himself as the military had claimed.

At the time of writing the first edition, there was no questioning of the 1990 investigation into Allende's death. Previous disagreements had died down, and moreover, the Chilean government had just launched another enquiry into his death, and the early indications were that it would confirm the suicide thesis. Yet, in early 2014, one of the Supreme Court judges opposed the Court's decision, stating that the 'uncertainty around the intervention of third parties' meant that the case should not be closed definitively.[1] In 2016, a photograph emerged that purports to show Allende's dead body, wearing a bloodstained white shirt, which would at least indicate that Allende was not wearing the jumper and jacket of the official photograph. A well-known Chilean journalist, Rubén Adrián Valenzuela, confirmed the authenticity of this photograph and wrote about others that General Baeza had shown him shortly after the coup, which showed Allende's torso with a line of bullet holes across it.

Today, it seems we may never really know how Allende died, at least until the Chilean authorities release footage and photographs taken at the scene on the day of the coup (the one existing photo was leaked in December 1973, but we know of 29 others). Nevertheless, there are enough problems and contradictions with the official story — from the contradictions in the testimonies left by Doctor Patricio Guijón and others to the second-hand testimony of various military officers that claim that Allende was killed and the issues with the various investigations held in 1973, 1990, and 2014. Since question marks remain over exactly how Allende died, in the interests of truth, readers should be acquainted with the main problems with the official version.[2]

The junta's initial version of events was contradictory. For the first few hours, there was no official communication, but media reports falsely stated that Allende had surrendered. Then Pinochet and Palacios both mentioned that Allende had been fighting, and in the days after the coup, Palacios said that Allende had died in

---

[1] See Radio Universidad de Chile, 'Corte Suprema confirma tesis del suicidio de Salvador Allende', 7 January 2014, (accessed in 2020). https://radio.uchile.cl/2014/01/07/corte-suprema-confirma-sobreseimiento-total-y-definitivo-en-causa-por-muerte-de-salvador-allende/

[2] A summary of these can be found in Luis Ravanal and Francisco Marin, *Allende: yo no me rendire. La investigacion historica y forence que descarta el suicidio*, (Santiago: Ceibo, 2013).

combat. The junta's official version of Allende's suicide was not broadcast until 20 September 1973. The question is, why did it take all this time to agree to an official version?

According to Ravanal and Marin (one a historian, the other a forensic specialist), who have thoroughly researched the issue, the 1973 autopsy and crime scene investigation into Allende's death were not carried out properly. The autopsy was carried out during the night of 11 September by two medics — Dr Tobar, a forensic specialist and Dr Vasquez, a gynaecologist — later associated with false autopsies on victims of the dictatorship, including the Spanish diplomat Carmelo Soria, who Vasquez concluded had died after being run over, while he had, in fact, died under torture.[3] Allende's autopsy was carried out under military supervision in the military hospital, not in the specialised autopsy theatre in *Investigaciones* police headquarters, where it should have been carried out according to the law.

Contrary to the procedure, the written description of the autopsy failed to cover the whole body, and no photographs taken at the autopsy have ever been released. The original copy of the autopsy report has allegedly been lost, but the available copies make mention of 'part of an orifice with an external bevel' in one of the bones from the back of the skull.[4] In the report, this orifice was associated with the shot from Allende's AKM, but Dr Ravanal, a forensic expert, argues that a high-velocity bullet that destroys the skull cannot create an orifice in the bone while it does so. Therefore, according to Ravanal, the orifice must be from a different, low-velocity shot to the one that destroyed the skull, such as one fired from a pistol, which would appear to confirm General Palacios's claim to have shot Allende. To add to the mystery, Dr Tobar, the forensic specialist at the 1973 autopsy, later committed suicide during the dictatorship.

The ballistic and crime scene investigations carried out on

---

[3] Ravanal and Marin, p. 158.
[4] The report is transcribed in Ravanal and Marin, pp. 195-199.

the day of the coup were signed off at gunpoint. The crime scene investigation carried out by the police homicides department describes three wounds on Allende's body — one entry wound (under the chin), one exit wound towards the back of the skull, and one around the right eyebrow or eyelid (which the report states, could have been either an entry or exit wound). The investigators were not permitted to check Allende's AKMS, which was taken by General Palacios, so they did not know whether there was a bullet in the chamber or how many bullets, if any, were left in the magazine (although Palacios claimed it was empty). Afterwards, the military presented an AK-47 with a wooden butt that they said had been Allende's weapon, but photographs, the investigations and testimonies show he had actually fought with a later model AKMS with a folding metal butt, possibly the one Castro had given him during his visit to Chile. One of the characteristics of the AK family of assault rifles is that they have two settings — single shot and automatic. In automatic mode, the gun fires around ten bullets in a second. If Allende used this setting, how did only two bullets (according to Guijón) go through his head? If he used the single-shot setting, how did he fire two bullets?

Then, in 1990, Allende's remains were exhumed in extraordinary circumstances. Patricio Aylwin — the vociferous and hard-line enemy of the UP — had recently been elected president of a new Socialist-Christian Democrat alliance, gratefully receiving the presidential sash from the hands of General Pinochet. It was obvious that the government had to provide some form of truth and reconciliation in the wake of the dictatorship and that the foundation of this would be to establish the truth of what had happened to President Allende. Given the differing versions in existence, establishing the truth of Allende's death became an important political question. The new government decided that Allende would be buried in Santiago's main cemetery, following an official ceremony that would help put the related dramas of the UP and the dictatorship in the past.

Allende's remains had originally been buried on 12 September

1973 in a sealed zinc coffin in Viña del Mar, in the tomb of the Grove family — the old friends of the Allendes'. Hortensia Bussi, Allende's widow, was not permitted to see the body before it was buried. In 1990, Allende's remains were exhumed, but the way it was done left much to be desired. Firstly, the exhumation took place on the night of 17 August 1990. Why at night, unless it was to keep the public away? Allende's remains were exhumed by torchlight. They were removed from the coffin by the local gravediggers, who simply gathered fragments of bone and threw them into a bag before emptying it into a new coffin. The clothes and shoes, along with some of the remains, were bagged and, unbelievably, then thrown away. The entire event violated established procedures by discarding evidence and treating some of the remains as rubbish. Allende's remains were then raced to Santiago with minimal fuss and no publicity.

Allende, the lifelong atheist and freemason, was given funeral rites in Santiago's Catholic cathedral on 4 September 1990, the anniversary of his victory. There then followed a series of eulogies at the cemetery, presided over by Allende's political enemies, which were closed by President Patricio Aylwin, the Christian Democrat leader who had rejected Allende's political approaches in 1973. Aylwin gave a message of national reconciliation and the need to abide by the rules of democracy to avoid the traumas of the past. 'Those who want to make of this act a motive or pretext to reanimate grievances are mistaken and cause harm', he said. The horrors Chile experienced 'have taught us that those circumstances should never be repeated for any reason!' For Aylwin, the hatred and violence of the past needed to be 'uprooted', and national life needed to avoid 'ideological sectarianisms, personal or collective insults'. People needed to learn 'to respect difference and abide by the rules of democracy'. The time for blame was over, everyone shared responsibilities for what had happened, and everyone had made mistakes. 'For all Chileans of goodwill, today is an act of unity and peace', he claimed.

It sounded good. And it contained some truths. But underlying it was a set of assumptions about politics that have since been shown to be false and which Allende would have rejected. What Aylwin was really calling for was for the economic causes of things to be ignored, for blame to be dispersed, and for democracy to be conflated with civility. For Allende, this had not been what democracy was about. For him, democracy was the 'possibility of rebellion against injustice', and a 'conscious result arrived at through principles, ideas, and doctrines'; it was the honest competition between ideas aimed at national progress. It was not elite collusion at the expense of the people.

Aylwin's government reburied Allende with the minimum ceremonial that it could get away with. The masses were kept well away from the heart of the proceedings. Perhaps the shadowy presence of Pinochet contributed to this, but it is also true that if there was one thing the new government agreed with the military on, it was that the UP had been a disaster. The police beat back demonstrators trying to get into the cemetery. Nobody wanted Allende's ideological and combative example to become an obstacle so early in the transition.

In 2008, new court cases forced Allende's death to be reconsidered, and in 2011, the Chilean authorities decided to end the speculation by carrying out a new investigation with international forensic experts involved. Allende's remains were, therefore, again exhumed on 23 May 2011. Although the forensic specialists noted that much of the skull and other evidence had been lost in 1990, they eventually reconfirmed the suicide thesis. However, in the opinion of Dr Luís Ravanal and other critics, this was because the investigation took a selective approach to earlier evidence that contradicted the suicide version. For example, it did not seek to investigate the issue of the rounded orifice described in Tobar and Vasquez's 1973 autopsy report, nor did it properly engage with the way in which different witness statements contradicted each other. These and other problems mean that the official version of Allende's death will be questioned until further evidence appears. Therefore, it is entirely possible that Allende died in combat and that the suicide was set up by the members of Chile's military intelligence, who entered the Moneda before the police homicide teams were allowed in.

Chile After Allende: The Triumphant Counter-revolution?

> The problem of revolution as of war consists in breaking
> the will of the foe, forcing him to capitulate and to accept
> the conditions of the conqueror.
> — Leon Trotsky

Allende's death marked the beginning of a dark period in Chilean history. The military treated Chile like an occupied country. Football stadiums and army barracks became detention centres. Hundreds of thousands of people were arrested and detained over the next few months. Foreigners were particularly sought out as members of a supposed guerrilla army that had been assembled under Allende. Soldiers disobeying orders were shot, senior officers perceived as close to Allende were arrested and tortured, and some were killed. The ordinary members of Chile's left-wing parties and trade unions were hunted down, and many were killed and disappeared. Dozens of children were killed or tortured. Thousands were abandoned to their fate as parents disappeared into torture camps and prisons. In the countryside, landowners took violent revenge on peasants and the Mapuche indigenous people. Hundreds of thousands of Chileans were forced into exile. Allende had feared civil war, but Chile was subjected to a massacre in the end. The Left's strength in numbers was simply swept aside by violence.

On 18 September, Eduardo Frei went to the newly installed

junta's Independence Day blessing in Santiago Cathedral. His presence as President of the Senate, alongside two other former presidents, was a powerful legitimation of the new regime. In October, Patricio Aylwin, the president of the PDC, met with the military junta. Although what happened is disputed, events appear to support the version that asserts that Aylwin endorsed the coup and offered the cooperation of PDC members on an individual basis in the hope that power might yet be handed to him.[1] Other leading Christian Democrats, such as Radomiro Tomic and Bernardo Leighton, immediately condemned the coup. The PN dissolved itself. The Junta dissolved the Congress. While the priests incanted their blessing, Chile's democracy was being sacrificed along with the lives of thousands of anonymous people who had hoped for a better future.

Pinochet gradually consolidated his rule and began implementing a project intended to extirpate 'the Marxist cancer' from Chile. The education system was purged of Leftists, and military officers were placed in charge. Public figures that might have unified the opposition in exile were assassinated — General Prats was murdered in Buenos Aires in October 1974; PDC leader Bernardo Leighton was shot and crippled in Rome in 1975; and former Chilean ambassador to the US Orlando Letelier, murdered in a Washington car-bombing in September 1976. In 1982, Eduardo Frei, who had done so much to prevent a political agreement with Allende, was poisoned and killed after he threatened to unite the opposition to the dictatorship. It is symbolic that the military murdered both presidents who had striven to reform Chile, one within capitalism and the other through socialism.

In 1977, Pinochet laid the basis for a new constitution in a speech to a nocturnal congregation bearing burning torches.[2]

---

[1] See Chapter 3 of Pablo Politczer, *Los Modelos del horror: Represión e información en Chile bajo la Dictadura*, (Santiago: LOM, 2014).

[2] Several members of Chile's current right-wing government were present at this ceremony.

Three years later, it was enshrined after a military-controlled plebiscite. The 1980 constitution, although reformed, still forms the basis of the Chilean constitution to this day. Its eighth article outlawed Marxism. It made Pinochet president and guaranteed his rule until 1990, with the possibility of extending it to 1997. It enshrined a 'binomial' electoral system, which severely distorted the electoral process until 2015 and a Labour Code that severely weakened labour organisations; it re-privatised part of the copper mining industry and opened up other mining sectors to foreign companies. It also enshrined the private ownership of underground resources in perpetuity. The dictatorship lowered import tariffs, prompting a flood of imports and the subsequent closure of most of Chile's industry. Unemployment and poverty shot up, and wages collapsed, rolling back decades of social progress.

The Christian Democrats moved into the opposition, but despite myriad Communist concessions, the PDC leadership still refused to ally with them against the dictatorship, preferring a separate opposition. Time passed, and frustrations grew. Inside Chile, the Left began to organise to strike back. The MIR tried to install a guerrilla movement in the forests of the south, but it was destroyed. The PS split. The social impacts of the 1982 debt crisis sparked mass resistance to the regime, and a year later, the Communists launched a Manuel Rodríguez Patriotic Front (*Frente Patriótico Manuel Rodríguez*, FPMR) aimed at defending the popular mobilisations and building towards a 'national uprising'. In September 1986, Pinochet narrowly survived the FPMR ambush of his cavalcade, and amid growing fears of a revolutionary overthrow in both Washington and Santiago, the Reagan administration made strenuous efforts to identify and support 'moderate' sectors in the regime and among the opposition, who would be amenable to an alliance excluding the PC. The Catholic Church was recruited to the cause, alongside an array of foreign NGOs, who worked hard to promote a transition to democracy. With this amenable opposition guaranteed, after 1986, the regime began to implement a transition towards 'democracy'. The steady collapse of 'existing socialism' in Europe formed a potent backdrop that sucked strength from the Left.

The PS underwent an extraordinary transformation in these years. Carlos Altamirano escaped from Chile in an operation organised by the East German Stasi. Initially in exile, the Party continued to privilege the rather simplistic narrative that the Left had failed to properly develop a military force of its own. In the mid-1970s, the Party decided to overcome this failure and set up a 'Technical Commission' to develop what was envisioned as the backbone of future popular armed forces. Many former members of Allende's GAP and the Chilean ELN joined and underwent rigorous military training, mainly in Cuba and East Germany. At the same time, another group within the Party, led by Allende's former Foreign Minister, Clodomiro Almeyda, developed an analysis that was closer to that which was maturing within the PC — the Left had allowed the isolation of the working class.

Chile's Socialists had always been an ideological mixed bag, and in exile in Europe, many of them became increasingly influenced by Western European social democracy. Their existing Trotskyist and anarchist critiques of Soviet socialism were gradually deepened and broadened by the critiques predominant in Western Europe. Meanwhile, the experience of exile in Eastern Europe, particularly East Germany, led some to completely reject 'real existing socialism'. Carlos Altamirano was one of them. Altamirano rapidly shifted from the dogmatic Marxist firebrand of the UP towards the main articulator of the need for the Party to 'renovate' itself rightwards, in a process that echoed European 'Eurocommunism'. Superficially, the 'renovation' of the Altamirano wing of the PS seemed like a tardy adoption of Allende's ideas, but in essence, they stripped it of its revolutionary content, and it became the vehicle for a third-world social democracy, a little different from that tried years before, by Allende's friend Rómulo Betancourt. By the end of the 1970s, the PS within Chile had been almost completely eliminated; its leadership came to rest in the hands of youngsters just out of school.

The split in exile was reflected by fragmentation within Chile, and by the mid-1980s, there were several groups vying to claim the Party's mantle. The Party's fragmentation and renovation were of great interest to the US, which had begun to shift its policy in the wake of the overthrow of General Somoza in Nicaragua in 1979. Support for bloodthirsty dictators had undermined Carter's adoption of human rights as a foreign policy weapon, and the overthrow of Somoza showed that repression contributed to polarisation. Throughout the 1980s, the Reagan administration gradually shifted towards a much more sophisticated approach that combined all the political, military, social, and economic levers at the disposal of the US to promote 'democratisation'. One important plank of this policy was the efforts to identify and bring together moderates among the opposition to the dictatorship, as well as among the dictatorship's supporters. US power was used to create and sustain a new political force that excluded Communists on the Left and military hardliners on the right. US funding to think tanks, civil society organisations, NGOs, and academics played an important role. The two groups could eventually be brought together in such a way that guaranteed achieving US economic and foreign policy goals while replacing unpopular dictators with centrist regimes.[3]

The PC was not immune to the global pressures facing the Left in the 1980s. The Party had created the FPMR to combat the dictatorship with what Corvalán called 'acute violence', but as 'moderates' among the opposition and the regime grew closer,

---

[3] For more on this process, see Victor Figueroa Clark, 'The Forgotten History of the Chilean Transition: Armed Resistance Against Pinochet and US Policy Towards Chile in the 1980s', *Journal of Latin American Studies*, 47 No. 3 (2015); William Robinson, 'Promoting Polyarchy' (Cambridge: Cambridge University Press, 1996); and Robert Pee and William Michel Schmidli (eds), 'The Reagan Administration, the Cold War and the transition to Democracy Promotion', (Palgrave Macmillan, 2019).

the Party faced the danger of total isolation. It tried to shut down the armed resistance to the dictatorship. However, armed struggle cannot be switched on and off at will. The bulk of the Frente's leadership split from the Party and attempted to continue the struggle. Most of its leaders were killed and disappeared in 1987, although it struggled on into the early 1990s. Its best-known actions were a series of spectacular prison breaks (the subject of two recent Chilean films) and the assassination of one of the dictatorship's ideologues, Jaime Guzmán. Another group of Communists grew increasingly critical of the impact of the Party's military policy and of the new Party leadership associated with it. Many of them eventually left the Party, some joining the Party for Democracy (*Partido por la Democracia*, PPD), which the opposition had set up before the October 1988 plebiscite.

Gradually, under US pressure, Chile's 'moderate' Socialist and Christian Democrat opposition accepted Pinochet's 1980 constitution, while US support of moderates in the military encouraged engagement. Nonetheless, the democracy born of the transition was a mutation that served to preserve an unjust economic system. On the cusp of the handover of power in 1990, Pinochet added several articles to his constitution that ensured his control over the incoming civilian government. These included the creation of 'designated' senators and decentralising and privatising education. Pinochet retired and then appointed a new Supreme Court; he ensured Congress had no remit to investigate members of the 'military regime'. With everything in place, the civilian 'Concertacion' government took power, a new alliance of Christian Democrats and 'renovated' Socialists and ex-Communists.

Over the next twenty years, the Concertacion ruled Chile, implementing a sort of underdeveloped social democracy through coalition. Among its first measures was the demobilisation of the vast popular movement that had sprung up in resistance to the dictatorship. The Concertacion tried to diversify Chilean exports and agro-industry. Fishing, fruits and wood became important sectors. The economy grew, but it was recovering from a very low base. Foreign investment flooded in, and money from copper and mining flowed out.

Chile remained dependent on raw material exports. What growth was achieved was unevenly distributed. Instead of redistribution by taxation and wage increases, the Concertacion used income from copper mining to successfully target extreme poverty. Yet, inequality remained embedded in the system. With the remains of the Left largely excluded from the system — thanks to an ideological crisis and the intricacies of the binomial electoral system — and the trade unions crippled by a repressive Labour Code and a 'flexible' workforce, only in 2000 did average wages achieve their 1970 levels. Chile remained overwhelmingly dependent on what Allende had called 'the wage of Chile' — copper.

The Concertacion also failed to rigorously pursue human rights abusers, and it was not until Pinochet's arrest in London in 1998 that the curtain of impunity began to be lifted on any but the most notorious abusers. The civilian faces behind the military remained untouched. Popular discontent bubbled away, but it was held in check by the potent combination of a steady improvement in people's economic situation, the introduction of easily available credit, and a latent fear of a return to military rule. Together, credit cards, TV, the internet, mobile phones and the accoutrements of modernisation encouraged an I-don't-care-attitude.

In 2010, with discontent with the Concertacion mounting, the centrist coalition put forward an unpopular candidate, Eduardo Frei Junior, the son of Allende's old friend and rival who had already had a term in the 1990s. The result was that Sebastian Piñera, the billionaire brother of one of Pinochet's Interior Ministers, became President of Chile. Dozens of Pinochet supporters, among them notorious human rights abusers, stepped out of the shadows and back into the political limelight. The right saw it as a popular vindication, but during the same elections, the PC finally managed to win four congressional seats. The Concertacion suffered its first desertions, and the PS began to fracture again. Chilean politics had begun to polarise once more.

During Piñera's first term, Chile witnessed the largest demonstrations since the dictatorship, with Santiago and other cities seeing the return of the famous *cacerolazos* of the 1980s, when the urban population would take advantage of blackouts to beat pots and pans and beep car horns to demonstrate their discontent. In 2011, students mobilised, demanding that education be properly funded and, in effect, renationalised. Among their leaders were charismatic young women from the PC. However, most notable was the creation of new political movements, such as the Democratic Revolution and Autonomous Left, which were set up by student leaders from the 2011 protests to channel demands they felt the existing parties could not or would not pursue.

Organised workers also went out on strike, and there were large mobilisations by environmental activists and indigenous people. They were heavily repressed, and the indigenous regions of the south were put under police control. Several Mapuche activists were killed and many more imprisoned, where they periodically went on hunger strikes. As in the 1920s, a new generation of trade unionists, student leaders, and political activists was shaking the foundations of Chile's political structure, but was it enough?

Piñera's first government was followed in 2014 by a centre-left government called the 'New Majority' (*Nueva Mayoria*). For the first time since before the coup, the PC was admitted into the governing coalition. This led some of them to compare the New Majority to Allende's project for the UP and his efforts to bring the PDC into an alliance with the Left. However, even in the twenty-first century, this was too much for many leading Christian Democrats and they left the PDC. Nevertheless, the bulk of the Concertacion parties hoped that the Communists would help re-legitimise a governing coalition that had been heavily battered in recent years. The Communists hoped to channel the demands of the street in parliament and tried to recreate a symbiotic relationship between social mobilisation and political activism. Key to the New Majority's manifesto were constitutional reforms aimed primarily at changing the tax system, the education system, the Labour Code and the electoral system.

For many Leftists outside the New Majority, the Communists had betrayed the popular movement by engaging in the politics of a system that they viewed as irredeemably corrupt. It was true that corruption was affecting increasing areas of public life. Corruption scandals rocked the military ('Milicogate') and the police ('Pacogate'). Socialist President Michelle Bachelet's family was implicated in another scandal, where her son sold his political influence. The scandal also linked members of right-wing political parties. Moreover, in a country where the average income was around 400,000 Chilean pesos a month, ordinary people felt that politicians earning 12 million pesos were living in another country. They bitterly called the parliamentary Left the 'red set'. In a hostile media environment, it mattered little that the handful of Communist politicians exchanged their salaries for a party stipend linked to average wages. They were accused of becoming part of the system and tainted by association.

Bachelet's New Majority pushed for the changes it had promised but was stymied by a new emerging alliance between the right wing of the PDC and the right-wing National Renovation under former President Piñera. Leading foreign trade bodies such as the Anglo-Chilean and Chilean-American Chambers of Commerce vociferously opposed the reforms. Then, the constitutional court — labelled as 'the third chamber of parliament' by a leading constitutional expert — in which the right-wing dominated, struck down the central aspects of the labour reform, which had already been much watered down by political horse-trading in the New Majority, so much so that it was even criticised by the CUT trade union federation. In 2017, the weakened Labour Reform was passed, but it did little to resolve the power imbalance between employers and employees.

For much of the Left, outside the New Majority, the government had shown that it could not fulfil its promises, and the corruption scandals showed how far the political class as a whole was implicated in the exploitation of the people. Its leaders emphasised the need for a purer left-wing alliance, and in 2017, they created a political alliance known as the Broad Front (*Frente Amplio*, FA) inspired by the Uruguayan example. Rather than working with the established parties, the FA sought the creation of a powerful social and political bloc that would be able to force through the necessary political changes without relying on the rotten parties of the old guard.

The division in the Left was the latest manifestation of the age-old split over how to engage with the existing political institutions and whether to privilege politics in the institutions or social pressure on the streets. Layered on top of this were differing interpretations of recent history, of the causes of the defeats suffered by the Left in the overthrow of Allende and the struggle against Pinochet. It is also suffused with differing attitudes towards hierarchy and process and refracted by contrasting attitudes towards the importance of the environment and sectional struggles such as those of young people, women, sexual minorities, and indigenous peoples.

It was no surprise when the New Majority lost the presidential elections in 2018, allowing Sebastian Piñera to regain the Presidency. The bitter truth for the Chilean Left was that ideological crisis and the impact of the reigning socio-economic and political system had created a situation where political parties were no longer seen as the vehicle for change in society, nor were that other pillar of twentieth-century political activism — the trade unions. What is the point of political parties when political institutions exist to prevent change, not channel it? How can unions become an engine for change when they are barely strong enough to defend their members effectively or when most people no longer strongly identify as workers? The problem for the system comes when people become explicitly aware that the problem resides in the system itself. The problem becomes a crisis when people begin to experience worsening conditions that the elite escapes from.

At this point, the only avenue for change is mass protest.

This is what has happened. In October 2019, an ordinary protest by students against a fare hike on the public transport system in Santiago was severely repressed by the police firing rubber bullets and pellets. The repression sparked a mass response, and hundreds of thousands of people were soon out on the streets. Metro stations were attacked and burned down, as were some supermarkets. It is still unclear who was behind the mayhem, but videos surfaced showing masked men talking to police before setting barricades ablaze. Possibly, the government was seeking an excuse to bring out the army. Within two days, the government had called the army out onto the streets for the first time since the dictatorship. Many people were shot, killed or wounded, but the protests grew and spread from city to city. Even remote provincial towns saw rioting.

The demonstrations and the riots went on day after day, and it was clear that for many, Allende was present in this mass struggle. As one protest placard put it, 'Allende has returned in the form of millions'. The army was withdrawn from the streets as it became clear that they would need to start a large-scale massacre to stop the protests. After the arrest of Pinochet in London in 1998, no Chilean General was willing to risk an international tribunal to save the skin of an embattled politician. The protestors rapidly developed a series of socio-economic demands, which were the result of local gatherings known as *cabildos* at which people discussed what was wrong with the country and how it needed to be changed. The demands included an end to privatised pensions, decent free healthcare and education, nationalisation of natural resources, a new social contract and a new constitution. The demands cohered around the call for a constituent assembly.

In November 2019, the government agreed to a referendum on whether people wanted a new constitution. The referendum was set for April 2020, but the protests continued. Politics again barged its way into everyday life for the first time since the fight against the dictatorship. 'Chile has awoken!', the protestors cried. Society and families began to split along political lines. Fascist attitudes began to emerge from beneath the superficial decency of the rich neighbourhoods, where protestors were branded as 'fucking *rotos*' and Communists. The media and the elite consistently tried to blame the unrest on external forces, ostensibly linked to Venezuela, with the president's wife notoriously talking of 'an alien invasion'. Yet, they could not stop the protests that took place around the epicentre of Plaza Italia, which became known as the *Square of Dignity*.

Incredibly, the government was rescued by Covid-19, at least temporarily. The government decreed a National State of Catastrophe in March 2020, and the referendum was postponed until October. In the meantime, the virus made its deadly way into Chile's poor neighbourhoods, where people have no healthcare and live from day to day. Chile's quarantine measures caused hunger, and few trusted the government to spend the USD 23.8 billion loan granted by the International Monetary Fund to tackle the problems of ordinary people. In fact, the government was forced to allow people to access their pension funds in order to alleviate the economic impact.

In October 2020, the Chilean people voted en masse to support a new constitution to be written by a constituent assembly during 2021. The constituent convention, initially presided by a Mapuche activist, developed a draft outlining the path Chile must take in the future. The draft was built around gender parity and, recognised all ethnic, gender, and sexual diversities and included substantive democratic reforms in all areas of life. While there was great optimism that it would be approved, particularly after

Leftist former student leader Gabriel Boric was elected president in November 2021, the eventual vote in September 2022 resulted in a shocking popular rejection.

There were many reasons for this defeat: the lack of unity among the progressive members of the convention, the ambivalent attitude of centrist forces in the convention towards key economic issues, the narrow sectoral focus of too many social actors involved, the government's failure to energetically support the campaign to approve the draft, as well as a vast media and social media disinformation campaign, and the Left's failure to reach out to the masses as Allende used to. The Left was shocked and disoriented by this defeat, the government much weakened, and it now seems that Congress and the old professional politicians will be far more involved in the next stages of the constitutional process.

Nevertheless, the protests have killed Pinochet's constitution, for while it still reigns today, it is a 'zombie' as one constitutional expert has written. What exactly will replace it is yet to be decided, but it is obvious that it will be more progressive, and more democratic than the 1980 Constitution.

Allende's Revolutionary Legacy

> The past resembles the future more than
> one drop of water another.
> — Ibn Khaldun

Salvador Allende died at the age of sixty-five. By his own admission, he had lived a relatively long and fruitful life. It was a life dedicated to the struggle for democracy and a life defined by elections often contested in difficult circumstances. Allende's persistence in fighting elections was a testament to his belief that in Chile, because of its unique history and social context, this was the most viable and effective way of placing the country on the path to socialism.

Allende's conviction was not a wilful construct. He was born during the dying stages of the post-1891 system, and he became an adult as the democratic system (that lasted until 11 September 1973) was born. As the scion of a family with a distinguished history, Allende had lived a privileged childhood amid members of the Chilean political elite. As a student, he had mixed with many future political leaders and was witness to the growth and development of the popular organisations of the Left. As a young adult, he also witnessed the failure of the military-inspired 'Socialist Republic' of 1932, contrasted in 1938 by the successful election of a Popular Front government that began a process of radical reforms. All helped to shape his perception that in Chile, the revolution did not have to follow the 'traditional' violent path. Allende decided to act 'in accordance with the reality of my country, in conformity with its idiosyncrasies and needs', as he later said.[1] His concrete, practical and intimate knowledge of the political system convinced him that in Chile, it was possible to initiate deep structural change from within.

Learning from the experience of the Popular Front, Allende thought that this approach required the broadest possible coalition of people and organisations around proposals aimed at achieving democracy, social justice and economic as well as human development. The PC came to a similar conclusion. Fortunately for both, much of the PS, while sceptical of a multi-class alliance, was amenable to a narrow alliance of working-class organisations. However, for much of the 1940s and 1950s, the PS was itself divided. This was reflected in the division of the trade union movement as well. Allende played an important role in rebuilding socialist unity, and once this was achieved, sustaining the alliance with the PC took him to the Presidency after eighteen years of struggle.

Allende was one of the Left's best-known and most respected leaders among a generation of political stars forged during the Popular Front. Together, they helped to shape the Chilean Left — one of the most vibrant, best organised, and most effective in the world. Allende was, without doubt, the figure that stood tallest among them, thanks to his knowledge of the system, his work rate, combativeness, and his deep compassion for the people, his capacity to educate and gather bright minds around him, along with a public persona that was shaped over decades of public life. Additionally, Allende had the ability to think tactically and strategically, to grasp rapidly the essence of a situation and to look further forward than those around him. This ability showed the influence of a particular set of political ideas and guiding

---

[1] Interview in *El Clarin*, 13 September 1970.

principles. While it is true that Allende did not develop a universal political theory, it would be a mistake not to recognise a particular 'Allendista' set of principles. He had what Regis Debray called 'a firm conceptual foundation'. He read widely, especially about politics, and although he may not have read many of the more recent Marxist theoreticians, he had no doubt learned much about them from his conversations with those who had. In this sense, his intellectual legacy is a mixture of concepts drawn from a broad spectrum of sources and life experiences. In this, he was truly a 'heterodox' thinker. It was Allende's political vision, along with his fearlessness, his charisma, his international contacts, his national stature and his total dedication to the cause, that made him the irreplaceable leader of the Chilean Left.

Allende spent his life in the search for the unity of the Left without compromising its diversity. He did not seek the construction of a narrow vanguard but the development of a mass movement. This movement would seek points of agreement with the political centre while maintaining a firm commitment to anti-imperialism and to socialism. Allende's UP government was the culmination of this fifty-year-long effort to build the broadest possible coalition. During election campaign after campaign Allende, the CUT trade union federation and the parties of the Left sought to spread their analysis of Chile's problems and their solutions to the people, evolving and adapting their programme as they went. Gradually and against the odds, they convinced a majority of Chileans. The growth of the Left's influence dragged the entire political spectrum leftwards to such an extent that the PDC, its main competition, aped its programme and its language.

The UP was the culmination of Allende's efforts to forge a broad coalition. Just as the UP was the triumph of his methods and message as president of the country, Allende also bears some responsibility for the ultimate failure of the UP. There are a variety of explanations usually given for this defeat. Those critical from the Left have tended to emphasize his underestimation of the threat from the United States and the inevitability of the failure of an unarmed revolution. Other radical critiques focus on his unwillingness to arm the people or mobilise them in defence of the process, or upon the government's failure to support the new political organisations that began to form outside the traditional institutions. The Communist critique centred on the failure to deal with the 'ultra-left' within and outside the UP coalition and on Allende's failure to use coercion against the more extreme right-wing opposition, which together resulted in the 'isolation of the working class'. Liberal critiques have, in turn, emphasized that economic chaos and political polarisation, along with the structural restrictions of the political system, created an unworkable situation and that Allende's failure to retreat from his revolutionary goals, therefore, made the coup inevitable. Perhaps each of these rather general explanations contains some truth at particular points during the UP. None, however, explains why Allende acted as he did. To find the answer, we must look into the mind of the man who led the process and who, therefore, had the greatest potential to change the course of events.

Key to understanding Allende's actions is understanding what he meant by 'revolution'. Some, including Carlos Altamirano, have argued that Allende was a reformist who became a revolutionary in later years. However, Allende always sought to transform Chilean society and do away with capitalism. Those who accused him of being a social democrat mistakenly confused the non-violent methods of his struggle with the desired outcome. Allende did not want to destroy his opponents but to liberate them. Allende wanted to build on the solid foundations of the past, not upon its smoking ruins. Allende sought to avoid the social costs of other revolutionary processes, and he tried to maintain Chile's social cohesion, but he did not want to preserve capitalism. Allende aimed to create the conditions for a transition away from dependent capitalism towards independent, sovereign, and democratic socialism. Crucially, Allende saw Chile and Latin

America's underdevelopment as the result of the combination between exploitative upper classes and their subordination of the region to the US. Internationally, it was vital that Chile throw off US domination because it distorted politics, crippled the economy, and severely limited Chile's international relations. It was, therefore vital that Chile develop good relations with other countries seeking a similar independence and with those of the socialist world. This struggle was not just in Chile's interests — it was necessary to end exploitation and inequality internationally because this would liberate the exploiters from their 'sentence of despotism'. Therefore, from Allende's perspective, the failure of Latin American nationalists like Rómulo Betancourt in Venezuela was due to their failure to challenge the basis of elite power in imperialism.[2] For Allende, socialism was true patriotism, and the solution to Chile's problems required linked national and international action. This was what shaped Allende's thinking and prevented him from being another reformist nationalist.

For Allende, socialism was both a strategy for socio-economic development and a means to achieve human fulfilment. It was a way to make real the promise of the slogan 'liberty, equality and fraternity', which inspired the Latin American independence struggles. Under the influence of these ideas, Allende's socialism had to include tolerance of diversity within the Left and tolerance of the opposition. The way to combine this with a revolutionary transformation of state and society was through participatory democracy; through it, pluralism of opinion and, thus, true liberty could be achieved. Yet, in order for democracy to function effectively, social justice is also required. For Allende, democracy and socialism were, therefore, two halves of the same coin. This concern with democracy and the realities of the Chilean political system translated into an almost obsessive search for the support of the majority and a rejection of the coercive role of the state.

---

[2] Debray, p. 69.

In order to achieve social justice, it was vital to provide preventative healthcare, quality education, and decent living conditions for all Chileans so as to end the hidden violence caused by malnutrition, ill health and poor housing. Development had to be funded by public control of Chile's natural resources and by a programme of agrarian reform and industrialisation that would give the state a principal role in the economy. However, it was not enough simply to enable the state to play a major role — the very purpose of the state needed to be transformed to serve the interests of ordinary working people. Yes, the state had been created by the oligarchy, but it could act against it if enough 'social force' could be applied. Allende thus understood the state to have some autonomy from its origins as an instrument of the ruling class.[3] The subsequent economic development would provide the resources to achieve the 'most noble potential' of each and allow Chileans to 'join civilisation' as masters of their destiny. Economic development and state control of resources were thus a precondition for the creation of socialism. In a similar way, Allende saw the existing legal and constitutional system as an incomplete conquest by the people. Therefore, this legal system based on liberalism could and needed to be *transformed* into a more advanced socialist form, not completely destroyed.

Allende's socialism was democratic and undogmatic; he spoke of the need to develop the theories and the practice of the new forms of organisation that would develop. He did not already have a clear vision of what would happen and how; rather, his government would begin to provide the spaces in which these new forms would develop democratically. This approach also envisioned the long period of time needed for people, if necessary, over generations, to adjust to socialist ethics and values. Therefore, the gradual reformism of the Chilean road was also the way to guarantee socialism. Together, anti-imperialism, participatory

---

[3] Jorge Arrate, *Salvador Allende, ¿sueño o proyecto?*, (Santiago: LOM, 2008), p. 42.

democracy, pluralism, and the transformation of the state made Allende's road a truly unique revolutionary method. These concepts explain why Allende rejected the use of force during the UP since violence would itself alter the kind of socialism being built. Unfortunately for Allende and for the UP, the global context of the 1960s and 1970s created an environment where many came to fetishize violence and dogmatic ideas about the seizure of power. As a result, Allende's road was misunderstood by many, who otherwise shared his goals.

After so many years in opposition, when Allende won the 1970 elections, he knew that his government would face strong opposition from the Chilean elite as well as from the US government. The example of US pressure and interference on Chilean governments and society since the late 1940s, the US interventions against Guatemala and Cuba — all served to make Allende aware of the probability of such an intervention against his government. Furthermore, he was familiar with the Marxist observation that each revolution provoked a counter-revolution, often with foreign support. Allende's government also received multiple warnings of the Nixon administration's hostility towards the UP. Therefore, Allende was not naïve about the probability of US hostility. In fact, the construction of a broad alliance for change was both a method to achieve democratic socialism and a way of ensuring the security of the process in the face of US hostility.

Therefore, Allende's political strategy depended upon the construction of a solid social and political majority with the support of the Christian Democrat grassroots and of its parliamentary representatives. The only way for the UP project to succeed was to continue bringing more and more people together in support of the goals of the revolution, turning the national majority for change into a political majority within Congress. The problem was, thus, Allende's main area of concern, and he sought to bring together the two political movements that argued for a transformation towards socialism in Chile — the 'popular movement' embodied in the UP and those within the PDC, who supported the ideals of 'communitarian socialism' and much of the UP programme. Only then could the legislative framework for the socio-economic changes necessary be created. This explains Allende's unwavering commitment to a policy of alliances with the centre. The problem was that his own coalition was not fully behind him in this.

Allende doggedly sought to create an alliance with the PDC throughout his time in office. At first, he sought such an alliance in Congress, seeking to force the PDC to make good its Leftist and nationalist rhetoric by becoming co-sponsors of a package of reforms nationalising copper and simultaneously creating the mechanisms for institutional change. Unfortunately, Allende's efforts were stymied by resistance and incomprehension within both the UP and the PDC.[4] The referendum package idea sank when the UP leadership preferred to separate the proposed economic and political reforms. The UP thus failed to consolidate its victory and eventually allowed the opposition to take the initiative. However, Allende never stopped trying to achieve a deal.

It is a testament to Allende's vision that this strategy came close to success on several occasions. Among those that share responsibility for its ultimate failure are those leaders of the PDC, who preferred to help destroy Chile's democratic system rather than allow Allende's process to continue. To a lesser extent, the extremist leaders of the PS and other groups who sought a confrontation and the military officers, whose loyalty to the constitution did not stretch to defending it, also bear some responsibility. Though the greatest responsibility lies with the US government, since without the US intervention, not only was the Chilean elite too small and too weak to hold back Allende and the UP's revolutionary process, but it is highly likely that the PDC would have eventually allied with the UP. US intervention did much to remove the incentives for this alliance, and it did much to finance and link together

---

[4] Corvalán, *El Gobierno de Salvador Allende*, p. 264.

the forces of opposition. Yet, even with this intervention, it took three years of sabotage to break Chile's institutionality, destroy its democratic traditions and undermine the constitutionalists within the Chilean armed forces.

Allende could arguably have done more from his position as president to deal with the problems his government faced, such as the disunity within the PS and the UP leadership. His commitment to democracy and his hostility to individual leadership became an impediment to effective decision-making in his government. In the past, Allende had shown himself able to both lead and leave the PS to help eliminate opposition within it. Yet, in government, he failed to take the measures needed to discipline it. Allende repeatedly tried to clearly state the necessity of his path forward, but he failed to demand loyalty to this path, this method of achieving the socialist goal, loyalty and unity in thought, word and deed. Once it was obvious that the disagreement over the methods of revolution was going to become an issue, those in leadership positions — who, in essence, opposed his road — could have been dealt with through expulsion or demotion. They did not need destroying, but to paraphrase Corvalán, they needed to be on a different train. As president, Allende became the figurehead of a Left that was bigger than the individual parties of the UP, and he needed to use this position to stamp his methods and objectives more firmly onto the Chilean Revolution. If the PS had split, perhaps Allende could have led his fraction forward more effectively, and it would have forced those Socialists in parliament, such as Altamirano, to decide whether they stood for or against the UP. It was a political tactic that Allende had used before.

Once it became clear that the coup plotters were increasingly active in state institutions, Allende could have taken measures to seize the initiative and, by doing so, disrupt their plans. Modern methods of dealing with similar forms of subversion provide an indication of what they could have consisted of. For example, Allende could have expelled the US military advisory teams, expelled a number of US diplomats, or even broken off diplomatic relations completely. Allende could have issued a decree requiring the financing of media, social, and civil society organisations to be made transparent and mired them in accounting and accountability procedures. Of course, such measures would have had some political repercussions, but they would also have directly impacted the US's ability to coordinate and finance the opposition. Other options Allende could have used included measures intended to distract the coup plotters within the military. Allende could have ordered military exercises far from Santiago or contributed a large contingent to UN peacekeeping forces, or taken any other measure to keep the military busy and out of politics.

Allende could perhaps have used methods drawn from Chile's own history or from the experiences of previous revolutions. Allende was arguably too unwilling to use coercion of any form, whether against his own coalition or against the opposition, to the detriment of his ability to govern. Allende's government could have supported popular efforts to dominate the streets, forcing the opposition to choose between more violent radicalisation or retreat to institutional forms. For example, Allende could have backed the creation of a popular militia, as had been called for during the Popular Front, or to counter the opposition's women's demonstrations, the UP could have formed a women's militia. These did not need to be armed; they just needed to prevent the opposition from enjoying an uncontested ability to mobilise and organise in public.

Of course, such actions were not without risks, and some would have been seen as threats to 'order', but arguably, this mattered less than the capacity to disorganise the opposition and, by doing so, seize the initiative. Such methods could also be seen as undemocratic, but as Lenin argued, 'Why should a revolutionary state allow democracy for the exploiters?' Even today, we routinely witness capitalist regimes' use of violence to preserve stability and governability. This issue was at the heart of the Marxist-Leninist perspective on the necessity of a dictatorship of the proletariat since the exploiters, even after the revolution, remained stronger (nationally and internationally), remained hopeful of restoration, and remained active in fighting for restoration.[5] This reality, Lenin argued, made Marx and Engels aware that some form of dictatorship of the exploited was necessary.

In theoretical terms, the question was whether Allende's institutional transition towards socialism could fit with this perspective on the revolution and its methods. For the MIR and those ultra-leftists in the UP, the answer was that it could not. But, the methods indicated above show that there was some middle way through which Allende could have defended the UP more effectively without adopting the strategy of direct confrontation with the Chilean state that he led. We know that some of these methods had been used by the Chilean Left at other stages in its history or were proposed during the UP, but they were not given serious consideration by Allende because democratic legitimacy was key to the success of the institutional road, but also because blows below the belt were not in his being. Allende's politics was one of Queensbury rules, of honourable and chivalric contest, not of cage fighting.

The question, therefore, has to be asked: Was Allende, despite all his skills, ideas and experience, simply too decent to succeed once the rules of the game began to shift away from institutional politics? Allende was probably the perfect politician for the path chosen by the Chilean Left; the relationships he had and the trust he commanded were key components in the UP's ability to reach an understanding with the PDC and, therefore, the key to the potential success of the UP process. Allende's weakness lay in his inability to adapt his methods once the dynamics of the political

---

[5] For Lenin's discussion on this, see *The Proletarian Revolution and the Renegade Kautsky, State and Revolution, and Democracy and Dictatorship,* all can be found on
https://www.marxists.org/

contest began to shift, and the root of this inability was in part due to his decency as a person but mostly due to a rather binary understanding of the concept of coercion — one that the Left as a whole struggled with throughout this period, as is evident in the debates around Chile's being an 'unarmed', 'peaceful' or 'non-armed' road to socialism. As subsequent theorists have shown, coercion can take many forms.

Other critics have asked whether Allende's humanism was a bourgeoise luxury. After all, unlike so many revolutionaries, Allende kept his hands clean of blood, but the ultimate failure of his government was nevertheless measured in lives taken, lives destroyed, uprooted and ruined, not just during the dictatorship but also by the system that has outlived it until now. It is likely that this question underestimates the limitations Allende was working within — the constitutional guarantees and the fact that Allende could not order the institutions to act against the plotters without damaging his legitimacy in the eyes of those same institutions. Let us suppose that Allende had cracked down on the coup plotters and the ultra-left, and he had used indirect means to repress the social movements of the opposition and, by doing so, had saved the process. Would this have been more humane in the long run? Possibly, in merely quantitative terms, but it would have been fatal to Allende's democratic reputation (even if capitalist democratic governments routinely use these forms of coercion in times of emergency). Variations of the question of what to do with the internal opposition have been faced by revolutionaries everywhere at all times, as Domenico Losurdo's work shows.[6] At root, the issue is that while it takes two to make peace, it only takes one to make war. If the opposition becomes bent on conflict, how can a government react? It is a dilemma as old as time, even reflected in the Old and New Testaments of the Bible — to take an eye for an eye or to turn the other cheek. But Allende believed in the unity of

---

[6] Domenico Losurdo, *War and Revolution*, (London: Verso, 2015).

ends and means, and he believed that democracy was vital to the success of the Chilean project at a stage when the popular forces did not yet dominate all the levers of political, social or economic power. Therefore, in effect, he had to 'turn the other cheek' since it was the only way he could see that would preserve the chance of a deal with the Christian Democrats and the Chilean road to socialism.

The result was that Allende's main counter to the coercion being meted out by the opposition was the hazard of what he called a 'moral punishment' — the fact that in order to overthrow him, they would need to kill him, kill the constitutionally elected President of Chile and by doing so, become criminals. This act could never be legitimate and would condemn whoever gained power from it. However, it was a punishment that came at the price of Allende's own life. If the opposition were bent on his overthrow, there was little Allende could do about it without abandoning the path he had spent his life building. Nor could Allende realistically alter the fate of the thousands of Chileans and foreigners killed after the coup. However, it cannot be doubted that Allende strained every sinew to seek a bloodless solution to the impasse. Nor did he shirk from his final sacrifice. In the end, it was this dogged commitment, along with the laying down of his own life, that helped to preserve the political and moral legitimacy of the UP.

While it took three years of active subversion at home and abroad to bring down the UP and destroy the 1925 constitution, today, it is the internal contradictions of the post-coup model that are weakening Chile's institutionality. It is no accident that Allende's legacy is gathering interest at the same time as capitalism endures its most serious crisis since the collapse of the Soviet Union. During the years that socialism was seen as a pipe dream, Allende's legacy could be brushed under the carpet as a relic from a bygone age. Today, however, it is becoming increasingly clear that Chile and the world need an alternative to neoliberalism and the failures of social democracy. Capitalism is the crisis. At the same time, in the rest of Latin America, left-wing governments are developing processes bearing striking similarities to UP. In this context, people are beginning to look back at Allende's ideas in search of guidance.

The idea of the need for public control of natural resources is again becoming widespread in Chile as people search for ways to fund improvements to education and public services. At the same time, many are criticising high levels of inequality, arguing for a fairer distribution of wealth. Interestingly, the mass mobilisations of recent years have shown a remarkable similarity with those of the early twentieth century. While many within the social movements question the need for broad alliances or participation in what they argue is an illegitimate system, the future will likely see movements and parties coming together to change the most pernicious aspects of Pinochet's legacy. It is also likely that initially, as in the 1930s and 1940s, these alliances will not be led by the Left but by the centre. Just as likely as before, the Left in some new form will come to dominate again since, as Allende argued, social democracy cannot resolve the problems of countries in the 'over-exploited' world. While it may take time, the political experience will show that the path chosen by Recabarren and by Allende, that of building unity — in method and objectives, between the social and the political — and using this unity to struggle both within and outside the institutions of the political system is the most effective way of achieving profound and lasting social change without using revolutionary violence.

The early twenty-first century has seen the election of governments across Latin America with goals and methods remarkably similar to Allende's. They share a heavy emphasis on Latin American and Third World solidarity, a lack of dogmatic ideological solutions, an acknowledgement of the importance of the state in the economy, and an emphasis on democracy, pluralism and participation in both economy and politics. These progressive processes in Venezuela and elsewhere have all come to power through elections. In each of them, the development of supportive mass movements was crucial to victory, as has been the educating role of the principal charismatic leaders such as Rafael Correa, Hugo Chávez, Daniel Ortega, Cristina Fernández, and Evo Morales.

In the wake of Allende's overthrow, the Left in Latin America and throughout the world sought to draw lessons from defeat. Allende's defeat was illustrative of the methods that imperialism would use against any Leftist process. The new generation of progressive governments demonstrated an appreciation both of the importance of what they call 'military patriots' in their survival, as is most notable in Venezuela and of the importance of popular mobilisation in defence of the revolution, which enabled them to respond with flexibility to the aggression unleashed by their domestic-foreign opposition. Also, in the modern processes, the revolutionaries have put constitutional reform at the centre of their political projects and by doing so, they have sought to create new mechanisms of popular power at the same time as they transform the structures and the purpose of the state. These have ranged from Venezuela's 'missions', which circumvented the established bureaucracy and the various 'communal' initiatives that have sought to decentralise and democratise local government to the creation of militias and the rewriting of military doctrines. This combination of methods and tools enables these processes to be, in the words of Hugo Chávez, 'peaceful, but not unarmed'.[7]

The US political and institutional elite also learned from the overthrow of Allende. Chile was not the first country where the United States had promoted and helped to foment a coup against a democratically elected government. In Guatemala, Iran, Brazil, and elsewhere, the United States used similar tools to put in place governments responsive to US priorities. US decision-makers, intelligence services, the military and private enterprises

---

[7] Luis Bonilla-Molina and Haiman El Troudi, *Historia de la revolucion Bolivariana*, (Caracas: Ministerio de Cultura, 2004), p. 52.

learned from these experiences to gradually create a well-oiled and practised, if somewhat 'clumsy' regime-change machine.[8] After 1973, what became clear to the institutions of imperialism (which were mainly in the US, although they were informed by international discussions in various elite and political forums) was that while their destabilisation efforts and military coups were effective, they were highly unpopular and carried significant political costs for the US at home and international level. The resulting regimes, such as Pinochet's, carried little domestic or international legitimacy, which made them vulnerable to social upheaval, as the cases of Portugal, Iran, and Nicaragua had shown. At the same time, the defeat in Vietnam had brought home to decision-makers in the US military and political institutions that 'unconventional war' was a mainly political conflict. This led to several conclusions. Firstly, the main target of conflict was the population of the country in question. Second, it was not enough to destroy the enemy's organised forces; the US needed to build alternative forces that were responsive to US interests. Thirdly, new organisations and institutions needed to be created to do this, and finally, the US domestic constituency needed to be supportive.[9] The US had realised, as had Lenin and Allende much earlier, that 'democracy is a vital, even revolutionary force', as George P. Shultz put it.[10] All they needed to do was redefine democracy to make it suit their own agenda.

When Reagan came to power in 1981, he adopted what was called the 'Kirkpatrick Doctrine' to help roll back the gains that 'communism' was perceived to have made in the preceding decade. This doctrine posited that right-wing dictatorships or 'authoritarian regimes' were preferable to 'totalitarian' regimes

---

[8] William I. Robinson, *Promoting Polyarchy*, (Cambridge: CUP, 1996), p. 87.

[9] William I. Robinson, *Promoting Polyarchy*, (Cambridge: CUP, 1996), p. 81.

[10] W.M. Schmidli, 'Recreating the Cold War Consensus: Democracy Promotion and the Crisis of American Hegemony', in *The Reagan Administration, the Cold War and the Transition to Democracy Promotion*, eds. R. Pee and W.M. Schmidli, p. 84.

because they could evolve into (pro-western) democracies, whereas the latter ostensibly could not. It was a shaky intellectual distinction that hid a basic truth — 'authoritarian' regimes were not generally hostile to US interests, and therefore, while they might be an embarrassment to the US, there was no fundamental conflict of interest. Therefore, Reagan's government increased support to regimes such as Pinochet's while also increasing US backing for 'freedom fighters' confronting supposedly 'totalitarian' socialist-oriented governments in Afghanistan, Nicaragua, Angola, and elsewhere. At the same time, the US sought to reorganise its regime change structures and the language and justifications it used to justify US interventions. Reagan's National Security Council developed 'Project Democracy', overseen by the CIA, to 'foster the infrastructure of democracy'. Reagan also began a reorganisation of the US military around 'rapid response' and what they called 'low-intensity conflict' as well as beginning the process of privatising US military and intelligence, contracting, creating a vast array of 'para-institutional forces' that together increased US capacity to intimidate and coerce Third World states.[11] Reagan, therefore, used 'the lexicon of human rights to justify aggressive US Cold War policies' with the objective of making security interests and human rights concerns 'mutually reinforcing'.[12]

In 1983, the National Endowment for Democracy (NED) was inaugurated in order to better combine overt and covert operations to create and support groups responsive to US interests by providing funding and coordinating activities among political parties, trade unions, business groups, media and civil society.[13] Other institutions followed, specialising in monitoring elections,

---

[11] Andrew Thompson, *Outsourced Empire: How Militias, Mercenaries and Contractors Support US Statecraft*, (London: Pluto Press, 2018), p. 92.

[12] W.M. Schmidli, 'Recreating the Cold War Consensus: Democracy Promotion and the Crisis of American Hegemony', in *The Reagan Administration, the Cold War and the Transition to Democracy Promotion*, eds. R. Pee and W.M. Schmidli, p. 80.

[13] William I. Robinson, *Promoting Polyarchy*, (Cambridge: CUP, 1996), p. 88.

building connections in media and so on. These institutions helped build up an accurate picture of the target society, meeting, training and coordinating local leaders and activists and using US funding to guide their activity towards objectives that aligned with US interests. The ability to use means widely seen as legitimate enabled the US to achieve its foreign policy objectives in ways that concealed the coercion that was at its heart.

Alongside these institutional developments, the US developed a theory for regime change that was based on the ideas of defence functionaries, including Gene Sharp — 'one of the most important US defence intellectuals of the latter twentieth century' — who had published 'The Politics of Non-Violent Action' in the year Allende was overthrown.[14] Sharp's doctorate was funded by the US Department of Defense [sic]. While the Albert Einstein Institute (AEI) he founded in 1983 was funded by the NED and its Republican Party offshoot — the International Republican Institute (IRI).[15] Sharp believed that states were the main cause of violence and that all societies were, in essence, divided between rulers and subjects, and he understood that no government could keep everybody happy. No matter the form of government, all government was by consent, and yet, the gap between aspiration and reality meant that there was always a potential social base for an opposition.

Sharp's genius was to identify the pillars upon which any government stood and to theorise how these pillars could be undermined through what today would be called 'information war' and non-violent struggle.[16] Sharp later declared, ' ... non-

---

[14] Marcie Smith, 'Change Agent: Gene Sharp's Neoliberal Non-Violence. Part Two', *Non-site.org*, 29 December 2019, Issue 30.
https://nonsite.org/change-agent-gene-sharps-neoliberal-nonviolence-part-two/

[15] Marcie Smith, 'Change Agent: Gene Sharp's Neoliberal Non-Violence. Part One', *Non-Site.org*, 10 May 2019, Issue 28.
https://nonsite.org/category/issue-28-2/

[16] Brian Martin, 'Gene Sharp's Theory of Power', *Journal of Peace Research*, 26, No. 2, (May 1989).

violent struggle is armed struggle. And we have to take back that term from those advocates of violence, who try to justify with pretty words that kind of combat. Only with this type of struggle one fights with psychological weapons, social weapons, economic weapons, and political weapons'. It was the perfect mix for a 'renovated' US regime change policy around which a methodology began to be developed during the mid-1980s.

Ironically, the initial targets of these new regime change efforts were the dictatorships the US had helped install in the 1960s and 1970s. The previous US support they had enjoyed, their economic exposure to the US and their pro-US ideological orientation made them particularly vulnerable to US meddling. In Chile and the Philippines, the United States used a human rights-centred discourse to support the overthrow of Pinochet and Marcos increasingly. Here, the US expanded upon its support for opposition social groups that it had tested in Allende's Chile. The US used all the political, economic, cultural, and intellectual tools at its disposal — it threatened to block arms deals and credits, and it funded unions, social organisations, NGOs, academic conferences, journalism and legal campaigns that focused narrowly on the objective of regime change while tending to ignore the political and economic structures the dictatorship had put in place. The US corralled and stimulated international backing through the State Department, the cooperation of intelligence agencies, through the activity of transnational corporations and even through religious organisations. No violence against these dictatorial regimes would be tolerated.[17] The new centrist opposition would condemn violence 'wherever it came from'. The strategy was effective; by the end of the 1980s, the US had largely eliminated the right-wing dictatorships that it had helped into existence in earlier decades, and it had helped force the Sandinistas from power, replacing all of them with pliant, US-friendly 'democracies'.

[17] William I. Robinson, *Promoting Polyarchy*, (Cambridge: CUP, 1996).

By their nature, many aspects of these operations were covert, but we know from US institutional sources (such as the AEI and the NED) that through the 1990s, the focus of their efforts shifted to Eastern Europe, to the former socialist states, on to the Balkans in the late 1990s and then onwards into the Caucasus and Central Asia. Along the way, the methods and tools were honed and perfected. One among them was the identification of a colour and symbols associated with the movement for change, which earned them the label of 'colour revolutions'.

It was not long before the new 'colour revolution' method was used in Latin America. The experience here showed that modifications had been made to the original 'non-violent' programme for change. Social media were brought into the mix to spread opposition messages and help coordinate actions. In Caracas, Nicaragua, and Bolivia, as in Ukraine in 2014, violent groups among opposition protestors targeted members of state forces and political leaders. The violence was hidden from international view by US-friendly international media, but it helped to demoralise state workers, create a sense of crisis and justified international pressure. The key was for the opposition to see itself and be seen by others as the shiny-faced and bright-eyed underdog, and in this, international media played a key role. Opposition violence had to be ignored, while regime use of coercion had to be exaggerated because it would undermine the 'social consent' needed to govern. Incredibly, using these methods, the forces of reaction could even claim to be 'revolutionary'. Soon, the methodology was adapted again, this time to include the creation of alternative national leaders, such as Juan Guaidó (later, Sviatlana Tsikhanouskaya from Belarus), who were recognised by the US and its allies but effectively powerless. Their purpose was to challenge the legitimacy of the government, act as the international face of the opposition and legitimate US aggression with the Western public.

Despite the innovations, these 'colour revolutions' used

many methods and tools that Allende would have recognised — economic blockade, enemies 'operating from the shadows', funding and coordination of the political opposition, media campaigns, and the like. In Latin America, these 'colour revolutions' were largely stymied by a combination of vast social support for the governments, economic growth and the US distracted by its wars in the Middle East and Central Asia. Only in Honduras and Paraguay were progressive governments overthrown. Yet, years of progress were followed by difficulties as the price of oil plummeted in 2014, and the US once again turned its attention to Latin America.

The conflict in Colombia, which had consumed much US attention in the region since the late 1990s, entered a peace process in 2013, allowing the US to expand its attention elsewhere. Venezuela and Cuba, in particular, have been and are being subjected to a combination of pressures similar to those faced by Allende, including sanctions and terrorism by neo-fascists and foreign agents. Nicaragua and Bolivia also experienced uprisings with a similar social composition. In Bolivia, with support from the OAS, the attempt was temporarily successful. The Sandinistas survived largely, thanks to the loyalty of the military and police forged in the revolutionary war of the 1980s and the autonomous organisation of the people against the rebellion. In both Venezuela and Nicaragua, survival has also been due to consistent openness to dialogue with the 'systemic' opposition. This, along with the government's political and social hegemony, has forced the opposition into the kind of conflicts between extremists and moderates that beset the Chilean Left in the 1960s and 1970s. It has also exposed the relationship between the most extreme groups and the US.

While the Left has since been betrayed in Ecuador (2018) and overthrown in a 'judicial-legislative coup' in Brazil (2015), and briefly overthrown in Bolivia (2019), there are many reasons for optimism. In Bolivia, a strong social movement managed to force new elections, which saw the MAS re-elected under President Luís

Arce. In Brazil, former President Lula is back in office. In Colombia and Mexico, progressive presidents have also been elected.

The search by Latin America's Left for an independent and non-aligned foreign policy and for the political and economic integration of Latin America continue to echo Allende's policies, and in all of this, Allende is recognised and hailed as their precursor. Allende is thus as yet more recognised abroad, where politicians seek to implement his methods in order to achieve similar goals and where schools, streets, and squares are named after him than he is at home, where a solitary statue stands outside the Moneda palace. At least for now.

In Chile itself, the recent mobilisations promise an awakening from the long night following September 1973. The people of Chile are discussing a new constitution, and during the UP, there is everything to gain. Perhaps soon, as Allende predicted on that grim September morning, 'the great avenues' that Chileans will walk in order to build a better society will open up again. In order to do so, Chileans will need to build upon the revolutionary legacy left to them by Salvador Allende and the UP.

Organisation Names

1. Christian Left (*Izquierda Cristiana*, IC).
2. Councils of Supply and Prices (*juntas de Abastecimientos y Precios*, JAP).
3. Broad Front (*Frente Amplio*, FA).
4. Communist Party (*Partido Comunista*, PC).
5. Communist Party of Chile (*Partido Comunista de Chile*, PCCh).
6. Fatherland and Liberty Nationalist Front (*Frente Nacionalista Patria y Libertad* or simply *Patria y Libertad*, PyL).
7. Federation of Chilean Workers (*Federación Obrera de Chile*, FOCH).
8. People's Front (*Frente del Pueblo*).
9. Group of Personal Friends (*Grupo de Amigos Personales*, GAP).
10. Independent Progressive Alliance (*Alianza Progresista Independiente*, API).
11. National Party (*Partido Nacional*, PN).
12. Popular Action Front (*Frente de Acción Popular*, FRAP).
13. Popular Socialist Party (*Partido Socialista Popular*, PSP).
14. Popular Unitary Action Movement (*Movimiento de Acción Popular Unitario*, MAPU).
15. Popular Unity (*Unidad Popular*, UP).
16. Revolutionary Left Movement (*Movimiento de Izquierda Revolucionaria*, MIR).
17. Socialist Party of Chile (*Partido Socialista de Chile*, PS).
18. Socialist Workers' Party (*Partido Obrero Socialista*, POS).
19. Socialist Workers' Party (*Partido Socialista de Trabajadores*, PST).

Victor Figueroa Clark

lectures at the London School of Economics

and is the editor of the Left History website.

His previous works include a history of the Chilean

volunteers who fought for the Sandinistas and

Salvador Allende (Pluto, 2013).